ARIANA

A Glimpse of Eternity

a novel

Rachel Ann Nunes

Covenant Communications, Inc.

Covenant

Cover photograph by "Picture This...by Sara Staker"

Published by Covenant Communications, Inc.
American Fork, Utah

Printed in the United States of America
First Printing: January 1999

06 05 04 03 02 01 00 99   10 9 8 7 6 5 4 3 2 1

ISBN 1-57734-436-7

For being there whenever I need you,
Mary, this one's for you.

CHAPTER ONE

The confrontation took place in the sitting room. Marie-Thérèse watched as a deep crimson flushed her sister's face. The color traveled from Josette's neck up to her deep brown eyes, where Marie-Thérèse imagined she could see red-hot sparks leaping out, burning whatever they touched.

For a long moment their parents, Ariana and Jean-Marc Perrault, said nothing, but regarded Josette quietly from their seat on the long blue couch. Marie-Thérèse could hear the tick-tock of the grandfather clock that stood near the window. She shifted nervously on the chair, her fingers drumming on a table beside her. Outside the window, the twilight crept steadily on, enveloping the world with its diffused light.

"I tell you, I'm not going!" Josette repeated into the silence. It was the third time she had said that exact phrase in the past two minutes. "I don't want to leave France."

"Now is rather late to be telling us this," their father said. "Fall classes start in eight days." His voice was mild, but his face was set firmly in a way Marie-Thérèse recognized all too well. He would not compromise, no matter what.

"You can still get your money back," Josette protested.

Their mother rose from the couch and put her hand on Josette's arm. "That's not the point," she said. "You committed to go, and we all agreed it was best."

"But America! It's too far away. I'll die without Alphonse!" Josette stomped her foot like a small child and glared at Ariana. Marie-Thérèse thought how alike mother and daughter appeared. Of course, there were notable differences: Josette had long hair while Ariana's was short; Josette's curvaceous figure was taller and slightly fuller than her mother's; and Josette was deeply tanned by an active outdoor life. The biggest dissimilarity came from the twenty-four years separating them. Josette was hot-tempered and flighty, while Ariana's passion had been tempered by a difficult but fulfilling life.

"Die without him?" Their mother laughed. "Oh, Josette, be serious! You only met him a month ago."

"But Alphonse is different."

"As was the boyfriend before this," Jean-Marc put in. "And he's not even a member of our church. You know how we feel about that."

"But Brigham Young University is so far away. Why can't I continue my education here?"

"You know very well why," Jean-Marc said. "Your mother and I both feel you need to gain some independence."

Josette turned to Marie-Thérèse. "Help me!" she demanded. "They'll listen to you."

Marie-Thérèse wanted to help her sister, but the truth was, she agreed with her parents. The twenty-year-old Josette needed a change in her life, and BYU just might be able to give it to her.

Josette herself had been the catalyst that had convinced Marie-Thérèse to side with their parents. Four months earlier, Marie-Thérèse had come home to find Josette and her latest boyfriend alone in the sitting room, kissing. Or necking, as their parents called it. No one else was in the house. Josette's twin brother Marc was on his mission, André and Pauline were at a church activity, and their parents had taken their youngest brother, Louis-Géralde, to a birthday party. The only reason Marie-Thérèse had come home early from her college study group was because she had forgotten her class notes.

She had opened the apartment door with her key and had almost immediately heard the giggling behind the wooden screen that separated the sitting room from the entryway. Slowly, she had pushed the partition open, already suspecting what she would find.

"Marie-Thérèse!" Josette had gasped from the couch. She pushed the boy away and sat up straight. "What are you doing home?"

"I should ask you the same thing."

Josette ran to her side. "Don't tell Mom and Dad, promise?" she whispered urgently. "I mean, it's not as if I'm sixteen anymore. We were just kissing a little."

Marie-Thérèse glanced at the boy who sat calmly back against the couch, grinning at her. She recognized Marcelin Cuvier from one of her classes at the private college she and Josette attended, and knew his reputation. A little kissing was not the only thing on his mind.

He stood up and sauntered over to Josette, giving her a long kiss on the mouth. "I'd better go. Catch you tomorrow."

Josette's full lips went into a fake pout. "Okay, I guess," she said.

When he left, she turned back to Marie-Thérèse. "You won't tell, will you?"

"That depends."

"On what?"

"On if you leave him alone."

Josette laughed. "What do you mean?"

Her tone made Marie-Thérèse angry. "You know exactly what I mean. He's a spoiled rich boy who's only out for a good time." *Just like you,* she wanted to add, but refrained by biting her tongue. She had learned to think before acting—one of them had to be responsible, and Josette was almost never that.

"Well, what's wrong with having fun?"

"His fun is not our kind of fun," Marie-Thérèse retorted. "What about your values? What about a temple marriage?"

Josette crossed to the couch and put her feet up on the coffee table. "Goodness, I'm not sleeping with him, I'm just fooling around!"

"You're playing with fire."

"What do you know about it?" scoffed Josette. "You hardly even go out."

"I do when I find someone worthy of my goals."

Josette impatiently pulled her waist-length hair up and over the back of the couch. "Maybe it's time you stop being so picky. You don't want to end up an old maid, like Aunt Lu-Lu almost did." Her hair tumbled forward again as she picked up a magazine from the table and began to thumb through it much faster than she could ever read.

"'Almost' doesn't count," Marie-Thérèse said, moving to sit beside her sister. "She found Jourdain and you know how wonderful he is.

What if she had settled for a nonmember and lost the chance of meeting him?"

"Is that what this is all about?—my dating a nonmember? That's strange, coming from little Miss-I'm-planning-to-go-on-a-mission. What about repentance? What about me converting him? It does happen. Why don't *you* look at Aunt Lu-Lu?"

"Uncle Jourdain is different. Special."

"So is Marcelin." There was no flexibility in Josette's eyes.

"All right," said Marie-Thérèse. "What if I can prove that he's not special? What if I can prove he's only out for what he can get? What then? Would you promise to drop him?"

Josette's eyes narrowed. "How?"

"What if I can get him to ask me out? Or meet me somewhere."

Josette threw back her head and laughed. "Oh, don't tell me you're interested in him. If that's the case, then—"

"I'm not interested in him," snapped Marie-Thérèse. "I've told you that I'll never let a man come between us. I'm just worried about you."

Her sister's laughter vanished. "I know, Marie-Thérèse. And I feel the same way. No man is worth our friendship."

"Then you'll let me do it?"

"Only if you'll agree to support me if he doesn't fail your test."

Marie-Thérèse hesitated only a second. "Okay then. But I get a few tries."

"Three." They shook on the deal.

The next day, Josette amazed Marie-Thérèse by throwing herself into the plan. She styled Marie-Thérèse's hair, spraying and scrunching until it looked like a picture from a magazine. She even let her wear her favorite perfume. "Marcelin loves this," she giggled.

"You'd think you want him to fail."

"I just want to be sure," Josette said. "No, not that blouse, wear this one. The green makes your eyes stand out. And this skirt." She pulled a tight-fitting emerald skirt out of their free-standing closet. "It goes with the blouse, and it makes you look very sexy."

Marie-Thérèse rolled her eyes. "Oh, great." She studied herself in the full-length mirror near the closet. She was taller than Josette by about ten centimeters. Her shoulder-length hair was a lighter brown than her sister's and cut at varying lengths along her thin face to give it fullness and to emphasize the small, upturned nose and pixie face.

"You look a little like Aunt Paulette," Josette said suddenly, her eyes darting to a picture above Marie-Thérèse's bed. In it, Paulette Perrault held a baby Marie-Thérèse.

Marie-Thérèse nodded absently. Except for her nose, she did favor her birth mother, who had died of AIDS when she was only four. They shared the same brown hair, the light-brown eyes, the lean body, and the many freckles. Marie-Thérèse's natural sister, Pauline, however, almost completely resembled their adoptive father. Marie-Thérèse often thought that her younger sister fit perfectly into her aunt and uncle's family—except for the fact that she was HIV positive. That didn't fit comfortably anywhere.

"I wish I was slim enough to wear that skirt," Josette said a little enviously.

Marie-Thérèse much preferred Josette's more womanly curves, but she did have to admit that she looked good today. She had always considered herself plain against the backdrop of Josette's passionate beauty, but maybe she judged herself too harshly. Regardless, she hoped her looks would be enough for the task.

"What's your plan?" Josette asked as they rode the elevator down the five flights to the street. The May air was still cool this early in the morning, and Marie-Thérèse felt goose bumps rise on her bare arms.

"Well, Mom and Dad have plans tonight, and I've already given André and Pauline money to take Louis-Géralde to a movie. I thought I'd test Marcelin at our apartment."

"But I have a date with him tonight!"

"So, I'm cancelling it. He'll come to pick you up and you won't be there. It's as simple as that."

"But I *will* be there," Josette said. "I want to hear for myself what he does."

Marie-Thérèse shrugged. "That's fine by me. I don't want to be alone with him anyway. I don't trust him. If you're there, I won't have to ask one of my friends over to hide and watch." With effort, she formed a stiff smile. "And that way you can see what kind of a man he really is."

"Humph!" Josette tossed her long hair over her shoulder. "*When* he passes your silly little test, I'm going to go out with him like I'd planned."

"Suit yourself. *If* he passes."

"He will," her sister insisted. "But I don't know why we went to all that work getting you ready this morning when he's not coming to get me until seven tonight." Josette's enthusiasm for the project had dimmed, but Marie-Thérèse became even more determined. Although her sister had agreed to give her three chances, she doubted there would be any more than just this one. That understanding was the reason she had taken such care with her appearance this morning. Tonight she would make her move on Marcelin, but during the day she would lay her groundwork.

They walked the rest of the way to the metro in silence, and Josette didn't speak at all to Marie-Thérèse on the train. When they arrived at school, she disappeared with a hasty wave of her hand. Marie-Thérèse stared after her, loving her sister and wishing for the millionth time that she was a little more stable. *When had it happened? When had Josette changed?* Marie-Thérèse's eyebrows scrunched together as she fell into her usual habit of analyzing the world around her. Today she found no answer. Her sister still had the strong sense of love and responsibility she had always felt for the family, but something else wasn't right.

Marie-Thérèse's plan came into play during the math class she shared with Marcelin. Both were finance majors, and in the same year. Since her childhood, Marie-Thérèse had wanted to follow her adopted father's footsteps and go into banking. Marcelin was there to learn how to make his rich family even richer—or so he told anyone who would listen.

She arrived early to class, relieved to see that Marcelin hadn't yet found a seat. It wouldn't pay to be too obvious. The gathering students murmured among themselves, and Marie-Thérèse didn't miss the fact that Marcelin's companions were all young women— and pretty ones at that. Ignoring her usual place in the front, she sat next to the chair Marcelin used each day without fail. The teacher entered, and the students quickly took their seats.

Without glancing her way, Marcelin settled into his accustomed spot. Marie-Thérèse felt her heart pounding so loudly that she was sure the whole class must hear. She waited until the teacher was well underway before pushing her pen off the desk with the edge of her book, praying silently that it would land near Marcelin.

It did. He leaned down and scooped it up, handing it back. *Now,* Marie-Thérèse told herself. She accepted the pen, but grabbed it farther up than necessary, touching his fingers. "Thanks," she said with a smile. He grinned, and Marie-Thérèse noticed for the first time how good-looking he was. Her pulse quickened now for quite another reason. She purposely held his eyes with her own in the way Josette was famous for doing. He grinned and stared insolently back.

Well, at least he saw me, Marie-Thérèse thought.

"You look great today," Marcelin whispered.

She smiled and lowered her eyes. "Thanks."

"Hey, uh, I missed class the other day," he added. "Do you think you could give me your notes?"

This was way too easy! "Sure," she said. "You have a date with my sister tonight, don't you? You can get them then."

Marcelin blinked in surprise, then his face showed nothing, but Marie-Thérèse knew that he hadn't realized who she was, much less her relationship to Josette. She was nothing but a backdrop, someone he had never noticed before. Her face flamed, but she turned it so he wouldn't see. Had her betraying face ruined her chance to save her sister?

Marie-Thérèse didn't dare look at Marcelin again. *Some femme fatale I am,* she thought with a silent sigh.

After class, Marcelin put his arm briefly on her shoulder. "See ya tonight," he said.

"Tonight," she agreed, startling herself by giving him a wink. He grinned and strode out of the room, a picture of confidence, while she leaned against the wall until her knees were no longer shaking. "I'm no good at this," she muttered. "Even though I've had the best teacher." Josette had been adept at charming the opposite sex since she was five; it seemed to come naturally for her.

Later that evening, Josette changed hiding places four times before Marcelin came to the door. First she stretched out behind the couch in the sitting room. Second, she crouched behind the chair. Then she decided to stay in the kitchen and sneak out to listen at the folding wood partition which Marie-Thérèse would close after bringing Marcelin into the sitting room. At the last minute, she hid behind the couch again. "That way you won't have to worry about closing the partition," she said.

From her flighty movements and quick speech, Marie-Thérèse could tell her sister was nervous, but that nervousness couldn't possibly equal the butterflies in her own stomach. She wished she could call the whole thing off.

Marcelin didn't arrive until ten minutes after the hour. Marie-Thérèse opened the door with a smile. "Come on in." She led the way to the sitting room and motioned for him to sit on the blue couch.

"Josette's not coming," she said, settling next to him a little closer than she would have normally liked. "She said to make her excuses, but it couldn't be helped. She'll explain later."

Marcelin didn't contain his surprise well. "Oh," he said, looking disgruntled.

"I thought we could go over these notes, if you want."

"Sure," he said. His voice was slightly sour.

Marie-Thérèse explained what she had written and the meaning of the abbreviations she commonly used. All too soon, she was done. "Well, that's it."

Marcelin leaned back against the couch, one arm spread across the top, and stared at her lazily. "I guess I'd better get going."

"I guess," Marie-Thérèse agreed reluctantly. What was she going to do? They'd been alone together a whole twenty minutes, and he had been a perfect gentleman. For her part, Marie-Thérèse felt she had made her pretend feelings for Marcelin obvious. Maybe Josette was right about him after all.

"How is it that you and Josette are the same age?" Marcelin asked. At least he didn't seem to be in too great a hurry to leave. "I thought she had a twin brother, not a sister."

"We're actually cousins. My parents died when I was young, and my aunt and uncle adopted my little sister and me. I'm four months older than Josette and Marc."

"Oh." Marcelin's face came suddenly close to hers. "I like you, Marie-Thérèse," he murmured. Then he kissed her, strongly and passionately.

She pushed him away, feeling anger kindling in her gut. "What about Josette?" she asked calmly. "You can't ask me to steal my sister's boyfriend."

"I won't tell her if you won't."

"You want to date us both!" Marie-Thérèse couldn't keep the incredulity from her voice.

"Why not? If you're game. We'll keep it our little secret."

He tried to kiss her again, but Marie-Thérèse punched his chest and leapt to her feet. "I want you to leave," she insisted.

Marcelin's face grew red. "I was under the impression you liked me," he grated.

His vehemence startled her into telling the truth. "I wanted to see for myself what kind of a man my sister dated. It was a test. And you failed."

Marcelin raised a fist, and Marie-Thérèse became suddenly afraid. But she didn't flinch. "Leave!" she repeated firmly.

To her relief, Marcelin dropped his hand and walked to the entryway. "It's your loss," he said. "You're too thin, anyway. I like my women to look like women, to be softer than dried up old bread." The comment stung, but Marie-Thérèse didn't let him see. "And forget about telling Josette," he added. "She'll never believe you. It's your word against mine."

"She'll believe me. We're sisters," Marie-Thérèse said, but she wondered if he wasn't right. Would Josette have believed her if she hadn't heard for herself what kind of man Marcelin was?

"Cousins," corrected Marcelin. With that, he turned on his heel and strode out the door, slamming it behind him.

Utter silence filled the room. *Why doesn't Josette come from behind the couch?* Marie-Thérèse made her way to where a small table with long legs and a gilt-edged mirror separated the wall from the couch. Josette lay under the table on her side.

"Josette, come out of there."

No answer.

Marie-Thérèse stooped down and reached tentatively toward her sister's hair. "I'm sorry," she murmured. And she was. She almost wished she hadn't challenged her sister's relationship with Marcelin. Almost.

Josette looked up. There were tears on her face. "Will I ever find someone?" she whispered. "Someone who loves me for me?"

"When it's time."

Her sister scrambled from under the table and to her feet. "It's okay for you!" she shouted. "You don't care. You want to go on a mission and convert the world. I just want a family. What's so wrong with that?"

"You're only twenty," Marie-Thérèse said dryly.

The words spurred Josette to further anger. "I'm going after him!" she declared. "We didn't play fair. We tricked him! You tricked him!"

"It could have been anyone," Marie-Thérèse began.

Josette wouldn't listen. "I don't care what you say!" she shouted. With that she ran to the door and was gone.

Marie-Thérèse thought for a long time, and she knew what she had to do. When her parents arrived home, she told them what had happened.

Jean-Marc's eyes met Ariana's as though communicating some private message. "I think it's time," he said.

She nodded. "I'd hoped she'd settle down, but ever since Marc left . . ."

That's it! thought Marie-Thérèse. *It was when Marc left on his mission a year ago that Josette began to change.* Her sister had always been passionate about everything, but only in her twin brother's absence had she become uncontrollable. Josette had seemed to be the one to keep the impulsive Marc out of trouble, but apparently he had stabilized her as well. The twins had been very close—closer even than she and Josette, the cousin-sisters.

"What did we do wrong?" Ariana asked. "We didn't let her date until she was sixteen, and then only in group dates. How can she be so careless of what we've taught?"

Marie-Thérèse watched her father put his arm around her mother. "Ari, we did the best we knew how."

"I feel like she's drowning and I can't save her," Ariana said. "I haven't felt that way since André hung out with those drug pushers when he was twelve."

Involuntarily, Marie-Thérèse shuddered. A youthful drug addiction on her mother's part had caused her birth parents' AIDS all those years ago.

"I think BYU is a good option," her father said. "Apparently Josette needs some time to decide what she believes in."

"But to send her away?" Ariana protested. "How can that be right? We won't be there to help her."

"Our prayers have been answered," Jean-Marc said gently. "Don't you think so?"

Marie-Thérèse saw the answer on her mother's face before she spoke. "Yes. This is our answer. But we can't send her alone."

As one, they turned toward Marie-Thérèse.

"What?" she asked warily. She had followed the conversation, but still didn't understand.

"We've decided to send Josette to Brigham Young University in Provo to finish college," Jean-Marc said. "We'd like you to go with her."

"But my mission."

"You won't be twenty-one until the end of November, and you weren't planning to submit your papers until then anyway. It would only delay you a month or so. Do you think you could do that? Josette will need you, especially since Marc is so far away."

Go to the United States? It was something Marie-Thérèse had thought about doing for a vacation, but never for an extended period of time. She knew without a doubt that France was where she belonged. Still, she loved her sister, and the time in America would be a learning experience for them both. Her parents had said that sending her was an answer to their prayers; shouldn't she be willing to do her part? "Sure," she said. "I'll go."

The relief was evident on her parents' faces. "Good," her father said. "You can start filling out the papers right now."

"You have them already?"

"Yes," Jean-Marc said. "And we've been in touch with the administration there. The missionary who baptized your mom already has things underway, just in case we decided to go this route. He's a professor there."

Marie-Thérèse realized that her parents had been aware of Josette's need all along, and had been searching for some way to help her. "What if she refuses?" Marie-Thérèse asked.

"She's an adult," Jean-Marc said, "even if she doesn't act like one most of the time. We can't force her, but I think that together we can convince her. Especially after what happened tonight."

Marie-Thérèse wasn't so sure. After all, Josette had gone after Marcelin. "Let me talk to her first, okay?"

Her parents smiled. "Thank you," Ariana said. "I knew you would help."

Marie-Thérèse was in the sitting room, filling out the application papers, when Josette came home a short time later. Josette said nothing, but threw herself on the end of the couch. Her face showed no signs of tears. "Where's everybody?" she asked as though nothing had happened.

"In the TV room." Marie-Thérèse wanted more than anything to ask about Marcelin, but she didn't dare.

"What ya doing?"

"Filling out papers for Dad to fax tomorrow. I'm going to BYU."

"You're what?" Josette leaned closer, suddenly interested.

"It'll be good to get away," Marie-Thérèse said cautiously. "It'll be a whole new experience."

"But your mission!"

"I'm only going to America until December. Then I'll come home."

Josette said nothing, but her expression was sad.

"How'd it go with Marcelin?" Marie-Thérèse asked softly.

Josette's luminous eyes met hers, and when she spoke the words came more slowly than Marie-Thérèse had ever heard them come from her sister. "He said you threw yourself at him, and that he had to fend you off."

"Did you tell him you were there?"

"No. I told him my sister would never lie. He denied it again, but I said he wasn't worth my relationship with my sister—that no man was."

Marie-Thérèse felt gratitude wash over her. Marcelin was put into his place, at least as far as they were concerned. "I'm sorry," she said.

"I'm not," Josette said fiercely. "I hate him."

Marie-Thérèse stifled a laugh. Her sister hated with the same intensity that she loved.

Josette touched the papers on the desk. "Are you really going away?"

"Not without my sister." Marie-Thérèse brought out the second application from under her own. Most of it she had already filled out in her precise script.

A slow smile spread over Josette's face, making her more lovely than ever. Marie-Thérèse hugged her. "Come with me?"

"Okay," Josette said. "Whatever."

They told their parents together, both of whom expressed pleasure in Josette's decision. "We feel this is an answer to prayer," Ariana said.

"For your own good," Jean-Marc added.

Josette acted as though she scarcely heard them. She threw herself into the planning with the same passion she showed about everything. "I'm going away to school in America," she told her friends. "And I might just have such a good time that I'll never come back! Maybe I'll even marry an American. I can't wait to get there!"

But things had abruptly changed when Josette met this new boyfriend, Alphonse, a month before they were to leave for Utah. Since then, she had been hinting about staying behind. Tonight, as they confronted one another in the sitting room, things had culminated in her blatant refusal to go.

"Marie-Thérèse, aren't you going to stick up for me?"

At Josette's plea, Marie-Thérèse's thoughts returned to the present. "But I *want* to go to BYU," Marie-Thérèse found herself saying. "It'll be fun."

"I don't want to go!"

"Your grades have slipped this past year," Jean-Marc said. "If you don't go now, you may never get in."

Josette's lower lip jutted out. "I don't care."

"You promised!" Marie-Thérèse said.

"But . . . Alphonse—"

"Will still be here when you come home for Christmas," Ariana said. She put her hand on Josette's shoulder. "I trust you will do what's best."

Josette shrugged off her mother's hand. "I hate it when you say that!"

Marie-Thérèse smiled inwardly. Their mother knew only too well how to appeal to their sense of honor.

Josette glared at her, but Marie-Thérèse easily met her eyes. It had come to her just now what to say, a silent whispering of the Spirit. "Is Alphonse worth letting me down?" she asked. "Is he coming between us?"

Air whooshed out of Josette's lungs as though from an untied balloon. "Oh, dang it," she said. "Of course not." She faced their parents. "Okay, I'll go, but only for one semester." She flounced to the door before turning and declaring, "But I'm going to hate every second."

CHAPTER TWO

Elder Marc Perrault felt the old scars on his stomach itching. His "battle wounds," as he called them, had been caused partly by the kidney transplant he had endured shortly after his sixteenth birthday, and partly by the explosion in the metro which had caused his kidney failure in the first place. He had been in the right place at the right time to help a stranger survive, but there had been a cost. He thought of Danielle Massoni's beautiful gray eyes and knew it had been worth it.

As with old farmers who knew it would rain because of the aching in their bones, the itching warned Marc that the investigator he and his new companion were teaching wasn't focusing on what they were saying, and that she was about to break their hearts.

"You see," Elder Zachary Fields was saying in his Americanized French, "being the perfect example, our Savior showed us the way back to our Father in Heaven." He spoke good French for only being in the country three months. Of course, the younger missionary had studied two months at the Missionary Training Center in Provo, and before that in high school. He told Marc he had always known he would be coming to France on his mission.

"Even though Jesus himself was pure," Elder Fields went on, "he was baptized, not only because it is a commandment, but so we would understand that everyone needs to accept baptism before they can return home to live with him."

Marc tried to catch his companion's eye to signal that something wasn't quite right, but Elder Fields didn't look his way. Marc wasn't surprised. They had only been together a month, and it usually took longer to become accustomed to a companion's body language.

"That's so nice," Madame Legrand said as Elder Fields paused for
breath. "You'll have to teach it all to my daughters when they come
back from vacationing with their grandparents—they go there every
summer, you know." They did know; she had told them each of the
other two times they had come to call—once when they knocked at
her door and the next day when they taught her the first discussion.
That had been three days ago, and they had hoped to commit her to
baptism during this second visit, but her mind was far away from
spiritual matters. This discussion was quickly going nowhere.

"You'd like my daughters," Madame Legrand said. "They're just
about your age, and they love anything to do with America." She
winked at Elder Fields. "They both cook and know how to keep
house. Oh, yes, I taught them, so they would make good wives. I bet
they'd love to hear your lessons when they return home next week."

"What about you?" Marc asked.

"I always enjoy hearing about Jesus," she said absently. "Did I
show you pictures of my daughters? They're very pretty."

Marc stifled his annoyance, praying silently. "You did, Madame
Legrand," he said, "and they seem like . . . uh, like nice girls, but how
do you feel about—"

"Then you'll come back and meet them? Maybe you could go see
a movie."

"We don't date while we're on our missions," Marc said.

Her eyes narrowed. "What kind of religion is this? Can't go out
with girls. You do like girls, don't you?"

Discouragement weighed heavily on Marc's heart. Apparently, this
woman's only interest in them was as husbands for her homely daughters. He was about to make their excuses and leave when Elder Fields
spoke, his blue eyes boring earnestly into Madame Legrand's. "Your
daughters are very important to you, I see," he said. "I know how you
feel. My family is very special to me as well. That's why what we're
teaching is so important. What if I told you that you and your daughters could be a family forever? In our church, we believe that marriage
is eternal, and that's why we have temples." He pulled out his flip
chart and showed her each of the temples, explaining how sacred and
important they were to him, and how the ordinances came about.
"When I get married, it will be in one of these temples," he said.

"Sealed forever. I want to know my family will be together forever, that the grandchildren I bounce on my knee will be as close to me in the next life as in this one."

Marc had opened his mouth to warn his companion not to skip too far ahead in the discussions, but stopped when he recognized the almost palpable touch of the Spirit in the room.

"What a beautiful thing," Madame Legrand murmured, her eyes soft.

"I want you to know that these principles are true," Elder Fields said. "I have prayed about them and have felt the Spirit tell me so. How did you feel when you read from the book we left you last time? What did you feel during your prayer?"

"Well, I . . .uh . . . didn't read it," she admitted, contradicting what she had said earlier. "I was busy, and I felt kind of funny praying like that. I'm used to memorized prayers."

Marc felt a slight smile tug at his lips. No wonder she had not been interested in their second discussion; she had not yet internalized the first. That usually meant an investigator hadn't understood the Book of Mormon's great importance. He took up where Elder Fields had left off.

"Remember what we talked about last time, about how Heavenly Father always calls prophets to bring his word to the people?" Marc asked. He started from the beginning, explaining the many reasons why she should want to know for herself that the book was true. "If it is true," he added, "then everything we've talked to you about, including how families can be together forever, is also true. Do you see how important this is?"

Elder Fields cast him a grateful smile, and for the first time Marc understood that the elder had been just as worried and frustrated as he had been. Marc was amazed at his junior companion's fortitude and his closeness to the Spirit. *I will learn from him and do better,* he vowed.

After bearing their testimonies of the Book of Mormon, the elders set up another appointment and left Madame Legrand holding her blue book to her chest.

"Whew!" said Elder Fields when they were outside the apartment building. "I was worried there for a minute."

"You did great," Marc said. Though he had never considered himself short, he had to crane his neck to meet his companion's eyes.

"So did you. Remember, it was you who told me that we had to care about what the investigator cared about before we could reach them."

"Yeah, but her daughters? In another minute, we both would have been engaged."

Elder Fields laughed. "We still might," he said. "The daughters come home next week."

"It'll be all right," Marc said confidently. "Once they go to church and talk with the members, they'll understand that we're off limits. At least *you* have nothing to worry about. After your mission, you'll go home to another country. They won't be able to follow you there!"

"They could always go to BYU," Elder Fields said. "Like your sisters."

"Yeah, that's right, they'll be leaving soon." As always when he thought of his twin sister, a warm feeling came to Marc's heart. The only thing he hated about being on a mission was being apart from her. She had always mothered him somewhat, telling him not to do dangerous things, but she was as guilty of carelessness as he had been. He hoped Marie-Thérèse was taking good care of her.

"Do you think they'd take a package to my parents for me?"

"I'm sure they would."

"She's a pretty girl," Elder Fields added.

Marc didn't have to ask who he was talking about. Ever since he had shown him Josette's picture, his companion had been infatuated. "Of course," he said, "she looks like me."

Elder Fields punched him in the shoulder. "Right. Well, what'll we do now?"

Marc considered for a moment. The setting sun sent a hazy red light echoing over the sky, but there was still time for knocking doors. It was probably the least effective way of finding investigators, but they had nothing else lined up for the evening. He made a knocking motion with his hand and his companion immediately understood.

"How about that building over there?" Marc said. "We didn't finish knocking all those doors yesterday."

They knocked at each apartment with no luck, moving to the building next door and then the one beyond. At each door the people shook their heads and sent them away. One young man seemed interested, but his father quickly appeared in the doorway behind him and pushed the boy firmly out of the way. One glance at the missionary tags was enough for him. "Excuse me, excuse me, excuse me," he said, and slammed the door in their faces so hard that Marc felt his short hair ruffle in the ensuing breeze.

He sighed. Some parts of missionary work he could definitely do without. Right now he would give almost anything for a bowl of his mother's vegetable stew and a soft bed.

They knocked on the rest of the doors with no better results. "We've got time for one more," Marc said, glancing at his watch. "If we hurry. It's almost curfew."

"I think we should try that pink building," Elder Fields said, pointing. "I've been wanting to go there for weeks." The building wasn't really pink, more of a dusty rose, but it did look incongruous among the other duller structures—perhaps some kind of a sign?

"Let's go." Marc knew enough to trust his companion's feeling. He was beginning to understand that Elder Fields was the most spiritually-attuned elder he had yet served with in the mission field.

As they walked toward their goal, two mongrel dogs sprang out of a dark corridor between two buildings and into the dim light of the street lamp. The first was big and black and ugly. The other was big and brown and just as ugly as the first. The mongrels bared their sharp teeth in ferocious growls. "Run!" Marc yelled to Elder Fields. They fled back the way they'd come, the pink building all but forgotten, keeping just ahead of the dogs. At last they spied their own apartment building. Elder Fields scooped up a few rocks and hurled them at the canines while Marc fumbled with the outside door key. They darted inside and pulled the lobby door shut as the dogs pawed on the outside.

"We've got to do something about those dogs," Elder Fields muttered.

Marc agreed. This was the third time in the last week these dogs had chased them. "Tomorrow I'll go talk to our landlady and see if she'll call somebody."

"Good idea," Elder Fields said. "This city has to have a dog catcher."

Uncharacteristically silent, they stumbled tiredly into the room they rented from the Vincent family, who were members in their ward. It had been a discouraging month for both of them. In fact, the discussion with Madame Legrand had been the most promising they had given together. Neither had seen a baptism in three months. For Elder Fields, that meant he had never had the opportunity to baptize someone he had taught.

"Can I see your sister's picture again?" Elder Fields asked.

Marc reluctantly handed it over, dreading the question he had been expecting the entire month. As expected, it came.

"I'd like to meet her someday. Do you think she'd write back if I sent her a letter?"

Marc quickly thought of an excuse. "I don't know. Her letters to me are rare enough, and I'm her twin. She might not make the effort for a stranger. She's really busy—she's usually got a lot of dates. And then there's school—"

"Yeah, you're probably right," Elder Fields said. "But she sure is pretty. There's something about her. It's obvious you are taken with her—and she's your sister. She must be a great person. Maybe I'll come to visit you after my mission and sweep her off her feet. How would you like that?"

Elder Fields had gotten down to the crux of the matter, but it wasn't him Marc worried about. He knew Josette well—she was much like he had been before missionary service changed him. She lived only for the presents people bought her, the expensive clothes, the glittering lights of the dance halls. His twin was warm, vivacious, and loving, but she was also light-minded and—Marc didn't like to admit it even to himself—frivolous. The spiritual Elder Fields could never love a woman like that, no matter how beautiful, and Marc wouldn't allow him to hurt her.

"You're not good enough for her," he said lightly. "Besides, she doesn't date younger men. You're a year younger than we are."

Elder Fields laughed. "Well, I guess I'd better work harder to impress you," he said. "The both of you. And I'm going to start with that pink building. Let's go ask Sister Vincent if she has any cayenne pepper. I've got a bone to pick with some dogs."

* * * * *

The next time they visited Madame Legrand, she had read the Book of Mormon passages, and during the ensuing discussion she accepted the idea of baptism. "I'll want to pray about it, of course," she said, blushing slightly at her own words. "But if this is true, I'll eventually accept it."

Elder Zachary Fields knew her reaction was a good sign, if not the complete conversion he and Elder Perrault had prayed for. He felt good about her tentative commitment and hoped he would be in the area to see her baptism.

"Next time the daughters will be there," Elder Perrault said, making a face. "I hope they don't destroy her testimony."

Zack hoped so, too. He put on a confident face. "Maybe on Sunday we can have a fast to help her."

"Good idea."

"Now, how about knocking that pink building we keep wanting to get to?"

His companion grimaced. "Shall we make a run for it?"

Grinning, Zack pulled a small spray bottle out of his pocket. "I don't plan on running. I have faith the dogs won't like this cayenne mixture Sister Vincent and I whipped up the other morning while you were popping pills." He held up the bottle and Elder Perrault laughed.

They walked briskly down the cobblestone sidewalk, keeping watch for the giant dogs. Night came steadily, and the missionaries jumped at each shadow. Zack's hand began to sweat around the bottle that had been in his pocket the entire day in preparation for this confrontation.

"I guess they aren't showing," Elder Perrault said with a nervous laugh. "We'll get to the pink building without a fight."

Zack knew it wouldn't be so easy; he had felt too strongly that they must visit the pink building. They went steadily on. Just when he was beginning to think his companion was right after all, the dogs jumped out in front of them, deep growls coming from the backs of their throats. Zack froze, and it seemed an eternity before he could talk his fingers into moving. The black dog circled, looking for a place to lunge, and Zack wondered how its canine mind understood that they planned to fight instead of run. Instinct, he supposed.

Elder Perrault turned with the circling dog, brandishing his scriptures like a sword. "Somehow I don't think this is what my sister had in mind when she bought these scriptures for me," he said in a shaky voice. "Uh, Elder, don't you think you should spray them now? Any closer and they'll be eating my scriptures as an appetizer."

Zack pressed the nozzle and directed the stream toward the brown dog. It snarled ferociously, but as the water and cayenne hit its unprotected eyes, the growls quickly turned into yelps of pain. The dog bounded down the street, howling. Zack didn't have time to let himself feel the unexpected pity that rushed to his heart.

The black dog attacked, but Elder Perrault blocked the slobbering mouth with his scriptures. Strong jaws closed over the edge of the books as Zack again sprayed his potion. Immediately the dog released its hold and scuttled away, whining as loud as it had ever barked.

Elder Perrault's face slowly regained its color. "Good timing," he said, pulling a tissue from his shirt pocket. Holding his scriptures gingerly, he wiped off the slobber left by the dog. Zack leaned over and saw the impressive teeth marks. "Good investment, those scriptures," he said. "They just saved you another operation."

Elder Perrault laughed. "That's one way to look at it, I guess. But next time, *I'll* do the spraying and *you* fend off the dogs."

"Deal." Zack turned his head toward the pink building. "Let's go find whoever it was we were supposed to find."

"It better be someone very special to have gone through that," his companion muttered.

"They will be," Zack said, and felt the Spirit confirm his thought.

On the third floor they met Pedro Leandro. He opened the door, his chestnut-colored face smiling. "Yes?" he asked with raised eyebrows.

"We're missionaries of the Church of Jesus Christ," Elder Perrault began, "and we have an important message to share."

"Do you believe in Christ?" Zack picked up on his cue. As they spoke, dark head after dark head appeared behind the man. There were four children in all, and a grandmother.

"I do," the man said.

"Could we share our message with you?" Zack asked. The children clapped their hands at his accent and begged their father to let them in.

"It's just a message, isn't it?" he asked. "Without obligations?"

"Yes," Elder Perrault said. "We just want everyone to hear for themselves about Jesus."

"Well . . . ," the man said, vacillating.

"Are these all your children?" asked Zack. In France he had discovered that most people had only a few children; but he had also noticed that those of African descent, like this man, tended to have more children—as if their desire for family took precedence over their desire for wealth.

"They certainly are." The man's words held a trace of pride. He introduced each of the four children by name, and his wife's mother as well.

"It reminds me of my house," Elder Perrault said. "I have five brothers and sisters."

"I have four sisters," Zack put in, "and I sure do miss them."

"You're not from around here, are you?" one of the kids asked.

Zack bent down to speak to the child on eye level. "No, I'm from America. And I miss my family. But maybe I can come back and play with you guys when we come to give your parents our message. What do you say?" He glanced up at their father.

"My wife isn't home right now," the man said. "But come back when she's here."

"How about Saturday at one?" Elder Perrault asked, pulling out his appointment book.

"That'll be fine. But with no obligation, you understand."

"Oh, yes. See? I've written it right here." Elder Perrault held out the book.

"Without obligations," read the man. He smiled, showing a row of white teeth that seemed even brighter by contrast with his dark skin.

"Good-bye then." Zack waved to the children. "See you on Saturday."

They left the building, heading for home to beat their curfew. Zack kept a look out, but the dogs didn't return.

"Without obligations," Elder Perrault said sadly as he undressed for the night.

Zack understood how his companion was feeling. Too many times he had seen people react that way, and usually they wouldn't keep their appointment. But something was different about this family; Zack could feel it. He had learned in the Missionary Training Center to heed those feelings.

"Remember the dogs," he said. "Monsieur Leandro will be there."

Elder Perrault's face brightened. "I hope so. I really liked the children. Especially the little girl—Sofia, wasn't it? She is so full of excitement and, well, innocent joy. She reminds me a little of my sister Pauline." He hit his chest near his heart, his voice becoming gruff with emotion. "I can't explain it exactly, but the idea that they might not accept hurts right here. Sofia deserves to know her Savior. They all do."

Zack put his hand on Elder Perrault's shoulder. "I know," he said. "And we're going to help them. I think that feeling you're having is the Lord's way of letting you know how important they are to him. I feel it too."

Elder Perrault's gaze shifted to the family picture on the dresser, and Zack felt his companion's homesickness as if it were his own—with one difference. Zack missed his family, especially his little sister, Brionney, but strangely his thoughts turned more and more to Elder Perrault's twin. She was beautiful, but there was something else in her face, some quality that called to Zack's heart and soul. He knew her name—Josette—but his companion was remarkably close-mouthed about anything else. Zack wished he could ask to see the close-up picture Elder Perrault carried in his wallet, but every time he did, his companion became defensive.

Zack shook off the frustration and knelt with Elder Perrault for their companion prayer, forcing himself to focus on the task to which he had willingly pledged two years of his life. However potent, his feelings for this woman he had never met would have to wait.

CHAPTER THREE

Josette stared at the array of clothing piled on her bed, mostly warm-looking items. Six tall stacks to take, two smaller ones to leave behind. Her heart felt heavy as she lifted a handful of blouses and plopped them into the suitcase, blinking back the tears stinging her eyes.

I don't want to go! she cried silently. *Oh, Marc, where are you when I need you?* She felt angry and sad all at once. *Who am I? Why don't I know that when I'm not with Marc?* He had been with her since their conception—was that why she hated being alone?

In front of the other single bed against the far wall, Marie-Thérèse's two suitcases were already neatly packed, ready for tomorrow's flight. Josette slumped to her bed and let her chin drop to her chest, but a rustling sound made her look up again.

Her little sister Pauline stood quietly in the doorway. She was almost exactly Josette's height, and her eyes and short hair were just as dark, but there the comparison ended. Pauline was infinitely thinner than anyone Josette had ever known. Her face was pleasant to look at, but it held obvious marks of the many illnesses she had survived. She was often sick, especially of late, and spent a good deal of time at the AIDS clinic. Her HIV wasn't yet officially AIDS, but the line grew thinner each year. At sixteen, Pauline had already lived longer than the doctors had predicted at her birth. A miracle? Josette thought so.

Pauline came over and began to take Josette's clothes out of the suitcase and repack them carefully. "You don't want them to get wrinkled," she said with her ever-ready smile. "I know how you hate to iron."

"Marie-Thérèse will be there," Josette said.

Pauline snorted. "She doesn't like to iron either."

"But she'll do it."

As Josette watched her sister pack, emotion overwhelmed her, and she put her face in her hands, sobbing. Pauline dropped the clothes and stepped in front of her, reaching to push Josette's hands away from her face. "What's wrong?" she asked.

"I can't do this," Josette wailed.

Pauline hugged her sister's head, pulling it against her stomach. Josette's arms came up around Pauline's thin body. "Can't do what?" Pauline asked.

Josette sniffed. "Go to America."

Pauline pulled away slightly to look down at her. "I thought you were excited to go."

"At first I was," Josette confessed. It was easy to talk with Pauline; it had always been so. She was a light that lit up every room, and her quick smile always showed her love. "But I think . . . well . . ." Her voice lowered. "I was so ready to leave, but I'm a little afraid. I'm scared to leave my family."

"But we'll be right here when you come back."

"Will you?" Josette sat up straight and gazed earnestly at her little sister. "Will all of you? Do we ever know?"

Pauline sat on the bed beside her. "I guess we don't ever know for certain, but we can't stop living because we're afraid. You know what I think? I think you're just missing Marc. If he were going with you, he'd have you laughing at yourself so fast, you'd forget you were scared."

Josette smiled in spite of herself. "Yeah, he would, wouldn't he?" She sighed. "Oh, I guess I'm being stupid. I just keep wondering what it's going to be like. I mean, here I have lots of friends and boyfriends—even if most aren't in the Church. But there? I don't know what to expect."

Pauline's face lit up, and her laugh echoed through the room. "You're worried about guys, aren't you? That's the real reason you don't want to go. Why, that's funny!" If it had been anyone else, Josette would have been defensive, but Pauline's amusement lacked even the slightest trace of malice.

Pauline laid her head on Josette's shoulder. "Men will be men whatever their nationality, won't they? Those American boys don't stand a chance. I think you'll be a star with a hoard of worshippers in no time." She fingered Josette's straight hair. "You're so pretty; I wish I could look like you."

Josette hugged her sister, thinking that her inner beauty made up for the ravages of the HIV. "Thank you," she whispered. "I love you."

Pauline smiled. "So are we going to pack or not?"

* * * * *

Later that night as the family was finishing dinner, their mother brought out a square package and placed it on the table. "Will one of you have space for this?" she asked.

Josette eyed the parcel doubtfully, thinking of all the things she would already be leaving behind. "What is it?"

"A package from Marc—or from his American companion. You know, the new one, Elder Fields. He sent it in the hopes that you'd have room to take it to his family in America. They live in Provo, he says, not too far away from BYU."

"I don't have a centimeter of room left," Josette said. "What does Marc's companion think we are, the postal service?"

Ariana's eyes closed, but before she could say anything, Marie-Thérèse said, "He just wants to send his family some presents without it costing him his food money." She picked up the package. "I have room. It's not very big."

"Look, Elder Fields sent a picture of his family," their father said, handing a photograph to Marie-Thérèse.

"I suppose they want us to take the package right to their house," Josette grumbled. "And they'll probably want us to look at family pictures for hours."

Marie-Thérèse stared at the picture. "That wouldn't be too fun," she agreed. "Even if he is cute."

Josette grabbed the picture. A blond-headed family stared out at her: parents, four daughters, and one son. She looked again. One very handsome son, tall, with broad shoulders, blue eyes, and brilliant white hair. "This is Elder Fields? Well, maybe looking at his pictures wouldn't be so bad. I could stand to look at him for a while, couldn't you, Marie-Thérèse?"

Pauline giggled, and seventeen-year-old André rolled his eyes. "And they say men are bad for judging by looks," he said.

The buzzer in the hallway interrupted any retorts the girls might have come up with. Louis-Géralde pushed back his chair and scrambled into the entryway. "I got it, I got it!" he squealed with all the excitement of a four-year-old. Josette followed him, hoping Alphonse had come to say good-bye. This would be their last chance to be together until Christmas.

Jumping onto a wooden stool that Louis-Géralde kept in the spacious entryway for just such occasions, he jabbed at the black intercom button with his chubby fingers. "Who is it?" he called.

"Aunt Lu-Lu," came a crackly voice.

"Who?" Louis-Géralde said. "I don't have an Aunt Lu-Lu." He threw back his head and laughed with abandon.

Josette reached around his small head and pushed the button. Her brother jumped from the stool and landed on the polished wood floor with a loud crash. He opened the door to the hall and waited for the elevator to bring the visitors, dancing excitedly from one foot to the other.

When Lu-Lu arrived, she wasn't alone. Not only was her two-year-old daughter Mimi with her, but also her best friend Danielle Massoni and her two children, Raoul and Rebekka. Both women were striking, and Josette openly admired them.

"We've come to say good-bye," Lu-Lu said in heavily accented English. She had short brown hair dyed with red highlights, and beautiful green-brown eyes like Josette's father, who was her brother. Normally she was thin, but now her figure swelled with a new pregnancy.

"Thank you," Josette replied in the same language. Those two words at least came easily. Ever since she was small, she had taken English in their private school and had practiced with the missionaries. She felt she knew the language passably well, though her French accent was much heavier than Marie-Thérèse's.

"Play!" Mimi tugged, freeing her hand from her mother's. She toddled toward Louis-Géralde, who motioned to Danielle's children to follow him. Though Raoul was twelve and Rebekka ten, they were his favorite playmates.

"Behave yourselves," Danielle said to them. Josette thought the warning useless because Raoul and Rebekka were the most well-behaved children she had ever known, perhaps because their father insisted on strict obedience. Josette had never liked him, and she couldn't understand why Danielle put up with him at all—especially since he still refused to take the missionary discussions. At least he had allowed his wife and children to become members.

"I'm so excited for you, Josette!" Danielle said when the children had vanished. She was also slender like Lu-Lu, but her thick auburn hair fell mid-way down her back, almost as long as Josette's own. Her large gray eyes held an undeniable childlike quality, despite her thirty-three years. She had sculpted eyebrows that set off her eyes even further, drawing so much attention that one hardly had time to notice the stylish clothing she always wore. "America! Ever since I joined the Church I've wanted to see it. Just think! You'll be able to go to conference and see the prophet in person! And the Salt Lake Temple! I'm so jealous!"

Josette found herself being swept up in Danielle's enthusiasm. "I'll send you pictures," she volunteered.

"Oh, would you? Thank you so much! But speaking of pictures"—she fumbled in her alligator skin bag—"I wanted you to see what Mathieu looked like, since he's going to pick you up at the airport in Salt Lake City. Oh, I can't find it."

"Don't worry about it," said Lu-Lu. "He'll probably be the only French man at the airport."

Danielle laughed. "You're right. Just remember that besides the dark hair, he looks kind of German. Our grandmother was from Germany. We named Rebekka after her."

"That's why you spell it funny," Josette said.

"The girls did meet Mathieu once before," Lu-Lu interjected. "Don't you remember?"

"Oh, that's right," Danielle said. "It was at my baptism."

Josette remembered—faintly. She had been sixteen then. Mathieu had been twenty-one and a new member himself; his cousin's bubbly eagerness to share the gospel had already brought fruits, even before her husband agreed to her own baptism. Mathieu had seemed nice enough to Josette, but had been gangling and awkward and too shy for good conversation. She had given him up after a few minutes for someone more interesting.

"Anyway, would you take this package to him?" Danielle asked. It was the size of a shoe box.

Josette sighed. "I guess so."

"So what are you doing out there?" Ariana called from the kitchen. "Come on in here. We have plenty of dessert."

Josette followed the women into the kitchen, where the children were already elbow-deep in huge bowls of bread pudding. She handed the package Danielle had given her to Marie-Thérèse. "Could you squeeze this in?" she asked. "It's for Mathieu."

Marie-Thérèse made a face, but she set the package next to the one Elder Fields had sent.

Josette watched her family, feeling oddly detached. She didn't know how to describe the aching pain she felt in her heart, the hurt she had been feeling for so long. There seemed no purpose in life, no joy that she could hold inside forever. Was something wrong with her?

The only thing that chased the melancholy feeling away was to keep busy, to have fun. But that glittering world washed away too easily when she was alone.

Alone. *I miss Marc so much!* she thought. She squeezed her eyes as the emotions washed over her. Such severe feelings of sadness hadn't overcome her since her brother had almost died in the explosion shortly before their sixteenth birthday. Marie-Thérèse was her best friend and confidante, but her twin brother was part of her soul. Could there be any closer bond? Even in a marriage? If the men she had dated were any indication, Josette didn't think so.

To Josette's delight, Alphonse arrived before eight, and he took her out to dinner. She didn't confess that she had already eaten earlier with her family. Besides, she had only picked at the food to please her mother.

"Why so sad?" he asked as they finished their meal. He moved his thick eyebrows expressively as he talked. Josette enjoyed his dark good looks, but his nearness no longer made her tremble.

"I'm going to miss you," she said. It was true, yet not quite.

"But of course you'll miss me," he said. "And I you. We've had fun together. But we can't stop the rest of our lives for a little fun. If we are both still around at Christmas . . ." His comments made

Josette even more depressed. She knew he wouldn't be waiting around for her.

"Look," he said, bringing a hand from his pocket, "I brought you a present."

Josette clapped her hands together, the sadness vanishing. "Oh, Alphonse, you shouldn't have!"

He chuckled. "I know how you enjoy presents. Besides, now that I'm graduated and working at my grandfather's hotel, I can afford it."

She opened the small box to reveal a gold butterfly brooch, sparkling with diamond dust. "It's beautiful," she said, jumping up to kiss him lingeringly on the mouth. Heads turned their way, but she enjoyed the attention. For all the onlookers knew, Alphonse could have just proposed.

And why hadn't he? He had said many times that he loved her. Josette guessed it was not the marrying kind of love. Besides, what would she have said if he had asked her to marry him? She knew she didn't love him—not that much. He was simply an excuse she had used to try and convince her parents to let her stay in France.

"I love it," she added, slightly more subdued.

"Of course you do," he said. He tried to fasten it to her dress. "It's the one we saw in the store last week."

"How wonderful of you to remember!" He was right, she loved presents, and he had bought her enough of them to have realized just how much. "Here, let me do that," she said. She wore her black spaghetti strap dress, and his fingers were embarrassingly close to her skin.

When they left the restaurant and returned to his car, Alphonse kissed her hand repeatedly, then began working his way up her arm to her neck. "I can make you happy," he said, huskily. "And you can show me just how much you like your new bauble, and how much you're going to miss me in America."

"Don't," Josette said, pushing him back. He sounded more idiotic than a character in a poorly made film. Today she had been crying about leaving him, but now she wanted only to get away. "I need to get home."

Alphonse's black eyes narrowed in anger, but he submitted to her request. "I don't understand you," he said as he dropped her off outside her apartment building. "One moment you're hot, the next cold. Are you simply playing with me?" Before she could reply, he went on. "I hope you have a good life in America. I hope you find whatever it is you're looking for."

Josette wanted to throw the pin at him, but it was so pretty that she restrained herself. *It's mine,* she thought. *And I don't owe him anything for it!* But she felt that she did. Was that the only reason he had given it to her—to make her feel obligated?

Feeling numb, she watched Alphonse speed off. It was always the same. Men treated her like a queen at first, but it quickly degenerated into what she would or would not do with them. She smoothed the tight-fitting column dress her mother had not approved of. She knew she looked good—more than good. But why did she feel so empty?

"What is it I'm looking for?" she wondered aloud. "Alphonse doesn't know what he's talking about. I have everything I need. The only thing that's missing is . . . Oh, I think I hate you, Alphonse."

She rode up the elevator and unlocked the door quietly, not wanting to disturb her family. There was a light in the kitchen and she approached it, driven like a moth.

"She shouldn't have left tonight," her father was saying. "She should have stayed here with her family. She didn't even say good-bye to her grandparents."

"They said they'd come by tomorrow," her mother replied.

"They shouldn't have to. Josette needs to think more about others."

"She's young yet," Ariana said.

"So is Marie-Thérèse."

"Josette's not Marie-Thérèse. She has different problems and challenges."

"Well, I hope BYU straightens her out," Jean-Marc said. "Her grades have been terrible, and it doesn't help that she keeps changing her major. She doesn't know what she wants."

Josette bit her lip and pushed the hair out of her eyes. Anger and humiliation spread through her heart. How dare they talk about her this way! She was an adult, not a child! And she couldn't help it that Marie-Thérèse had always known exactly what she would do with her life—a mission, a finance degree, a home and children. Except for marriage and a baby, Josette didn't see the joy in any of her sister's goals.

As for the rest of her siblings, they also had blueprints for their lives. André and Marc planned to go into engineering, Pauline wanted to work with people who had AIDS, and even Louis-Géralde said he was going to be a letter carrier. Her littlest brother thought it must be the "funnest" job in the whole world, and he met the mailman each day in the lobby of their apartment building to practice putting the letters in the boxes. As for Josette, she wanted to live, to . . . to . . .

She didn't know what she wanted. At BYU she had signed up to learn about interior decorating. Maybe that would be her niche.

"Josette's going to BYU is the right thing to do," her mother said. "Some of us need a little extra push." Ariana's voice had a faraway quality. Josette heard a rustling, and she assumed her father was taking her mother into his arms.

"I'm so lucky to have you," Jean-Marc whispered.

"We are both lucky," Ariana said.

The love in their voices made Josette want to sob. *That's what I want,* she thought. *But why can't I find it?* She had dated at least a hundred boys and men, but not one had loved her like that.

Slowly, she walked back to the door to the apartment, opened it noisily, then slammed it for good measure. Her parents' faces appeared in the kitchen doorway, framed by light from behind.

"Your grandparents were here," Jean-Marc said.

"I'm sorry I missed them." Josette hesitated, knowing what they wanted to hear, but not wanting to give in. *I'm not a child!* "I know I shouldn't have gone," she said. "I'm sorry."

Her parents exchanged a pleased look and Josette was glad she had said the words, even if she hadn't meant them. Jean-Marc kissed her on both cheeks. "I'm going to bed," he said. "We all have an early day tomorrow." He grinned, and Josette felt herself smile back mechanically. "Not all of us will spend the day sleeping on a plane." He touched Ariana's shoulder, letting his hand linger.

"I'll be there in a minute," she said. Jean-Marc let the hand drop and went down the hall.

Ariana put her arm around Josette's back, eyeing the thin spaghetti straps. "You're not taking that to America, are you?" she asked.

Josette didn't answer. "Do you ever miss your brother?" she asked.

Ariana watched her for a full minute in silence. "Come in here and let's talk about it," she said finally. "I'll make some hot choco-late." As Josette sat at the table, Ariana pulled out two mugs, filled them with milk, and put them in the microwave Jean-Marc had bought when Louis-Géralde was born.

"Ouch," she said, bringing the steaming mugs to the table. "Careful, it's hot." She put a spoon of chocolate in her milk and mixed methodically, then passed the container to Josette. "My brother was very much like your brother," she said after taking a sip. "I loved him every bit as much as you love Marc, maybe more. You have other brothers and sisters, and I had only Antoine. But someday you will find a relationship even better than the one you share with him. And he will find that also."

"Like you and Dad."

"Yes, but—"Ariana's voice broke off as if she was uncertain how to continue. "But to find that, you have to remember what your destiny is. You are a princess, destined to be a royal queen."

Josette stifled a sigh. For as long as she could remember, her mother had told her these same words, but they didn't seem to have meaning in this life, only in death. And why would she want to think about death? She knew her mother's crusade had something to do with the death of her half sister, Nette, the child born to Ariana during her first marriage before she joined the Church. Her mother wanted them to be righteous enough to be reunited with her one day. It was a worthy goal, but so remote. An unattainable dream.

"You have to insist on being treated like a queen," her mother continued.

"Okay," Josette said dully, wanting only to wipe the anxiety from her mother's face. "I'll be good."

Ariana smiled. "I know. And I love you."

Josette wished she had said she was proud instead.

She kissed her mother good night and headed for the room she had shared with Marie-Thérèse since they were four. Her sister was sound asleep, and Josette undressed quietly in the dark. She smiled grimly, then rolled up the black silk dress and slipped it into the only spot left in her suitcase.

Inside, her hand touched the photograph of Elder Fields and his family, and she pulled it out. Though it was too dark to make out the faces, she saw his white hair and blue eyes vividly in her mind. He appeared so nice, not to mention good-looking. But appearances could be deceiving. Deep in his heart, was he like Alphonse? Or more like the stuffy young men in her stake, who couldn't seem to choose what socks to wear without praying about it?

She flung herself into bed, still clutching the photograph, but it was a long time before sleep came.

CHAPTER FOUR

A somber pall settled over the van, completely blotting out any joy—or at least Ariana thought so before she looked around and realized that it was only she and Josette who seemed to feel the gloom. Marie-Thérèse sat in the middle seat next to the brooding Josette, busily practicing her English phrases, a smile on her narrow face. André and Pauline sat in the back, heads close together as usual, giggling and laughing. Louis-Géralde sat between them, enjoying their attention if not understanding everything they said.

Ariana found herself looking for her oldest son, Marc, before she remembered that he was serving a mission. The army had rejected him for the year of mandatory service, but the Lord hadn't cared about Marc's kidney transplant, despite the immunosuppression medicine he took daily. For her part, Ariana was content that her son was serving in France so he would be close in case something happened.

Thank you, Jacques, she thought, *for saving my son. For giving him your kidney.* Briefly, Ariana wondered how her ex-husband and his new wife were doing. Since the birth of their baby boy in Nice three years earlier, she had heard nothing. They had received the missionaries and his wife had been baptized, but had Jacques joined the Church?

Jean-Marc's hand reached out and caressed her arm. "It's all right," he mouthed. "We're doing the right thing."

She hoped he was right. Josette was floundering, and Ariana didn't know how to help her. *What did I do wrong?* she asked herself repeatedly. But she knew Josette had to make her own choices, had to somehow develop her own testimony. Ariana had seen her decline, and she worried constantly that the passion and inconsistencies in her daughter would lead her to a life of sadness and despair. Each night she and Jean-Marc knelt and prayed fervently for help—and this was the answer. How could sending her away be the answer? *I must trust in the Lord*, she thought.

She kissed her daughters good-bye at the airport, not bothering to hide the tears in her eyes. "I love you," she whispered as she hugged them.

Then they were gone. André led the way back to the car with Louis-Géralde on his shoulders, both laughing. Pauline put her skinny arm around Ariana. "I love you, Mom." Her smile sent a ray of light into Ariana's heart, while at the same time bringing a dread.

"I still think we should have told them," Ariana said.

Pauline shook her head, her smile never dimming. "They wouldn't have gone."

She was right. But Ariana hoped Josette and Marie-Thérèse would forgive her later.

"Come on, Mom," Pauline said. "We always knew it would happen one day, didn't we? And I'm not too sick yet. I don't want people waiting around and watching. When the time comes, we'll send for them." She squeezed Ariana's arm and bounded to catch up with her brothers.

Ariana stumbled, and Jean-Marc put his arm around her. She sighed and leaned into him. "She's wrong," she said softly. "I *didn't* know it would happen. I kept waiting for her to be cured. For a miracle. You've heard the stories of the children born with AIDS, who months or even years later have no trace of the virus in their bodies. It does happen. I thought it would happen to her. And when it didn't, I—I still kept praying." She broke off. "I've grown too comfortable with the postponement, so much so that I thought it was suspended forever, even without the full miracle."

Her husband's arm tightened. "I know just how you feel."

Ariana was grateful for his support. He hadn't been with her last month when the doctor had informed her that Pauline's HIV had become AIDS, that it was only a matter of time until the new tumor in her stomach would kill her, but he hadn't let her go to the doctor alone since. Still, it was as though the world had ended that day, and they now lived in a strange suspension . . . waiting.

She wanted to scream and cry and yell. There was so much good in her life: Marc serving a mission, Marie-Thérèse doing well in college, André active at church, and her relationship with Jean-Marc growing ever sweeter. But now suddenly the joy was scrunched into a small place, locked away by the knowledge that Pauline would soon die.

Ariana had known sixteen years ago, when she had first held a premature Pauline in her arms, that this day would come. She remembered vividly the undeniable bond she had shared with the newborn infant, along with the insufferable fear, the all-encompassing ache in her heart that came with knowing that she was setting herself up for this experience. Yet she had taken Pauline into her home and had done the thing that would cause her both the most pain and the most joy: she had loved the HIV-positive baby as her own.

How could she let Pauline go now?

A traitorous part of her recognized that at least the sword had finally fallen, the worst had been realized. There was some minuscule relief in knowing that nothing worse could happen. Now she had to reach out to the Lord and into her soul to find the strength to face Pauline's impending death and the words to help her daughter be ready.

She had done it before long ago with Paulette, Pauline's birth mother; it didn't get any easier with time.

* * * * *

Later that night Ariana awoke, hearing something that didn't match the usual night sounds. At first she thought Louis-Géralde might be having another attack of the stomach flu he had suffered the week before, but the sounds came from Pauline's room.

"Jean-Marc!"

Without waiting for a reply, Ariana jumped from the bed and ran to the next room, her heart pounding in alarm. Quickly switching on the light, she found Pauline sitting up in bed, heaving. Her frightened eyes blinked at the sudden brightness. Ariana rushed to the bed and put her arms around Pauline, who moaned softly.

"I'm sorry, Mom. I couldn't make it to the bathroom. My stomach hurt so bad. I couldn't move."

Ariana held Pauline's head against her breast, smoothing her hair.

"It's all right. Don't worry about it. It'll wash." How easy it was to be nice to her. Ariana would gladly clean up after her daughter for a lifetime if that meant she would live.

Jean-Marc appeared in the doorway, his hair tousled. "Are you all right?" he asked anxiously, coming toward the bed.

"I feel a little better now," Pauline murmured weakly.

"We'd still better take you to the doctor first thing in the morning," Ariana said.

"It's just the flu, like Louis-Géralde had," Pauline said. "I'll be okay."

But Ariana knew that a sickness like this could kill her daughter as surely as the cancerous tumor. With Acquired Immune Deficiency Syndrome, nothing was minor. "It's just to be sure," she said lightly. Jean-Marc met her gaze, and his finger reached out and caught the tear on her cheek. Ariana pressed her face against his hand.

"Why don't you two get cleaned up and go to our bed?" Jean-Marc said. "I'll take care of things in here."

Pauline looked embarrassed. "Thanks, Dad."

Ariana found a new nightshirt in Pauline's drawer and helped her to the bathtub. When Jean-Marc finished cleaning, he gave Pauline a blessing. The three then spent the rest of the night sleeping in the hall next to the bathroom, so Pauline could throw up in the toilet if necessary. In the morning Ariana felt sick herself, but she wouldn't let Jean-Marc take Pauline to the doctor alone.

"We'll have to keep her in the hospital for a few days to be sure," the doctor said. "Even though she's not throwing up anymore, she's still losing a lot of fluids through her bowels. We have to make sure her body is getting enough liquids so she doesn't get too weak."

"Don't worry, Mom," Pauline said after the doctor left. "I'm going to be fine." Though she looked fragile, her face was its normal ray of sunshine. But despite the brave words and the smile, the way Pauline's hands clenched the thin blanket told Ariana how frightened she felt inside.

"Of course you're going to be fine," Ariana said. "But it's okay to be afraid."

"I'm not," Pauline insisted.

"Then why don't you try to sleep? You need to gain some strength."

A shadow passed over Pauline's face. "Where will you be?"

"Right here," Ariana said. "And Dad will stay too. André is with Louis-Géralde, so we don't have to hurry home."

Pauline settled obediently down in the hospital bed and closed her eyes. Ariana sat in the chair next to the bed and put her hand over Pauline's. With a silent prayer, she began a fast. When Jean-Marc brought her breakfast, she refused to eat, but by lunchtime she was shaking and could hardly think. Her muscles ached and her head felt light.

"You must eat, Ari," Jean-Marc said, kneeling beside her chair. "You're not doing Pauline or any of us any good."

"I'm fasting."

"You're sick yourself. You've had little sleep in the past week, being up with Louis-Géralde and worrying about Josette. I don't think now's the time to fast."

Ariana bristled. "I have to get Pauline well." She darted a glance at the pale face of their sleeping daughter. "You know as well as I do that she could die from this. Why didn't I keep her away from Louise-Géralde?"

"You sent her to your mother's for a week. What more could you have done?" Jean-Marc grabbed her hand. "Don't do this to yourself, Ari. Your daughter needs you, and you shouldn't fast when you're sick. Let me and the rest of our family do it. Please."

Ariana looked at the food he had brought from the hospital cafeteria. Though she couldn't tell what kind of meat lay next to the rice and french fries, it looked and smelled much better than any hospital food she could remember. Her stomach growled, and she hated herself for her weakness.

"Ari, your body is a temple and you have to take care of it. The Lord will understand. Remember that you are only required to run as fast as you are able."

The logical side of her knew Jean-Marc was right. *Please forgive me, Lord,* she prayed. *I promise, I'll fast next week when I'm better. And please, help Pauline.*

After eating lunch, Ariana felt considerably better, but she worried that her lack of sacrifice would bode ill for Pauline. Then she chided herself, knowing that the Lord did not ask for more than she was able to give. Besides, sending Josette to America had been right, and surely the Lord didn't mean for Pauline to die without her sisters present. Or did he?

Don't second-guess your inspiration, she told herself. But why did everything seem out of her control?

The next day Pauline was much stronger, and Jean-Marc returned to work. "The doctors said I could probably take you home tomorrow," Ariana said to her daughter.

Pauline hugged Ariana. "See? I told you. But thanks for staying with me, Mom."

"I'll be here whenever you need me," Ariana replied.

For a fleeting moment, Pauline looked sad, but she kept her thoughts to herself. "I know," she said with a bright smile.

Ariana laid her head on the pillow next to Pauline's, filled with gratefulness to the Lord for the additional moments they had been given. There was still time for a miracle.

CHAPTER FIVE

The flight to New York was long, but not very tedious. Marie-Thérèse kept busy studying her English dictionary, reading the American classic *To Kill a Mockingbird,* or simply watching the other passengers on the plane. Everything was new and exciting. She had flown before, but had never been outside France except for traveling to either the Swiss or German temples to do baptisms for the dead.

At first she tried to talk with Josette, but her sister slumped morosely in the aisle seat, an ugly scowl on her pretty face. Marie-Thérèse left her alone, knowing that Josette's temper would fade as the miles passed below them.

Shortly before they arrived in New York, a young man walked down the aisle, and Josette perked up. Before Marie-Thérèse realized what was happening, he had switched seats with the woman across from Josette, and they leaned over the aisle conversing in English. Josette had a fairly strong accent, and the words came slowly, but she improved with each try. Her smile flashed, bright like the sun, and her laughter made those around join in.

Marie-Thérèse shifted uncomfortably in the coach seat. Her flight bag and the package for Mathieu stuck awkwardly out from under the seat. There hadn't been space in her luggage, but she didn't mind taking the package. If only it weren't so cumbersome.

In New York they passed through Customs, and Marie-Thérèse had to open her luggage. As she did, she realized that half of one of her suitcases carried items that should have been divided between her and Josette—the goodies their mother had sent, the hangers for their clothes, the books on American culture their grandparents had purchased, Elder Fields' package, and finally the stuffed bear that Louis-Géralde had sent with them so they wouldn't miss him.

No wonder she didn't have room for Mathieu's package! She stifled the resentment before it built. Josette, completely oblivious, flirted with the man at Customs. He waved her along without opening her cases.

With relief, they finally checked their luggage and settled to wait for their domestic flight. "Maybe this isn't so bad," Josette said.

"Did you give him your number?" Marie-Thérèse asked.

"Who?"

"The boy on the plane."

Josette snorted scornfully. "Not him. He's too young. I wouldn't date someone younger than me. Besides, he lives in someplace called Montana. It's not on my itinerary." She giggled. "But he was cute."

Marie-Thérèse sighed and looked away, wishing she could have stayed in France and prepared for her mission. Twice a week she had been going on divisions with the missionaries, and she had learned the discussions well. In her purse, she had a Book of Mormon the missionaries had challenged her to give away on her flight. Now who could she give—

"Hi again."

They looked up to see the boy from the plane. "Hi," Marie-Thérèse said. Could it be she was to give the book to him?

"Oh, Braden, how wonderful," Josette said. "I was just about to get something to eat. Will you join me?" She waved a hand at the fast food restaurants lining the wall. "Marie-Thérèse can watch our bags." She smiled sweetly. "We'll bring you something back."

"Don't be late," Marie-Thérèse said. It would be just like Josette to miss the plane.

The pair came back as their flight was boarding. "Just in time," Josette said breezily, shoving a carton of french fries at Marie-Thérèse. "Thank you so much for lunch, Braden."

"But—"

Josette kissed his cheek, picked up her single carry-on bag, and started for the gate. Braden's mouth stayed open and his face flushed. Marie-Thérèse had no doubt that he was considerably poorer than he had been before meeting her sister, and had not even her telephone number to show for it.

"Here," Marie-Thérèse said softly, placing the book in his hands. "It's my gift to you." Embarrassed, she turned and fled the way Josette had gone, juggling her flight bag, purse, and french fries in one hand and her ticket and Mathieu's package in the other.

The flight was a repeat of the first one, except now the food served was American. Marie-Thérèse tried to sleep a little as it was bedtime in France, but Josette had come to life and there was no stopping the incessant words pouring from her mouth. Marie-Thérèse listened, even laughing occasionally. She loved her sister despite her lack of . . . She pushed the thought aside. It wasn't hers to judge, not really. Whatever made Josette happy was all right by her.

They arrived in Salt Lake City after ten, local time, and stumbled down the ramp searching for Mathieu, hoping they would recognize him. As the crowd of people cleared, Marie-Thérèse saw a young man with black hair and impressive dark eyes. He lounged in a chair, a relaxed smile on his face. "There he is," she said.

Josette stopped and stared, unmindful of the people who jostled past her. "I don't remember him looking this way," she said. "He's gorgeous."

Marie-Thérèse laughed. Mathieu's lanky figure had filled out since they had seen him last, but he had always been good-looking to her. "Come on," she said to Josette, who surreptitiously checked her face in her compact. "You look fine."

"I look a mess," Josette said, snapping the compact shut and popping it into her bag. "Hey, where is that package, anyway? I'll give it to him." She snatched the parcel out of Marie-Thérèse's hands and shot forward, an alluring smile on her face.

"Mathieu," she said, putting her face forward for the customary kisses. "How good to see you again!" Marie-Thérèse thought her sister exaggerated the amount of kisses. "Look what I've brought you from France," Josette continued. "Or rather," she added when she saw her sister's face, "what *we've* brought you. Marie-Thérèse carried it most of the way."

Marie-Thérèse's annoyance ended with her sister's confession. Mathieu met her gaze, taking her hand and kissing her cheeks as he had her sister's, and she found his closeness affected her in a way she hadn't expected. Why did her heart beat so fast?

"Marie-Thérèse," he said warmly, "I've been looking forward to seeing you again ever since our long conversation at my cousin's baptism. Tell me how you've been. Do you still plan on serving a mission?"

"Yes," she said. "I'll be putting in my papers soon. I'm excited to go."

"So was I. It was a wonderful experience."

"You went on a mission?" Josette asked, a slight pout to her lips.

Mathieu laughed. "Yes, I just got back last year. And I came back to BYU to finish my degree. This'll be my last semester."

"You were here before?" Josette asked.

"Of course he was; don't you *ever* listen?" Marie-Thérèse said, exasperated. "At Danielle's baptism he said he was coming to Provo for his third year in college, his first at BYU."

"I had some time before I could serve a mission," Mathieu said, picking up their bags. "I was twenty-one, but I hadn't been a member long enough to go on a mission at the time."

"That makes you twenty-five now," Josette said.

Mathieu's laugh was warm. "Guilty as charged."

"It seems like a lot of time to finish a degree," Josette said. "Wasn't it hard to come back to it after the interruption?"

"It wasn't exactly an interruption, just a different vein of study. I wouldn't change one bit of it. My mission taught me things I could never learn in school."

Marie-Thérèse liked his easy confidence and the words he obviously meant. He didn't think of missionary service as having slowed his career, but rather having enhanced and prepared him for life, while at the same time giving him an opportunity to help people. That's exactly how she thought of a mission.

"I'm glad we came here to study," Josette said, surprising Marie-Thérèse.

"So am I," Mathieu returned, but he looked at Marie-Thérèse as he spoke. Her insides churned and suddenly her knees felt strangely weak, making it hard to stand. Not for anything could she tear her eyes away from his.

"Let's go get our luggage, huh?" she said to break the spell.

Mathieu nodded in agreement and Josette hooked a proprietary arm through his, urging him on. Marie-Thérèse followed a step behind, feeling a loss she couldn't pinpoint. But Mathieu slowed slightly and matched his step with hers.

"Have you been waiting for us long?" Josette asked, gazing up at him with a captivating smile.

"Not too long," he said. "And seeing the two of you, it was well worth the wait."

* * * * *

Mathieu took them to the apartment he had found for them off State Street in Provo. "It's within walking distance of campus," he said after carrying their suitcases up to the fourth floor apartment. "I'll leave you to settle in, but I'll come around tomorrow and give you a tour so you'll be able to find your classes next week."

"Thank you so much," Josette said, pleased with Mathieu's thoughtfulness. And he was so good-looking!

He handed her a piece of paper. "Here's my number if you need anything. I just live a couple of buildings over."

"I'm so glad you're here, Mathieu." Josette gave him a hug. "What would we do without you?"

He grinned. "You'd think of something. For someone with your looks, I'm sure you could find a hoard of willing males."

Josette smiled doubtfully, uncertain whether he had given her a compliment or not. "Hmmm," she said.

"And as to the kissing, they don't do it here," Mathieu said. "So remember that, or people might think you're forward."

Marie-Thérèse laughed. "Did we scare you? Have you been among these Americans too long?"

"I thought Americans were warm-blooded," Josette said.

Mathieu chuckled. "I'll say they are. Wait until it gets cold and people are still wearing shorts and short-sleeved shirts to school. They're a bunch of nuts if I ever saw them."

"Dang, and I only brought one pair of shorts!" Josette said. She felt like dancing. What had she been worried about? This was going to be a lot of fun—exactly like in the movies, only a little more Mormonized.

After Mathieu left, they made their beds with the linens they had brought in their suitcases and then talked far into the night, too pent-up for sleep. Noni and Rosellen, the other girls who shared their apartment, seemed excited to have foreign roommates.

"I've never even been out of Idaho before," confessed Rosellen, "and now here I am sitting with two exotic French women!" Her giggle bubbled up and over, making Josette smile.

"It's my second year here," said Noni from her seat on Josette's bed. She pulled her knees to her chest, revealing pink underwear sticking out from her high-cut shorts. One finger twisted the frizzy bleached curls framing her pretty face. "You'll love this place. It has an outdoor and indoor swimming pool, and so many people live here that something fun is always happening."

"What are you studying?" Marie-Thérèse asked Noni. The young and innocent Rosellen had already admitted to not knowing what her major would be.

"Me?" Noni laughed. "I don't go to school. I'm just here to have fun. This is where all the single guys come."

Marie-Thérèse had an odd look on her face—one that Josette recognized all too well. "Don't," Josette said in French. "Don't start judging her."

"I'm not—"

"Good." Josette found herself admiring the tight-fitting ribbed shirt Noni had on, and she wanted to buy one for herself. Now she wished she had worked a few more years at the cafe where she had once worked when her father had lost his job. She had dropped the position when she entered college, unlike Marie-Thérèse, who had stayed on for two days each week.

"Is something wrong?" Noni asked.

"Nothing," Josette said, stumbling over the *th* sound in the word. "But I just love your top. Can you show me where to buy one?"

* * * * *

The day after they arrived in Provo, Mathieu showed them around as promised. Josette couldn't believe how large the BYU campus actually was. And all that grass, with students sitting on it— talking, reading, or simply soaking up the warm rays of the sun. She insisted on stopping and taking off her sandals, spreading herself out on the luscious green.

"I know," Mathieu said with a laugh. "All that grass, and people on it."

"And the school doesn't mind?" asked Marie-Thérèse.

"Not at all, unless you're cutting the corners and using it as a path," he said. "In America, they like using the grass. They have parks full of it for kids to romp on."

"Very smart of them," Josette said. "I think I'll stay here forever."

Marie-Thérèse laughed. "Listening to her, you would never know that I practically had to drag her to the plane, kicking and screaming."

Josette glowered at her sister. "You're just mad because you had to bring the packages," she said.

"Oh, then it's you I should thank for my cousin's package," Mathieu said to Marie-Thérèse.

"It was nothing."

"Do you like Swiss chocolate?" Josette asked.

"Josette!" protested Marie-Thérèse.

"I just wondered." Why did her sister have to be so stuffy?

"We had to know what was in it for Customs," Marie-Thérèse explained. "And they still opened your package even after I told them what it was."

"They always do that to me, too," Mathieu said.

Josette watched him, realizing again how handsome he had become. She would wait for a few weeks to see if anything more interesting came up, and if it didn't, maybe she would decide to date him.

She settled back on the grass, feeling happier than she had since Marcelin had betrayed her by trying to date Marie-Thérèse. How lucky she was that she had seen through him!

"Speaking of packages," Marie-Thérèse said, "hadn't we better take the one Marc sent to the Fields?"

Josette yawned lazily. "Let's do it next week."

"We could, but what if we get busy? Tomorrow's Sunday, and on Monday school begins. If we take it today, then we won't have to worry about it."

"Let's just call them and let them worry about coming to pick it up," Josette insisted. She wasn't anyone's messenger girl.

"What, and miss all the family pictures?" Mathieu laughed. "Why don't I take you, and then we'll go out to eat. My treat. They have a place in Orem with tons of food, all you can eat."

"You'll spoil us," Marie-Thérèse said.

"Spoil you, nothing. You're worth it. Or, if it would make you feel better, we'll go dutch." Mathieu and Marie-Thérèse laughed, and inwardly Josette sighed. Leave it to Marie-Thérèse to protest a free meal. At this rate, Josette would use up her savings quickly. Her parents had made it clear that their monthly allowance was only for food—prepared at home—and necessities. Her father had agreed to an additional amount for spending, dependent upon proof of maintaining good grades. Josette had planned to let her dates pay for any meals she ate out, but what if all were as willing to let her pay as Mathieu seemed to be?

"Oh, all right," she said, jumping to her feet. "Let's get this over with already. Take us home to get that stupid package."

"Yes, your highness," Mathieu teased.

He waited in the car while they went to retrieve the package. "He really should pay for dinner," Josette grumbled. "It was his idea."

"It's not as if it's a date," Marie-Thérèse said. "I bet he'd pay if you asked him. What, don't tell me you've fallen for him already. That's a new record—even for you."

Josette smiled grudgingly.

"Are you ready?" Marie-Thérèse asked.

Josette glanced down at her shorts and her thin top. In a brief flash she recalled the picture her brother's missionary companion had sent, especially the white-blond hair and blue, blue eyes of Elder Fields. "No, I think I'll change," she said. For some reason, one she couldn't even explain to herself, she wanted to make a good impression on the Fields family. "I'll just be a minute." She changed quickly to a purple rayon pantsuit her mother had bought her for her last birthday. It set off her dark hair and eyes to perfection.

Marie-Thérèse's eyebrows raised, but she smoothed her camel skirt and said nothing. Josette glanced in the mirror, checking her makeup, and ran a brush through her hair. "Okay," she said at last.

"You look nice," Mathieu said to her in the car. "Older."

Josette grimaced. "That I could do without, I think."

"Nonsense. The older I get, the younger the older people seem," he said. "And I like older people."

Josette felt in her purse and pulled out the picture of the Fields family. Elder Fields stared back at her.

"They're all married except Marc's companion and his sister," Marie-Thérèse said, pointing over Josette's shoulder from her seat in the back. "Brionney, I think her name is."

"She looks like him," Mathieu said, starting the engine. "The little sister."

He was right. Except for a few too many pounds, Brionney looked the most like her brother. All the Fields family had blond hair, but only the two youngest had that remarkable white-blond color. Likewise, the eyes were all some shade of blue, but only Elder Fields and Brionney had the color of the sky on a clear day. It was all Josette could do to tear her eyes away. "I hope they're home," she said.

"You mean you didn't call?" Mathieu asked.

"Elder Fields must have forgotten the phone number, and I couldn't find a phone book," said Marie-Thérèse.

"Well, no matter. We'll just throw it on their porch," Josette said, feeling better. "Then we won't have to look at family photographs." The others laughed, and Josette felt her own spirits soar. She couldn't help thinking that something important was about to happen.

They pulled up at the Fields' house in the foothills, and Josette felt taken aback by the beautiful landscaping. It wasn't the biggest house she had seen, not even close, but so well-loved that it seemed to welcome her. She practically skipped up the long, curving sidewalk, her heart pounding as they waited on the porch.

A chubby young girl answered the door. "Yes?" She looked at them questioningly. Her eyes were more startling than in the picture, and Josette thought her cute, even with all the extra weight.

"You are Brionney?" Marie-Thérèse asked in English. "I recognize you from your picture. Your brother sent this package from France." She handed it to the girl.

The girl's face lit up. "You're from France? Yes, I can tell by your beautiful accent. How neat to meet you! You have to come in." She turned and called over her shoulder. "Mom, Dad, some people from France are here. They know Zack."

She ushered them into an elegantly furnished living room with gold shag carpet and a long green couch. Mr. and Mrs. Fields stood up to greet them. "I'm Irene," said the mother, "and this is my husband, Terrell. You've already met Brionney. She's our youngest."

"It's a pretty name," Josette said awkwardly. Would they even understand her English?

"Thank you," said Irene. "Please, sit down. Tell us, how do you know our son?"

"We don't know him for ourselves," Marie-Thérèse said. "He's the companion of our brother."

"Your brother's companion," said Brionney. "How cool."

Marie-Thérèse grinned. "Yes, my brother's companion. You'll have to excuse if we don't speak perfect English. We learned only in school and with the missionaries."

"You're doing just fine," said Terrell. "What would really be funny is to hear us speak French."

Josette laughed. She liked Terrell Fields!

"Are you Elder Perrault's twin?" Brionney asked Josette. She pronounced the "l" and the "t" on their last name.

"Perrault," Josette corrected. "And yes, Marc is my twin."

"You look like him," Brionney said. "I always wanted to be a twin. But maybe someday I'll have them myself. Twins are special."

Josette nodded, feeling unbidden tears sting her eyes. "I miss Marc very much." But it went beyond that. It was almost as if a piece of her were missing.

Brionney's smile dimmed. "I miss my brother, too. I wish he could come home. Two years is a long time."

"Don't let her fool you," Irene said. "Zack teases her mercilessly when they're together. They fight like crazy."

Brionney shrugged and began to open the package in her lap. "Oh, look!" she exclaimed. "These are so cute!" She held up a long, tooth-shaped object dangling on a silver chain. "He sent a whole bunch of these."

"They're monkeys carved on a tooth," Mathieu said. "See? Hear no evil, see no evil, and speak no evil." Each monkey had his hands clapped over his ears, eyes, or mouth. "They sell these at all the flea markets. They're very popular with the tourists."

Also in the package were treats from France, a large stack of post-cards, and a dozen small Eiffel Tower statues. "He must mean one for each of his sisters and the grandchildren," Irene said with misty eyes. "Thank you very much. It helps having you visit like this."

"So who are you?" Terrell asked Mathieu. "A brother?"

Mathieu laughed. "Oh, no. My cousin is a friend of their family. But since we're all members of the Church, we're like family."

Terrell's smile nearly split his face. "Oh, yes. I remember how it was in the mission field. I served in England, you know."

There was a brief, awkward silence. Marie-Thérèse slid forward on the couch. "I think we had better be going," she said. "We are glad you were home."

Josette felt an odd panic rise in her chest. "What about pictures?" she blurted out. "Are you not going to show us pictures?"

Mathieu and Marie-Thérèse stared at her, their mouths open, but Brionney jumped to her feet and hauled a huge photo album from the bookcase. She settled on the couch next to Josette. "These are my parents when they were married. Here's their first baby—Talia. She has three boys now."

While Brionney and Josette pored over the pictures, Terrell and Irene Fields kept up a steady conversation with Marie-Thérèse and Mathieu, asking them about their families and school. Josette grew bored, but she knew she had no one to blame but herself.

On Brionney went, from Talia to Lauren and Mickelle, the other sisters. Finally, Zack was born. He was as cute a baby as Josette had ever seen. In each picture his eyes seemed to stare right at her.

"This was when Zack jumped into the pool to save me from drowning," Brionney said. "He was only six, but he knew how to swim like a fish. Mom was talking to a friend and didn't see me jump into the pool behind her. Dad saw, but he was clear across the pool and would never have gotten to me in time. Zack jumped in and pushed me to the side." It wasn't the only story Brionney told, and with every word her voice told of her love and admiration.

"I can see he is very special," Josette said.

Brionney's eyes widened. "Hey, I have an idea. You could help me with my French. Would you? It's not my best subject, but I want to impress my brother."

Josette hesitated. It was one thing to look at family pictures, but quite another to agree to teach Brionney. She had come to BYU for fun, not for work.

"You could be her tutor," Irene put in. "We'd pay you."

"I guess so," Josette said, thinking of her small allowance. If they paid her, it might be worth it. "Let us try it. Will Saturday mornings be okay? Not too early. Maybe eleven."

Brionney practically bounced on the couch with excitement. "Oh, yes! I would love it! I can't believe I'm going to learn French from a real French person!"

Josette smiled. It might not be so bad having her own personal fan club of one.

"We must be leaving for dinner," Mathieu said, standing. "I'm taking these lovely ladies out for some American food." He grinned at Josette and added, "My treat, of course."

"Oh, please won't you stay?" Irene asked. "I have plenty of food in the oven. And it's as American as it gets."

"Yes, do!" Brionney said.

"We do not want to intrude," said Marie-Thérèse.

"It's no intrusion," Irene insisted. "Tell me, wouldn't your mother do the same if we visited?"

She would, Josette thought. *In fact, she would be hurt if they didn't stay.* There was also the fact that the dinner wouldn't cost a thing—Mathieu couldn't be trusted to pay after what he'd said that afternoon. "I would like to stay," she said.

So they did. Josette was amazed at how comfortable she felt there, despite the odd foods and unfamiliar atmosphere. The Fields were interesting and kind, and the love they felt for each other was apparent. Talk centered upon daily events, but everything was related somehow to the gospel. *It reminds me of home,* thought Josette, and the uncomfortable knot she had felt in the pit of her stomach ever since leaving France relaxed.

When they finally left the Fields' home, darkness had fallen. Spotlights along the sidewalk lit both the bushes and their path to Mathieu's old car. Brionney walked with them, and hugged Marie-Thérèse and Josette as they left. "I'm so glad to meet you," she whispered.

"I too," Josette said, meaning it. "And we will see you next Saturday." Brionney skipped back up the walk.

"You could have at least offered to do the lessons for free," Marie-Thérèse said once they were in the car.

"Why?" Josette asked. "I'm going to need the cash." She turned her gaze to Mathieu. "So where to now, oh-he-who-drives? Shall we go dancing?"

He shook his head. "No. I'm not sure what time your ward starts, but mine starts early and I've a priesthood lesson to give."

"Do you go to a French-speaking ward?" Marie-Thérèse asked.

"No, I wanted to learn better English."

"Me too," she said.

"But the night is still young," Josette protested in disbelief.

"We could watch a little TV," Mathieu said. "They have a few good programs. But going dancing would keep us too late."

Josette sighed. She could have stayed in France to watch television. For all his good looks and charm, Mathieu was a little boring. She would have to fix that if they were going to date.

When they arrived at their apartment, Noni, dressed in a navy bikini, was leaving with a man. "We're going swimming," she said with a giggle. "Want to come?"

Josette eyed her companion. He wasn't good-looking in the same clean-cut sense as Mathieu or Elder Fields, but with his shaggy brown hair and the sharp curves of his face, he had a more dangerous, impulsive attraction. He grinned, openly looking her up and down. "I'm Grady," he said, pushing his long bangs from his light-colored eyes. "Nice to meet you."

"He's my ex-boyfriend," Noni confided in a whisper. "But he's loaded and fun, so I still go out with him when he comes around. He actually lives a few buildings over. Come on, you'll like him."

Josette made a rapid decision. "I'm going swimming," she said to her sister.

"What time will you be back?"

"When they kick us out," Noni answered for her. "Now hurry up, Josette, and change."

Josette threw her one-piece suit on, wishing she had a two-piece like Noni. Finally, a woman who knew how to have fun!

She blew Mathieu a kiss before she left, and he winked back at her. "Have fun," he said. Did she imagine his voice was strained? *Good, it'll serve him right to be jealous,* she thought.

Grady put one arm around her and the other around Noni as they made their way to the pool. "You look great," he whispered in

Josette's ear. "I'm sure glad we met. Say something so I can hear that gorgeous French accent. Maybe we'll dump yellow-head and get to know each other better."

All thoughts of Mathieu and Elder Zachary Fields fled from Josette's mind. *Now this is more like it,* she thought. *Maybe Grady is the man I've been searching for.*

* * * * *

The apartment seemed suddenly empty and small without Josette doing all the talking. Marie-Thérèse was all too aware of Mathieu's presence. He was so good-looking! Marie-Thérèse felt glad that Josette had deserted them. Mathieu had such great ideas, ones she would love to discuss without Josette's constant inane interruptions. On the other hand, she would now have to hold up her end of the conversation. What if he didn't like her? And why did it matter so much? She had never cared before what a man thought.

She glanced at Mathieu from beneath her lashes to see what he was doing. He seemed to be waiting for something.

"If you don't want to watch TV, I understand," he said.

Stifling an exclamation of surprise, Marie-Thérèse grabbed the remote and clicked it on. "Oh, I was just thinking about something else—sorry."

Mathieu sat on the couch and pulled out a coin from his pocket, tossing it to her.

"What's this?" she asked.

"For your thoughts."

Marie-Thérèse felt her face color and hoped he didn't notice. There was no way she would tell him how glad she was that they were finally alone! "Uh, I was thinking about Josette," she said. That much was true.

"She sure is a lively one."

Marie-Thérèse sat on the couch, a comfortable distance from Mathieu. "She's always been that way. She does everything with her whole self, that's for sure." She tossed the coin back to Mathieu. "Your turn. What are you thinking?"

He grimaced. "Do I dare say? I was thinking that I'd hate to be on Josette's bad side."

Marie-Thérèse laughed. "It's not pretty, I can tell you. But it passes quickly, and she doesn't bring it up again. She has a short memory for offenses—a good thing. And she has a sense of fairness. She's a pretty great sister." Marie-Thérèse clamped her mouth shut. Here she was alone with Mathieu, and all they did was talk about her sister. He must like Josette. The disappointment in Marie-Thérèse's heart surprised her.

"And so are you, I can see that," Mathieu said. "Every sister as crazy as Josette should have someone to look after them."

"Oh, I know how to have fun," Marie-Thérèse protested. She didn't like the picture of the matronly chaperone he had painted.

Mathieu grinned. "I know—haven't I been with you all day? I haven't had this much fun since I don't know when."

Marie-Thérèse stifled the urge to ask if his enjoyment had more to do with her or Josette.

"Except for those pictures," he said. "I couldn't believe it when Josette wanted to look at them. We should have just dropped her off."

"We would have missed a good dinner."

"We could have found something else." Mathieu's eyes locked onto hers, and Marie-Thérèse swallowed hard. What were these feelings? Why was she so attracted to him? Was this how Josette felt before she kissed a man?

The thought sobered Marie-Thérèse instantly. She wasn't like Josette and she wouldn't let herself get carried away, even if Mathieu was that type of guy—which he wasn't. She took a steadying breath. "Do you have brothers or sisters?"

"Not a one," Mathieu said. "My dad died when I was a baby, and my mom never remarried."

"That's crazy! Tell me, what's it like to grow up without fighting for the bathroom?"

"And you can tell me what it's like to leave the house without your mom asking you a hundred detailed questions!"

They both laughed, and the tense moment was forgotten. They talked about their families and lives until the late show came on. "Can you believe how the time went?" Mathieu looked at the TV, shaking his head. "And I didn't even see the movie."

"It was news, I think," Marie-Thérèse replied, though she couldn't say for sure.

"We'd better call it a night."

"Yes, we'd better."

Mathieu came to his feet reluctantly, and Marie-Thérèse walked with him to the door. "Thanks for staying," she said lightly. "It was fun." The tense excitement in her stomach had returned, and she quickly opened the door to hide her feelings.

Mathieu paused in the doorway. "I'm glad you came, Marie-Thérèse. I think we're going to have a great semester." He leaned over, and for a moment Marie-Thérèse thought he was going to kiss her. She wondered what she would do. Would she back away and remind him of her mission plans, driving him away forever? Or would she kiss him back?

To her intense relief and frustration, Mathieu's kiss brushed first one cheek and then the other as any of her friends in France might do. It was the proper thing. But the fire in his touch was different from anything she had experienced, leaving her oddly unsatisfied. "Good night," he whispered.

She smiled and watched him leave, silently chiding herself for wanting something more. They hadn't been on a date, and even if they had been she would expect him to act like a gentleman.

She sighed and put her hands to her face where her cheeks still burned.

CHAPTER SIX

The small room was fuller than normal for the weekly AIDS support meeting. Everyone in the youth group had come, and Pauline noticed that two new members had joined the group. One of the boys was very young—perhaps between the ages of ten and twelve—and had his mother with him, but the second was older and sat alone, leaning back on his chair and staring at the others with a mocking smile. He had extremely short dark-blond hair, hard brown eyes, and a lanky figure that often marked those with AIDS.

"Should I stay?" André said in Pauline's ear.

"Oh, don't bother," she replied, fighting the constant tiredness that tugged at her body. "It's too crowded in here as it is. Go on and play your basketball game. I'll meet you there afterwards."

Her brother squeezed her hand. "Have fun, Dolly," he said, calling her by the old nickname only he still used.

Pauline flashed him her smile. "We always do, and there are new members tonight."

"Go easy on them, huh?"

"The sooner they realize that what they have won't go away, the better it will be for them." Her words were mild, but for an instant there was agony in André's eyes, quickly masked. Pauline laid her hand on his cheek. "I'm so lucky to have you as my brother."

"Don't go all mushy on me," André said flippantly, "or I won't come here with you anymore." Pauline laughed. Her brother had been coming with her since they had been old enough to use the metro alone. Originally he had attended the sessions, but recently he had taken to playing basketball in the connecting gym. She had noted the withdrawal but didn't blame him. Since she had crossed the line between HIV and AIDS, he wasn't capable of staying with her; it hurt him too much.

He also hadn't agreed with her decision to hide her increasing illness from the rest of their siblings. But since his parents had agreed for the time being, he had finally acquiesced to her wishes. "Get going," she told him, "or they'll start playing without you."

After he left, she smiled and waved at her old friends, feeling as comfortable here as she felt at home with her family—in some ways even more so. Here she could be blunt about her feelings of fear without worrying about hurting those she loved most.

"Where'd your boyfriend go?" asked a lazy voice as she sat down. It was the older boy she had noticed earlier, except now he had changed seats, apparently to torture her.

She cocked her head at the newcomer. "Boyfriend? Oh, you mean André."

"He's not your boyfriend?" Again the mocking smile.

"And what if he is?" Pauline countered. She almost giggled, thinking that it was something Josette might have said.

"I'd say he was a wimp, leaving you here alone."

Anger flared. "My brother's been taking care of me ever since I can remember! If playing basketball in the next room helps him forget for a moment that I'm sick, then I want him to play!"

For the first time the smile reached his eyes. "Then he's not your boyfriend!" He held out his hand. "Hello, nice to meet you. I'm Emeri Fauré."

Pauline took his hand firmly. "I'm Pauline, and I'm glad you came. We have fun here."

"I've probably only got a few months left, according to the doctors," Emeri said carelessly, "so don't get too attached to me."

Pauline put a hand to her mouth and turned away. Something in his words hurt her very soul. While she had come here to help others face their illness, she hadn't faced the recent change in her own diagnosis.

Emeri touched her shoulder. "Hey there, now. I'm sorry. I didn't mean anything by it. I just wanted to get things out in the open. Isn't that what these sessions are for? I'm sorry. I didn't mean to make you sad. Please, look at me!"

He changed chairs again so he could see into her face. All traces of the mocking had vanished, and she saw a vulnerable young man who was afraid to die.

Like she was.

"It's not only you," she said. "I've had HIV since before I was born. I'm sixteen now. I've been on the border between HIV and AIDS for the past year or more, but last month they found a malignant tumor along with all my other problems. And you know what that means: more than one opportunistic disease and the HIV is considered—"

"AIDS." He swore, making Pauline wince. "I know the drill. That's all I've heard for the past two years. Do you think I like this short haircut? My hair's only just growing back."

"I like it short." Without the hardness in his expression, he could have passed for a missionary. She swallowed hard. "You know, I've had HIV for so long that I just figured I'd always have it, that it wouldn't go any further."

"Sixteen years is a long time," Emeri said. "I was diagnosed with AIDS two years ago. I didn't know before then."

"How did you get it?"

"I don't know. I tried some drugs once. I think that might have been it. I wish I had listened to my parents."

"How does your family feel?"

He shrugged, his face dispassionate. "I left home when I found out. I never told them. I'm eighteen now, and I'm living with some buddies. They're nice, but they don't understand what it's like. That's why I finally came here. Dr. Medard recommended the youth group."

Pauline understood all too well. "That's why I come. I have to always be happy around my family. They love me so much, and I'm afraid to show any sadness because it'll hurt them." She stared at the carpet, wondering why she was telling her deepest thoughts to this complete stranger. "I'm not afraid, really. I know where I'm going after I die. You know why I'm really afraid?"

He shook his head.

"I'm worried about who's going to take care of my family. They need me."

Emeri laughed, a dry, hollow sound. "That's nice to know," he said. "When I die, no one will even care."

"I will," Pauline whispered, and found it was true.

Emeri stared at her for a long moment. "I know this may sound like a line," he said, "but I feel I know you. From the moment you walked in the door, I couldn't take my eyes off your face."

He took her hand and Pauline let him, feeling her heartbeat quicken in her chest. She knew exactly how he felt. Being with him was somehow like spending time with an old friend. "Maybe we knew each other in the preexistence," she said.

"The what?"

"Where we lived with our Heavenly Father before our birth."

"Don't tell me you still believe in God." The mocking smile was back, and bitterness filled his eyes.

"Yes, I do. And I'd like to tell you why."

Emeri stared at her for a long moment without speaking. "Then you'll go out with me?" he asked. "I know a cafe by a park that we could go to."

"Yes, I'll go," Pauline said.

The bitterness in his gaze faded slightly, and Pauline knew now why she had felt so strongly that she should come tonight, though she had only wanted to go to bed early. She had been led here to help Emeri Fauré.

* * * * *

When Pauline came home from her support meeting, Ariana immediately noticed something in her daughter's face. Beneath the weariness that had become a constant since Pauline's bout with the flu, there was an underlying glow.

"How'd it go?" she asked casually, lifting her cheek for Pauline's kiss.

Pauline sat next to her on the couch. "There were two new kids tonight."

"And she wants to go on a date with one of them." André slumped on the floor in front of Pauline.

"André!" Pauline slapped his arm, wincing as though it brought her more pain than she had expected. "It's not a date. He's just a guy, and he's pretty nice."

"I heard everyone else saying he was rude," André said.

"Not to me. Abrupt maybe, but not rude. He's just having a hard time because he doesn't believe in God." She turned earnestly to Ariana. "Don't you see, Mom? How horrible it would be not to know where you go after this life! He's so sad. I have to teach him."

Ariana studied her daughter. Was there something more to this glow than missionary work? With a flash she had a glimpse of the vision she had seen many years earlier—of Pauline kneeling at an altar in the temple across from a blond man whose face radiated love. But now Ariana knew that Pauline would never live to see another birthday; she recognized the weakness in her body, the death in her weariness. It reminded Ariana of Pauline's father a few months before he died.

"Couldn't you talk with him at the meetings?" Ariana asked. "Or send the missionaries?"

Pauline laughed. "Oh, Mom, right. There's no way he'd see the missionaries. Come on, I'm sixteen. I'm old enough to go out, even according to the prophet."

"But we don't know this boy."

"That's what I told her," André said.

"I'll let André go with us if you want," Pauline said. "I don't think Emeri would mind."

Ariana wasn't so sure. Pauline was thin and ill, but she was still a pretty girl. Her positive attitude and ready smile had been a beacon for more than one dying friend, several of whom had been boys who had fallen half in love with her. But if Pauline felt she had the strength to help one more person, then how could Ariana refuse? "I think that would be all right," she said. "But I'd like to meet him soon." Her heart rebelled as she said it. One more person to love and lose.

"Thanks, Mom."

"I don't know," André said grumpily. "The next thing I know, you'll want to go on *my* dates."

"Ha! Like you go on any!" Pauline said.

"Well, that's 'cause I'm always with you!"

"What's going on?" Jean-Marc said, coming from the kitchen.

"I'll let Mom tell you," Pauline said, coming to her feet. She kissed his cheeks. "I have to go to bed. I'm going on a date tomorrow. André's coming with me so I can show him how it's done." She glanced impishly at her brother, who chased her out of the room.

Ariana noticed that André's motions were slower than normal in obvious deference to his sister's illness.

"She's going on a date?"

Ariana nodded and pulled Jean-Marc down to sit near her. "I haven't seen her this excited for a long time. I—I . . ."

"What?"

"I thought about that time when I saw her being married. I don't know. It gave me hope."

"That's something that's been in pretty short supply around here. It must be a good thing."

Ariana laid her head on his shoulder. "I wonder if he's blond."

* * * * *

Pauline brushed her hair very carefully, not wanting any more of it to fall out. Since she had started the chemotherapy a few weeks ago, she had noticed a lot of loose strands in her brush. The doctor had said hers wasn't the kind of chemotherapy that would make her hair fall out, but that she would probably have some thinning. She had thought she wouldn't mind, but found she did. What would she do if the doctor had to change her treatments and she lost all of her hair?

In her mind, she pictured Josette and her long, thick hair. Pauline had the same color and had been trying to grow it out, but it just didn't look the same. Now, she didn't dare wash it for her date because she was afraid of losing it altogether.

"Mom, maybe I should get a wig," she said, coming from the bathroom.

"Oh, brother!" André moaned. "It's just a date."

Ariana smiled. "Let's watch it and see if it gets any thinner. If it does, we'll go get a wig. It's just until the treatments are over and the hair comes back in."

Pauline grimaced but didn't say anything more for fear of upsetting them. She looked at André. "Are you ready?"

"I guess," André mumbled. "We might as well get this date over with."

"Isn't this boy coming to get you?" Ariana stopped with her late morning cup of warm chocolate halfway to her lips.

"We're going to meet him in town, Mom," Pauline said.

"That sounds a little strange for a date."

"He's shy, that's all." Pauline waved her hands in frustration. "Besides, I keep telling you this isn't really a date. I'm going to teach him about the gospel."

"Yeah, and you spend so much time on your hair every day," André said.

Ariana laughed. "I think you're in good hands, Pauline. Your brother sees it like it is." She took a drink. "You'd better get going then, before your *student* wonders where you are."

Pauline and André left the house and headed toward the metro. Pauline's step slowed, and she noted with irritation that André slowed to match her pace. Tears bit into the back of her eyes. Why did her body have to betray her at every step? For her entire life she had known she would die—but didn't everyone know that? Though she had long ago accepted her illness, it still held a quality of illusion. She had felt strong, mostly, up until this past year, and lately when she hadn't, her father's blessings had seen her through. Was the end really near?

"Am I going too fast?" André asked, turning to wait for her.

Pauline smiled. "Not a chance. I'm just nervous, that's all."

"I didn't mean what I said about the wig," André said. "I think you'll look cute. You always do anyway."

Pauline knew André didn't hand out compliments readily. "Thanks," she said.

A short time later, they came upon Emeri lounging at a table in the appointed cafe. "Hello," he said. He thumbed at André. "What's he doing here?"

André bristled. "I've come to check you out, that's all. Pauline's *my* sister."

"Well, have a seat, watchdog. But I'm not paying for you. Only for Pauline."

Pauline put her hands on her hips. "That's enough right now, Emeri Fauré. If that's how you're going to treat my brother, then I'm leaving right now."

Emeri shrugged. "Fine, he can stay."

Pauline didn't sit. "Well?" she said.

"Well, what?" Emeri asked.

André grabbed the chair and pulled it out. "Here, Pauline. If he doesn't know how to be a gentleman, I'll have to show him."

Pauline thought she saw a flash of embarrassment on Emeri's face. "You behave yourself, too, André," she warned. She picked up the menu and scanned the contents. From the look of Emeri's beat-up clothing, he didn't have much money. She wondered if there was some way she could pay for their drinks without offending him.

"So what'll you have?" Emeri asked.

"A lemonade, I guess. André and I love lemonade." Pauline kicked her brother under the table, daring him to defy her. The lemonade was the cheapest thing on the menu.

Emeri ordered lemonade for them and a beer for him. "Couldn't you just have lemonade?" she asked.

"Why?"

"You'll live longer, that's why."

Emeri gave a bitter snort. "Yeah, like it will make a big difference."

Pauline frowned. "I don't like it when you talk that way."

Emeri studied her for a full minute. "Okay, fine. A lemonade. Why not? It's cheaper anyway."

He turned to signal the waiter, and André made a face that said, "What do you see in this creep?"

Pauline glared. "You pay for the drinks," she mouthed. André shook his head. "Yes!" she emphasized silently.

"Am I interrupting something?" Emeri asked.

Pauline couldn't help but giggle. "No, sorry, Emeri. My brother's just a little stubborn. In a little while I'm going to send him home."

Emeri shot André a pleased look. "Okay by me."

"All right, all right," André said. "I'll be good. And in fact, I insist upon paying for all our drinks. But I'm staying."

Pauline grinned at him and said sweetly, "I think we should take him up on that, Emeri. What do you say?"

Emeri gave a wry laugh. "Maybe we should. That way he won't come next—"

"I love the clouds on days like this," Pauline interrupted. "See the big one up there? It looks like a teddy bear."

Emeri gazed up into the clouds. "Looks more like a shark to me."

"Hmm, I don't see that," she said. The silence grew long and deep, and under the table Pauline gave André a nudge. She had never had a problem finding something to say. Why was it so hard with Emeri?

"So, where are you from?" André asked.

"I live not too far from the clinic with some buddies. I work for Dr. Medard."

Pauline had heard that Dr. Medard had organized jobs at the AIDS clinic for many of the youthful patients, but for all his gentleness in his practice, he was rumored to be a hard taskmaster. "He's a nice guy," she said. "He's been my doctor since I was born."

Emeri shrugged and gave her a charming grin. "I get along okay with him—as long as I do what he wants. And I have to so he'll keep me in the program. I don't want to go back to public care. I like it here."

"Where's your family?" André asked.

Pauline waited for the answer. She hadn't told André about Emeri leaving his family.

Emeri glanced at her and then back to André. "I don't know. They could be anywhere. Frankly, I don't care." He drank down the rest of his lemonade. "Are you guys about ready? I'm feeling restless."

"Do you play basketball?" André asked.

Emeri shrugged. "Yeah. I do when I get a chance. Hey, why don't we go over to the clinic now and shoot a few?"

"I don't know. Are you sure you're up to it?"

Emeri's face darkened. "I may have AIDS, but I'm not dead yet. I'll run your butt all over the court." He added a couple of swear-words to emphasize his point.

Pauline stifled a sigh. Aside from the grin, she had seen nothing appealing in Emeri by the stark light of day. Was this the man with whom she had shared her innermost feelings? Had his vulnerability last night and the connection she had felt been only in her imagination?

André's face glowed an angry red. "I don't know where you came from," he said, "and it doesn't really matter. But I won't have you talking that way in front of my sister."

"Well, maybe you should use your energy for playing instead of talking," Emeri sneered. "Let's go play."

"Fine." André slapped his money on the tablecloth and vaulted to his feet.

Pauline had to hurry to catch up to them as they ran to the metro to catch the train for the clinic two stops over. She had made a big mistake in letting her brother come with her on this first date. How was she going to get close enough to Emeri to teach him if he and André were always at each other's throats?

During the basketball game, she noticed that André didn't cut Emeri any slack as he usually did when playing with other terminally ill opponents. He jumped, rebounded, and dribbled as though possessed. Emeri fought him every inch of the way until Pauline was sure he would collapse and die from the effort. His face was red, his chest heaving. At last he fell to the floor and didn't get up.

"So do I win?" André asked.

"Yes," Emeri gasped.

André shot Pauline a triumphant stare. She let her head drop into her hands and waited for what Emeri might do next. More swearing and bitterness? More hatred?

André held out a hand to the fallen figure. Emeri hesitated only slightly before accepting help up. He slapped André on the back. "Thanks," he said. "That was the best game I've had in a long time. Most people let me win."

"Any time," André said. "You're good."

André headed for the door. "Pauline, I'll be waiting outside. Take your time."

Pauline stared, unable to believe her eyes. What had just happened? Were all men total idiots?

Though she didn't look in his direction, she felt Emeri coming to sit on the hard floor beside her. She glanced over to find him staring at her, his dark eyes searching her face, as if drinking in her presence. "He's a great guy, your brother. I wish I'd had one like him." The softer man she had glimpsed last night had miraculously resurfaced.

"He's always been my favorite," she said tentatively.

Emeri lifted a hand as though to touch her arm, but let it fall to his lap instead. "Thank you for coming," he said stiffly. "I didn't expect that you would. It was fun."

She smiled. "Then I'm glad I came."

"Can we do it again?" he asked eagerly. "I promise I'll watch my language. You can bring your brother again too, if you want."

Pauline instinctively knew that he had once again opened himself to her, fearing rejection but holding enough hope to risk it. She found that she would rather do almost anything rather than hurt him or see that devastating mask of anger and fear return.

"Sure," she said. "I'd like that."

CHAPTER SEVEN

Brionney and Josette were in the front room, doing more laughing than practicing French verbs. In the kitchen, Marie-Thérèse tried to tune out their noise and concentrate on her math. She was finding the new concept difficult to understand, which was uncharacteristic for her, even though it had been explained in a different language.

They had been in Provo for one month, and Marie-Thérèse was happy she had come. She enjoyed school, her new ward, and the many new friends she had met. She would much rather be with any of them than doing homework!

She flipped the math pages in irritation, and a thin sheaf of papers fell out. She knew what they were without looking. Last week, when Bishop Denney had extended her a calling as ward chorister, she had told him of her mission plans and he had given her the application papers. "But I don't turn twenty-one until the end of November," she had said, gazing at him in astonishment.

"That's less than two months away," he replied. "If you don't want to turn them in now, keep them for a while and pray about your decision. Who knows? Maybe you'll meet someone special and change your mind."

"No way," Marie-Thérèse said with conviction. "I've been wanting to serve a mission for the past fifteen years. Marriage can wait."

Bishop Denney chuckled. "Can't fault you for that. Marriage will last an eternity. Many girls rush into it before they know what they want in a man." Marie-Thérèse had kept the papers, still blank, in her math book ever since.

Her thoughts wandered to Mathieu, as they always seemed to when he wasn't around. She had been with him a lot in the past weeks, but nearly always with Josette present. The few times they had been alone—usually studying or watching TV—the exciting tension she had felt on that first night returned. Marie-Thérèse didn't know what to make of it. Apparently neither did Mathieu. He didn't try to kiss her, not even on the cheeks, and kept a physical distance from her that he didn't usually maintain when Josette was in the room. Marie-Thérèse didn't know whether to be disappointed or relieved. She did notice that Mathieu had seemed irritated when she had mentioned receiving her mission papers. Was his reaction the reason she hadn't filled them in? *What am I waiting for?* she asked herself.

A knock at the door pulled Marie-Thérèse back to the present. She heard a male voice—another of Josette's many admirers. Though Marie-Thérèse wouldn't have dated the men her sister chose, she felt somewhat envious of her easy friendships.

"Some flowers for my French lady," the visitor said. "Now come and take a drive with me. The leaves are beautiful at this time—I bet you have nothing like it in France. The mountains are a kaleidoscope of color."

"Kaleidoscope?" Josette asked.

"A whole bunch of colors mixed together. Come on, you'll enjoy it."

"No, I cannot go with you, Grady," Josette said. "Maybe another day. Right now I am helping Brionney learn French."

"I want to learn French too," Grady said suggestively.

Josette laughed. "Go away. I will see you later."

The door slammed, and the silence was filled by the girls' laughter.

"Oh, Josette, I wish I could be like you," Brionney said. "I wish I had a whole bunch of boyfriends who brought me flowers."

"And why not? You are pretty."

"I'm fat," Brionney said. "That's always been my problem. Boys in America always like skinny girls."

"Then they are very stupid," Josette said.

Marie-Thérèse rolled her eyes. A lot Josette knew about being less than perfect. Her sister had always been disgustingly stunning, and her flirtatious manner attracted everyone.

Even Mathieu?

Marie-Thérèse groaned. Why on earth should she care who Mathieu liked?

She put her fingers in her ears and concentrated on her homework so hard that her head pounded. Pages and pages of problems lay before her. How would she ever get them all done by Monday?

A movement in the doorway caught her attention. She looked up, expecting to see Josette and Brionney, but instead Mathieu gazed down on her. Today he was unshaven, and his face was darker where the short hairs grew. She loved it when he looked like that. What would it be like to rub her cheek against his? She felt her face color at the thought. "Hi, Mathieu," she said.

"I've come to see if you guys want to ride up to Salt Lake and see Temple Square. We've been planning on doing it, and since next week is conference, I thought we could scope out where—"

"Oh, I can't! I've got stacks of math to do, and I can't figure out what I'm doing."

Mathieu leaned over. "Sorry. Can't help you. We geologists don't have to go *that* far into math. But let me translate the directions into French, and maybe that will help."

Marie-Thérèse was glad to let him. Mathieu had a much firmer grasp on the English language than she had. When he explained it in her native language, the concepts were clearer.

"I'm glad I only have to stay this semester," she said.

"You're going home at Christmas for good?"

"You knew that," she said.

"I thought maybe you would change your mind."

"No. France is the place for me. I only came for Josette. As much as I'm enjoying America, I want to be with my family."

He grinned. "That's how I feel. But we're in the minority. Many of the foreigners I know end up marrying and staying."

"Not me. Besides, I'm going on a mission, remember?" She touched the papers beside the math book.

Mathieu stared at her for a minute before picking up the papers and scanning them. "I thought maybe you would wait until your birthday," he said slowly.

She shrugged. "Why wait? I want to go more than anything."

His eyes met hers, searching, and Marie-Thérèse felt her senses reeling at his closeness. He bent closer . . . closer . . . then abruptly took a deep breath and pulled away. Had she imagined the moment?

She looked down at her homework, blinking away the smarting in her eyes.

Josette flounced into the room with Brionney tagging behind. "I'm ready," she said.

"You're going in shorts?" Mathieu asked, glancing down at his own casual slacks. "It's practically October."

"Why can't I wear shorts? All the Americans do it."

"Yeah, I've see the kids waiting for the school busses in the morning," Marie-Thérèse said, glad for the interruption. "They wear shorts and jackets tied around their waists and shiver in the cold. Not exactly smart."

Brionney laughed. "That sounds like the kids I know. Fashion over comfort, you know."

"What about your French lesson?" Marie-Thérèse asked her.

"I'm going to Temple Square too," she said. "I called my mom."

Josette tossed her dark head. "Don't worry," she said, switching languages, "we promised to speak only French, didn't we Mathieu?"

"If you change," he said.

Josette went up to him and touched his cheek with her hand. "Ooh," she squealed. "I just have to feel that with my face." Before Mathieu could object, she rubbed her cheek against his. "It feels like sandpaper," she said, giggling.

"You'd better go change, or I'll rub my face on your feet," Mathieu threatened.

"I might like it!" declared Josette, but she retreated a few steps.

Marie-Thérèse laughed with the others, but inside she felt miserable. *What is wrong with me?*

"Are you coming?" Josette asked.

"No, your sister is going to fill out her mission papers," Mathieu said. His voice lacked its usual warmth, but his face held no anger—or any other expression. A blank wall.

"Well, can I use your jeans then?" asked Josette. "The ones that are a bit loose on you?"

"Why not?" Marie-Thérèse said tartly. "They're in your drawer." Her only defense against her sister's borrowing tactics was her smaller size—and sometimes her good taste.

Brionney went with Josette, both oblivious to the tension between Marie-Thérèse and Mathieu. They waited in silence until

Mathieu finally said, "You're sure you want to go?"

"I've wanted to since I was little. Don't you recommend it?"

He sighed. "Yeah, I do. It was great. I just wish . . ." He stopped. "Oh, never mind. If anyone should go on a mission, it should be you. I think you'll be great."

Marie-Thérèse didn't know whether to laugh or cry. "Thanks. That means a lot coming from you."

"Hey, what are friends for?" His smile was back, and Marie-Thérèse found she could breathe again.

"Okay, is this better?" Josette came into the room and twirled.

"Lots," Mathieu said. "But speak French, remember?"

She bowed, sending her long hair flying. "Yes, indeed, oh-he-who-drives. Let's go then." She hooked her arm through Mathieu's and glanced at Marie-Thérèse. "Aren't you coming?"

Marie-Thérèse shook her head miserably. She watched them leave the apartment, feeling somehow betrayed. *I hope Josette and Mathieu do fall in love,* she thought. *He's the only man she's gone out with that I approve of. Mom and Dad will be happy. I've done what I came here to do.*

Resolutely, she began to fill out the mission papers. "I'll hand them in as soon as I get a physical," she said. At one time the idea had filled her soul with joy, but now the words echoed through the empty kitchen and back to her ears, sounding hollow and desolate.

You're not a missionary yet, she thought suddenly. She jumped up and ran from the apartment, plunging down the stairs and around the corner to the parking lot.

Mathieu's car was nowhere to be seen.

"It's just as well," she told herself. Her heart didn't agree.

Marie-Thérèse mechanically filled in the papers and made a note in her planner to schedule a physical. Then she returned to her math.

Concentration escaped her. She remembered Mathieu's face, the expressionless mask that had fallen into place when she had talked about her mission. What was he feeling? Why didn't he tell her? "Oh, right," she said aloud. "It's not as if he wants to marry you. 'What are friends for?'—wasn't that what he said?" Still . . .

Resolutely, she put all thoughts of Mathieu aside and began to work.

* * * * *

"So you're saying that up in this so-called heaven of yours, you'll see your parents again." Emeri leaned back in his chair and gave a little chuckle. "I hope you give them a lecture about doing drugs."

"Emeri, this is not funny!" Pauline punched him in the arm. The weekly AIDS support meeting was over, and they were the only ones left in the room. She could hear the thumping of a basketball game in the next room.

Counting three support meetings, it was the seventh time she had been with Emeri in the past two weeks. On each of the other four occasions they had been together, André and Emeri had played basketball before going with Pauline for a quick meal or a walk in the park. Pauline had seen a friendship spring up between André and Emeri, and she was glad for it. But Emeri never completely dropped his guard when André was present; only in the rare moments they were alone did she see his true self. In those moments, it was as though their souls communicated. Only one thing continued to plague her; each time she or André tried to talk with Emeri about God or his missing family, Emeri would withdraw into his mocking shell. Or he would tease, which she could stand better than the bitterness, but it still frustrated her.

"Life after death? Well, it seems like one of those science fiction novels André's been telling us about. And speaking of that, why don't we go see that new sci-fi movie tomorrow? We could even let André come along, if you insist, though I think it's high time we go out on our own. Oh, come on, Sunshine, don't stick your lip out that way, or I'll have to—" Emeri leaned forward to kiss her, but Pauline drew away.

"Stop that. I'm mad at you. Besides André will be here any minute, and he'll see us."

"So what? I thought you tell your brother everything. Besides, it's just a kiss."

Pauline blushed. She didn't know if she was ready for their relationship to go beyond the friendship line. "Darn you, Emeri, you're changing the subject."

"Darn? Pauline, don't you think that's rather close to swearing?"

"This means a lot to me!"

Emeri put his face close to hers, suddenly serious. "I know it does, but I can't think about any of that right now. I'm just going to enjoy being with you for every second we have. I can't think beyond that. I can't!" The urgency in his voice begged her not to continue, but Pauline couldn't let it go.

"But, Emeri, if you listened you might understand how much God loves you. You don't have to be afraid. He has a plan."

Emeri cocked his head back to look at her. He shook his head very slowly. "Oh, Pauline, then why are you afraid?" His voice was calm and matter-of-fact, but Pauline felt the words knife into her heart.

"I'm not afraid," she said.

Emeri took her hand. "Yes, you are. Oh, I know what you said to me the first night we met about your only fear being that your family wouldn't be able to get along without you. But that's not true. You're at least a little afraid of dying for its own sake. But you can't admit it. Your very life is a miracle to your family, yes, and they certainly expect you to live up to that grand idea. You have to be positive and happy every minute so you can spare their feelings. I've seen it in your relationship with André, and I'll bet it carries through to the rest of your family. And that may be great for them, but for you it stinks. If you're afraid, then you should be able to tell your family. They should comfort you." His voice lowered. "At least yours would try. They would never tell you to leave them alone."

Pauline felt angry at his words, but her curiosity ran deeper. "Did your family tell you to leave?" Emeri didn't answer, and Pauline knew from the look on his face that he wouldn't, at least not today.

"What are you really afraid of, Pauline?" he challenged. "Tell me." He still held her hand and she tried to pull away, but he squeezed tighter. "Please."

A tear escaped and slid down her cheek. "God loves me, and things are the way they are for a reason. A sin has to have a consequence."

"Even on the innocent?" he asked bitterly.

"Yes. Because they will stand as witnesses, as testimonies against that sin. We've talked about this before. And, yes, it does make me angry and afraid like you, but I know it's only for a little while. This life is so short, but eternity is forever."

He snorted. "And then, according to your beliefs, you'll live a life filled with glorious happiness and health." His voice became gentle, more so than Pauline had ever heard it. "So why are you really afraid?"

Pauline was touched enough by his perception to answer. "I'm afraid because I know it's true and I'm not good enough. How can I go to heaven when sometimes I feel so angry at God for not healing me? For seeing my mother suffer each time she takes me to the doctor? But those feelings are wrong, Emeri. I know the gospel is true, and I know God's plan! But still I get sad and angry and afraid inside, and I know it's wrong, and maybe I'm not good enough to go to heaven at all."

Emeri touched her face with his other hand, his eyes full of an emotion Pauline didn't recognize, but it made her heart pound. "Oh, Pauline. Dear, sweet Pauline. I can help you there. You are the most pure and wonderful person I have ever known. From the time I first saw you, I've felt that. I swear to you that if there is a God and a heaven, then you will go there. Don't you think that a God would know and understand and forgive all of the feelings you're having? The God you've been telling me about would. Just because you believe in God, and because of your belief you think your anger is wrong, doesn't mean he won't cut you just a little slack. If he won't, then I don't want to hear about such a Being. He wouldn't want to know me at all—not with all the hatred I have inside. Is that what you're saying?"

Pauline knew that Emeri was right. Each time she felt bitterness and anger, her Heavenly Father did understand. He had to! After all, she had been allowed to contract AIDS, but she had also been given spiritual experiences and blessings that equalled the agony. Blessings that included her family and Emeri. If God would forgive Emeri— and she knew he would—then he would also forgive her for her resentful thoughts.

"When Jesus prayed in Gethsemane, he felt our pain. Did you know that, Emeri?" she asked. "And he knew for himself what it was like to face death." She took her hand from his and wiped the tears from her face. She laughed self-consciously. "Thank you, and I'm sorry for being so emotional. I guess it's true we're always our own worst judges. I'm going to forget this stupid fear of mine and never mention it again."

Emeri frowned. "No, Pauline. We're dying. Dying! Whether you want to admit it or not, there's pain and bitterness in that. I want you to tell me everything. I don't want you to be happy and bright. Be honest. Tell me how things really are. I want you to treat me with the same honesty I treat you. Will you do that for me?"

She met his steady gaze. "Yes. I will, Emeri. I'll tell you how I really feel. But I won't stop talking about God or my church. They are also a part of who I am."

"I knew that already, Pauline. And I accept it. In fact, I wouldn't be honest if I didn't tell you there's a part of me that wishes you were right about this whole religion thing. It would make things easier." He stood, and taking both of her hands in his, pulled her to her feet. "Now let's go find that brother of yours before he works up another sermon on the evils of dating too young." He paused, his dark eyes dancing. "Or you could give me a kiss."

"He'll walk in on us."

"That at least would make his sermon more focused."

"All right." Pauline reached up and kissed him on the cheek.

"That," Emeri said, "was not exactly what I meant."

Pauline laughed. "Hi, André," she called to her brother as he walked through the door. "We were just going to look for you."

Emeri shook his head and sighed.

CHAPTER EIGHT

I should have come here ages ago, Josette thought as she lay stomach-down on her bed in the room she shared with Marie-Thérèse. *Nobody told me BYU was so fun!*

They were in the third week of November now; the months of school had whirled by in a rush of dates, shopping, and occasional study. Mathieu had taken them to see many things and to numerous activities, mostly paying for them himself on his credit card, and Josette found herself liking him more than she had expected. Except for his insistence on studying and going to bed early on Saturday nights, he was a lot of fun. During the evenings he and Marie-Thérèse stayed in to study, Josette went out with her other new American boyfriends—ones who saw life more like she did. Being a member of the Church didn't mean one had to be boring, did it? Marie-Thérèse frowned each time she left, but didn't object as long as Josette told her where she was going and what time she'd return.

"She's getting to be as bad as a mother," Josette mumbled aloud to the empty room. She stared at her English book, realizing she had read the same passage several times without understanding anything. Tomorrow she had a test, and if she wanted to keep the spending allowance her parents had promised, she had to get reasonable grades—either that or fall back on her own dwindling resources. Luckily, she had a good memory, and learning was generally a matter of reading the material a couple of times. Marie-Thérèse, on the other hand, had to study harder to internalize each lesson.

Josette's other classes were easy. Finally she had found something she was good at. Interior design came as naturally to her as shopping for clothes.

Yawning, she rose from her bed and stumbled to the kitchen. It was early for dinner, but she might be able to find something to snack on while she forced herself to read the dull material.

She waved to Marie-Thérèse as she passed the small front room where her sister sat on the couch with several books spread around her, frowning in concentration. Her hair was styled becomingly, and Josette wondered why she had bothered when they didn't plan on going anywhere this Thursday night. Was she hoping someone would drop by? She smiled. If someone did drop by, it would most likely be for her, not for her sister.

The doorbell rang, and she heard Marie-Thérèse answer it. She hoped it was someone who could manage to drag her away from the grind of studying. Maybe it was Ben from next door, who looked at her as if he couldn't live without gazing into her eyes. Or maybe the dangerous Grady, Noni's ex-boyfriend, who took her to expensive restaurants and teased her about her French accent.

She heard Mathieu's voice and dropped her half-eaten apple onto the counter, her daydreams vanishing. Mathieu was better than all of them, and she thought maybe he was starting to love her. He would be a man her parents would approve of, and he seemed to indulge her whims and flirtations with the other men. What more could she ask for?

"And I thought you might want to go with me," Mathieu was saying as she entered the front room.

Marie-Thérèse stood near the door, a silly smile on her face. "I've wanted to go," she said.

"Where are we going?" Josette asked. The other two looked uncomfortable, and for the first time Josette noticed that Mathieu held only two tickets in his hand.

"Uh, it's just a musical I happened to get a couple of tickets for at the last minute," Mathieu said. "I knew Marie-Thérèse was interested in going. I was going to try and get them next week for her birthday, but tonight they practically fell into my hands—my roommate's date cancelled on him and he decided not to go. I didn't think you would be interested, Jose." He called her by the nickname only her twin brother Marc used, and for some reason it rankled. "It's really not your style, but if you want to go, take my ticket. I'll even drive the both of you there and come back to pick you up."

Marie-Thérèse's smile dimmed slightly. "Oh, no, you and Josette can go," she said. "There's still time for me to get tickets. It'll be on for two more weeks."

"I don't know," Mathieu said. He looked at Josette, waiting.

Josette swallowed the lump in her throat. All this time she had thought Mathieu was interested in her, and yet he had come tonight to take her sister out. How many times had they gone out alone? Why hadn't Marie-Thérèse said anything? Josette felt her heart wilting, but she forced anger to replace the hurt.

"I don't like musicals," she said stiffly. "But thanks for asking." Her sister and Mathieu exchanged a hopeful look, twisting the knife in her heart. "Besides," she added, "I have a test tomorrow, and I have to at least read through the material. Good-bye. Have fun." She stalked down the corridor, silently hoping Mathieu's car would break down before they could leave the parking lot.

Marie-Thérèse came after her. "You can go," she said. "I've got studying to do, too."

Josette whirled on her sister. "He asked *you*."

"But that's only because I was there and he knew I wanted to go. It's not as if he likes me or anything."

"You like him."

Marie-Thérèse's cheeks burned a bright red. "No, I don't. I—I . . . We're just friends. We study together, that's all. You know I'm going on a mission. I'm not interested in a relationship."

"Well, I am," retorted Josette, flinging herself on the bed. Her book flipped shut and her notes went flying.

Her sister bit her lip, then cleared her throat. "Then you can have him," she said in an odd voice. "Remember our vow? No man to come between us—ever."

Josette softened. "I want a relationship, but I didn't say with Mathieu. You go ahead. I really don't like musicals, you know—all that singing. And besides, Mathieu isn't very exciting."

Then why do you want him? a silent voice mocked inside her head.

Marie-Thérèse pursed her lips, but didn't say anything for a long moment. "Go," Josette encouraged. "Go have a little fun before you sentence yourself to eighteen months with no men." She shuddered. "Yuck!"

Marie-Thérèse began to rapidly change her clothes. "If you're sure," she said pathetically. Josette could see that she wanted to go more than anything, and that bothered her even more.

"I'm sure." Josette picked up her papers from the floor and arranged them again on the bed.

Marie-Thérèse touched her shoulder. "I'll be home by ten, maybe sooner. I'll call if there's a change."

I'm not your mother, Josette almost said, but refrained. She wanted her sister to return early. The thought of her alone with Mathieu upset her more than she would admit.

When her sister had gone, Josette read the English passage, forcing herself to look up the words she didn't understand. "This is so awful," she thought. "I hate English."

"Josette! Are you here?" came an urgent voice.

"Yes!" she called, bouncing from the bed.

Noni appeared in the doorway, her tanned face flushed by the four-story climb to the apartment. "Some of the girls and I are going dancing in Salt Lake. Wanna come? I saw Rosellen downstairs, but you know how she is—too scared she's going to miss her beauty sleep or be late to a class. Come on! Get dressed."

Josette was changing before she realized what she was doing: tight-fitting black Levis with a form-flattering ribbed turtleneck in bold horizontal stripes. She glanced at her book and papers on the bed, but their call wasn't as loud or demanding as Noni's–and certainly not as enticing.

As she left the apartment, she thought fleetingly of leaving Marie-Thérèse a note to explain where she was going and what time she'd be back. Then she remembered her sister's desertion. "With my boyfriend!" she mumbled in French.

"What?" asked Noni.

"Nothing," she said in English. "I am ready."

* * * * *

Mathieu opened the car door for her as though they were on a real date. Marie-Thérèse admitted to herself that it seemed like a real date—more so than studying or watching a film. The drive to the theater was short and the silence comfortable.

"I heard from my Mom," Mathieu said. "She can't wait until I get home for Christmas. I'm looking forward to going. I've been away too long."

Marie-Thérèse knew what he meant. When she thought of her family, especially Pauline, she longed to be home. "Well, there's not much time left," she said brightly. "I mean, before we go back."

"No." His voice sounded sorrowful. "There's not much time left." Before Marie-Thérèse could ask what was wrong, he said, "Hey look, we're here. Let's hurry so we get good seats."

Marie-Thérèse didn't wait for him to open her door, but jumped out and bounded across the sidewalk. "I'll race you!" He laughed and ran with her to the building.

The musical was everything Marie-Thérèse had expected. She and Mathieu laughed during the humorous parts and watched solemnly as the characters passed through their trials. It seemed only natural for Mathieu to take her hand.

They continued to hold hands as they left the theater and walked slowly to the car. It was dark except for the moon and stars overhead and the weak lights in the parking lot. There was no snow on the ground, but Marie-Thérèse expected it any day. Their breath made warm clouds in the cool night air.

Mathieu paused when they reached the car. Instead of opening it, he stepped closer to her. She looked up, feeling an odd pounding in her ears. "Marie-Thérèse, I—" He stopped talking and kissed her.

Marie-Thérèse responded, enjoying his closeness as the passion swept through her body. Then she remembered that falling in love—even with Mathieu—didn't fit into her plans. With both hands she pushed at his chest. "Stop." It was a weak protest, but Mathieu drew away.

"I'm sorry," he said. "The night . . . I don't know . . . forgive me." His face creased with anger, but none of it seemed directed toward her. With precise movements, he opened the car door and helped her in.

He started the engine and drove home more quickly than usual. Marie-Thérèse felt guilty. Mathieu had apologized for kissing her, but it was just as much her fault. She had wanted to kiss him. Her chin rose in defiance. *And what was wrong with that?*

"So, did you turn in your papers?" Mathieu asked with nonchalance, as though nothing had happened.

Marie-Thérèse started. "No, I didn't. Yet."

He relaxed visibly. Or was it her imagination? "That was some show," he said. "We should catch another one. Would you like to?"

"Yes, I'd love to. I had a lot of fun." But Marie-Thérèse made a mental note to at least pay for the next one. If they were just friends, it was only fair. *Just friends, just friends, just friends.* That was all they were. And they had been carried away by the romance in the musical. Nothing more.

Mathieu walked her to the apartment. "It's early yet. Would you like to stay?" she asked.

He hesitated. "I should say no because I have an early class, but I would like to for a while. Maybe Josette would like to come and sit with us. We could help her with her homework."

"Come on in then, find a TV channel you like. I'll go check on her." *Why does he want Josette around?* she thought. *Could it be for the same reason I do—as a safeguard?*

Josette was nowhere to be seen, and Marie-Thérèse felt worried. Where could she be? Her sister always left a message if Marie-Thérèse wasn't home when she left. They both did. Was Josette angry about not going to the musical? Was something wrong?

"She's not in our room," she told Mathieu. "And there's no note. That's not like her. I'm worried."

"We'd better go look for her, just in case," Mathieu said.

"Good idea."

He held open the door. "Don't worry, she's probably just next door." Mathieu seemed as relieved as she was to leave the empty apartment.

Just friends, her inner voice taunted. She was willing to bet that Josette wouldn't draw such firm lines.

* * * *

Noni took Josette to a club she'd never been to before. The fact that Josette couldn't pronounce its name in English didn't stop her from dancing every dance with one admirer after another—a dozen in all. They loved her French accent, her wit, and her long hair. Josette rode a wave of approval until the drive home, when she felt abandoned and empty.

"You're a hit," Noni said. "We'll have to come back."

"Why?" Josette asked flippantly. "I gave to them my phone number."

"All of them?" Noni giggled.

"And why not? They liked me." *Or what they think is me,* she amended silently. That thought left her hurting. Was that the total of who she was—a beautiful face that men enjoyed looking at but never wanted to marry? Was she as empty-headed as Noni appeared to be? Josette wasn't sure she wanted to hear the answer.

Pushing the thoughts aside, she pretended to sleep on the way home. Noni and the two other girls who had gone with them chattered endlessly. For the first time, Josette found nothing appealing about their conversation.

She stumbled sleepily into the apartment after Noni opened the door. Marie-Thérèse rushed up to her. "Are you all right?" she asked in rapid French, for once ignoring politeness.

"Yes, of course I'm all right," Josette replied.

Her sister's freckled face flushed as anger overcame her concern. "Then where have you been? I've been frantic! I've been all over these apartments, looking everywhere. Everywhere! Mathieu is still searching. I called all your friends, even that grungy Grady, and nothing!"

Josette's fury matched her sister's. "You're not my keeper," she shouted. "I don't have to answer to you!" She stalked down the hall to their room, slamming the door behind her.

Marie-Thérèse followed. "You're my sister, for heaven's sake!" she yelled. "Of course I'm going to worry about you!"

"Well, I'm a big girl, so get over it. You had your date and I went dancing. Big deal!"

"You could have at least left a note!"

"You're not my mother!"

Marie-Thérèse sat down on her bed, breathing heavily and regularly, as if counting each deep breath. The scarlet slowly faded from her cheeks. "How would you feel if you were me?" she asked tensely. "I got home at nine-thirty, and there your book and papers were, just as when I left, your clothes on the floor. But there was no you. I was worried."

"I'm a big girl. I can take care of myself," Josette said, less angry now.

Marie-Thérèse stared at her. "I know that. And I can take care of myself. But that's not the point."

"We're not at home. We don't have to check in."

"Is that why you think we tell Mom where we're going? That's stupid. It's because we respect her and know she'll worry if she doesn't know where we are. And so if we're late, she'll know to look for us, in case we might be in trouble. Don't you understand? It's common courtesy, that's all. I don't want to keep track of your every move, but I also don't want to waste three hours worrying that you might be hurt and dying in some gutter. Wouldn't you be upset if I had been missing?"

Josette's fury abated at the love in her sister's voice. "Okay," she said reluctantly, "you're right, I guess. I'm sorry. I didn't mean to worry you, I was just in a hurry when we left."

"Well, tomorrow I'm going to subscribe to voice-mail so we can both leave messages from any pay phone if there isn't time to leave a note," Marie-Thérèse said.

Josette sat on her own bed, and for a while they said nothing. "So do you think you could spare just a minute to help me with this English?" Josette asked finally.

Marie-Thérèse frowned at the clock. "I suppose. But maybe we'd better find Mathieu and let him know you're okay."

Hope surged through Josette. "He was worried?"

"Of course he was, silly. We both were."

Josette smiled. Maybe the night hadn't been a total waste.

* * * * *

The next morning after her first class, Marie-Thérèse went home to get the mail at the same time she always did. She wondered if Mathieu would be there. For weeks they had both been coming to get the mail at the same time after having accidentally run into each other at the mailboxes. Marie-Thérèse tried never to vary the time she went because she enjoyed seeing Mathieu alone each day, if only for a few minutes. But would he come today after what had happened between them the night before? Had their kiss ruined their friendship?

"How are you?"

Marie-Thérèse nearly jumped as he came up behind her. "Mathieu!"

"Were you expecting someone else?"

"No, you just startled me."

He grinned. "Good. It'll keep you on your toes."

Marie-Thérèse felt relieved. They were still friends, even after last night's fiasco. She didn't know what she would have done if he hadn't been here.

They opened their mailboxes and scanned through their mail. "So how's Josette?" Mathieu asked.

"She was sleeping when I left this morning. I hope she got to her first class all right."

"Well, she seems to enjoy design, so I'll bet she went."

Marie-Thérèse nodded absently as she focused on the letters in her box. "Hey, a letter from Pauline!" She tore it open and scanned the first line. "Listen to this!"

"'Things are going better here than you might guess. I have to confess—I think I'm in love. His name in Emeri Fauré, and he has blond hair and a smile that makes me want to laugh. I met him at the AIDS clinic. He comes for the support group like I do. He's not a member of the Church, but I'm working on him. We talk a lot about God and dying, but it doesn't make me sad. I just realize how lucky I am to have been born in the Church and have the truth of the gospel. Emeri is so afraid of dying, but I know where I'm going after this life. It makes a great difference.'"

"How lucky she is?" Mathieu commented quietly. "How can she be so positive?"

"She's always that way." But Marie-Thérèse also wondered how Pauline could always be so happy. If someone asked her to describe her little sister in one word, she would say *sunshine*.

"I'm glad she found someone," Mathieu said. "She deserves it."

Marie-Thérèse found herself agreeing. It was good to have a relationship with a man who had common interests and challenges. Like with Mathieu. She swallowed hard and felt her face coloring, but he didn't appear to notice.

"Here's the rest," Marie-Thérèse said, focusing on the letter.

"'Emeri and André play basketball a lot, and we've taken to going out to eat afterward. André insists on coming with us and we let him. I think he likes Emeri. I haven't introduced Emeri to Mom and Dad yet. I'm worried about what they might say when they learn that he is more than just a friend. He doesn't get along well with most people, but he is very special to me, and I think they'll see that—if he finally agrees to meet them. He doesn't have any contact with his own parents, and he's nervous about meeting mine. Well, since I'm mailing this early, you should get this letter and card long before your birthday. Hope it's a nice one. We'll see you next month. Give my love to Josette. Love, Pauline.'"

"I can't wait to meet her again," Mathieu said. "When I saw her at my cousin's baptism, she was just a little thing. But full of life, if I remember correctly. Wasn't it she who—"

"Threw the punch on Marc?" finished Marie-Thérèse with a laugh. "Yes, it was. But he deserved it—he kept tying her ponytails in knots. That really was funny." Then she sobered. "There's something different about her letters now, but I can't really pinpoint what."

"Because she's in love?" Mathieu suggested.

"No, I don't think it's that. It's more of a resignation."

"Do you think she's become sicker?"

"That's what I worry about. I mean, all she ever talks about in her letters is her support meetings and the family. She doesn't even mention school or hiking or any of the activities she used to be involved in. I think maybe she's pulled out of all that now."

Several girls came to the mailboxes, and Mathieu took her arm and led her down the sidewalk. "You don't think your parents would hide anything from you, do you?"

"I wouldn't think so, but then they've also been so worried about Josette. Perhaps they are balancing out the two. You know, seeing where I'm needed the most." Marie-Thérèse sighed. "Pauline's one of the reasons I'm so anxious to get home."

"What about your mission?"

Marie-Thérèse's step faltered. "I don't know. I have to believe she'll be all right." She gazed at Mathieu and saw concern in his face. "Thank you for caring," she said, her voice falling to a whisper. "I've never told anyone before, but that's one of the things that really bothers me about serving a mission. I need to be there for Pauline, if something should happen. The rest of my family is important to me, but Pauline is all I have left of my real parents—I mean my birth parents." She shook her head impatiently. "It always bothers me when

I hear adopted people talk about their 'real parents.' I mean, real parents are those who've sat up with you when you were sick, who explained the gospel and life, who took pictures when you went on your first date. You know what I mean. But despite all that, Pauline is my blood sister, and I feel a special bond with her."

"I think I understand a little," Mathieu said. "I always wished I'd had someone like that. A brother." Mathieu put an arm around her. Marie-Thérèse knew it was meant for comfort, but her heart betrayed her with its rapid thumping.

"I just wish people would say what's really going on and not try to protect anyone," she said. Before the words came out, she didn't realize they were partly meant for Mathieu. Why didn't he tell her how he felt? But then, what did she expect? She had made it all too clear that she wanted to serve a mission, and he could do nothing but respect her wishes. That was the kind of man he was. So maybe the real question lay with her. What did she really want?

* * * * *

"We need to try a different series of treatments," Dr. Medard said. "This one just isn't working."

Pauline had known it would happen, and the words shouldn't have affected her so strongly. She brought her hand up to her hair. Dr. Medard saw the motion. "Yes, I'm afraid this time you'll lose your hair completely."

"It'll grow back," Ariana said. "What's important is that this treament gets rid of the tumor."

Pauline felt all her fears come to the surface. She leapt to her feet. "No, it won't grow back! It won't! And I'm not getting better!" Her voice changed to a quiet desperation. "Why won't either of you admit that?" Without another word, Pauline ran for the door. She made it down the hall past the nurses and to the bathroom before she crumpled into a sobbing heap. *Emeri*, she thought. *I need you!* He at least would be honest.

After a while, she heard someone come into the bathroom and knew without looking that it was her mother. Ariana said nothing, but came and sat on the floor next to Pauline. "Can I help?"

"I'm sorry, Mom," Pauline said, gulping for air. "I didn't sleep well, and I didn't eat much breakfast. I—"

"It's all right." Ariana put her arms around Pauline and held her tightly. "You don't have to pretend around me, Pauline. I know you're afraid. I'm afraid, too."

Pauline pressed her face into her mother's chest. It felt so good to be held and rocked as though she were a baby. In her mother's arms, nothing could touch or hurt her. Almost.

"Sometimes I wish I could just die and get it over with," Pauline said. "I'm tired of seeing you hurt, of feeling my body so weak. I'm tired of . . ." Her voice trailed off.

"Of being afraid."

Pauline hiccupped. "You knew?"

"Of course I knew. How could you not be afraid?"

Pauline poured out her heart to her mother, telling her all the things she had only told Emeri. Ariana didn't try to push her fears away or explain them, she simply listened. It was exactly what Pauline needed. Pauline already knew the answers. What she needed from her mother was love and understanding—and to be held and comforted.

"I love you so much," Ariana whispered.

Pauline smiled. "I love you, too."

* * * * *

Pauline leaned against the wall surrounding the edge of the Eiffel Tower, feeling the light breeze blow through the hair sticking out from under her hat. Below, she could see the Seine River and tiny people who seemed almost inhuman as they scurried about their daily activities. Beside her Emeri was silent, caught up in his own thoughts.

It was their first date completely alone. Emeri had been urging her to go with him for some time now, but she had been afraid. Of what? Her feelings for him? Of needing him too much? Both concerns were moot: she already needed him; she already cared.

Now she glanced over at Emeri and saw the vulnerability plainly in his face. No one else could see it, except André, perhaps, and only then on occasion. She stepped closer to Emeri until her arm touched his. He smiled and she felt content. His features were so familiar to her that she could shut her eyes and recall every detail. His hair had grown longer, but was still short enough to please even her parents if he would agree to meet them. And his eyes made her want to stare at him forever.

Without warning, Emeri stroked her hair. He hadn't tried to touch her since the support meeting when she had confessed her fears, and the act surprised her. "It's good to be alone with you," he said in a low voice.

Pauline winced as she saw a lock of her hair come away in his hand. Her hair had thinned so much in the past week that she had self-consciously begun wearing a hat every time she saw Emeri. He twirled the dark hair in his hands, refusing to meet her eyes.

"I'm getting a wig," she said brightly, gently tucking the rest of her hair up into her hat.

"Cancer!" Emeri spit the word out like a bit of phlegm.

"AIDS," she corrected automatically. "The cancer is just one of the opportunistic diseases." She felt stupid as she said it. Emeri knew the process as well as she did.

Emeri grabbed her and pulled her close, holding her so tightly that she found it difficult to breathe. He didn't say anything, he simply held her.

"Emeri, I'm sorry. Emeri, say something. Are you okay?"

She felt his chest heave several times before he spoke. "I didn't care about dying. I didn't care about any of it." There were rough, unshed tears in his voice now, and self-disdain as well. "Until I met you. I lived in the dark, but you are like the sun. Oh, dear God, there's no reason to this insanity!"

Pauline felt the pain in his words and wondered how long it had been since anyone had loved him as she was beginning to. She hugged him back with all her strength. "Emeri, I know this doesn't make much sense now, but I know God loves us both."

He drew away, blinking quickly, his face drawn tight. "How can you say that? After what he's done?" He beat his fists helplessly at the low wall in front of them.

Pauline forced herself to answer calmly. The fact that Emeri was talking about God as a real Being was progress from the abrupt denial he had given her at that first support meeting. "We've talked about this before. He didn't do this to me. My mom made a bad choice when she was young, that's all. She tried to make amends. She even gave up months of her own life so that I could be born."

"Into this?" Emeri scoffed. "What kind of a life is this?"

"Well, I've enjoyed a lot of stuff. I'm glad she didn't abort me." Pauline made a sweeping motion around her. "Emeri, there's so much more to life than what is here. Sure, there's a lot of pain and sadness where you and I are coming from, but we can still enjoy this life and plan for the next."

Emeri clenched his teeth. "I can't believe that," he said. "I won't."

"Why?"

He said nothing for a long time. "I don't want to hurt you, Pauline, but I believe religion is a crutch for people who can't face reality. Life is bad, so we'll wait for the next one. What a da—what a joke! Well, I don't want to wait for some pipe dream, Pauline. I want to act now! I want to feel! I want to . . ." He broke off and pulled her close again and kissed her, long and searchingly.

Pauline didn't have time to be surprised at her own reaction to this, her first real kiss, or to worry that she wasn't doing it right. All she wanted was for Emeri to keep kissing her. His mouth turned gentle, caressing, spreading a sweet warmth throughout her body. No wonder her parents had cautioned so strongly about physical intimacy. These feelings were potent!

Emeri stopped kissing her, but he didn't remove his arms. They stood, cheek to cheek, ignoring the tourists who had also come to see the Eiffel Tower. Pauline felt dampness on her face and knew that Emeri was crying.

"Oh, Sunshine," he whispered. "I want to live. Before I met you, I thought I didn't care. But now I want to live."

"So do I." Tears squeezed out of Pauline's eyes and trickled down her cheeks.

* * * * *

"Is something wrong?" her mother asked when Pauline arrived at the apartment. Emeri, of course, had refused to come up in case he might run into her parents.

"It's Emeri," Pauline said. She saw the concern in Ariana's face and hastened to reassure her mother. "I think he's beginning to see that maybe I'm right about God, but I don't like seeing him hurt. Why would believing make us—him, I mean—feel bad?"

Ariana took her hands. "The truth does that sometimes. When you realize, for example, that love can be eternal, it becomes more important than it was before. So much more hinges on working thing out, on growing and changing together. Hope can be painful without real faith. It's like seeing a treasure in front of you but never being able to hold or use it."

Pauline frowned. "I wish Emeri could believe. It's so easy."

"No, it's not, Pauline," Ariana said. "If Emeri has to admit that you're right, he'll have to let go of years of bitterness and pain. And from what you and André tell me, I think that's what he's hiding behind. That can be pretty scary for anyone."

"So if he gets rid of that, he'll have to face the truth straight on, right? Like us. Knowing that God loves me and still can let me . . ." Pauline saw the sadness in her mother's eyes and couldn't complete the sentence, despite the new openness they shared. She wondered if her mother's hope was something akin to the wall of bitterness Emeri had built around himself. But no, hope was not a surrender to the inevitable. It was a strength, a catapult to faith. Pauline felt like crying again. "Did you ever see something in someone that nobody else did?" she asked.

Ariana's eyes took on a faraway look. "Oh, yes."

"And did he change?"

"Yes, but it took a long time. And it was much too late to do me any good. But that doesn't have anything to do with what might happen to Emeri. Your life has been full of miracles, and I have no doubt they will continue."

Miracle baby. Miracle child. Miracle healing. If that was true, then her Heavenly Father would at least guide her to help Emeri. "Thanks, Mom." Pauline went to her own room and lay on her bed. With relish, she recalled each detail of her afternoon with Emeri. For the first time in her life, she knew she was in love.

CHAPTER NINE

The day of Marie-Thérèse's twenty-first birthday came with bright sunlight and no gray clouds. Outside, the air was crisp and clean. She pulled off her mittens to open the mailbox with the tiny key. Inside was a small stack of letters and paper. Eagerly, she searched through the junk mail and found two more birthday cards from friends and a letter from Marc.

She looked around for Mathieu, missing him. Why wasn't he here? It had been more than a week since their kiss, and things had seemed to return to normal—if you could count how his presence affected her as normal. Occasionally one of them would miss their daily two-minute rendezvous, but surely he wouldn't have made other plans on her birthday. She lingered for a few moments before walking back to the apartment alone.

"Josette, get up!" she called as she walked in the door of their room. "Marc wrote to me."

"It's Saturday," Josette whined. "Even Rosellen is still sleeping."

"Is not. She went to the library this morning. It's almost eleven. Brionney will be here for her lesson."

Josette pulled herself to a sitting position, her hair spilling every-where. "Marc hasn't written me for two months."

"Well, when's the last time you wrote to him?" Marie-Thérèse ripped open the envelope. Inside was a birthday card and a hastily written letter. Josette scooted close on the bed to read with her.

> *Dear sisters,*
> *I'm writing to you both even though you've neglected*

me horribly. What's going on at that university anyway? Have you both too much homework or too many boyfriends that you have to ignore your own brother?

Can you believe we're finally going to have some baptisms? Six to be exact. My first in over six months of diligent work and lots of prayer. After hearing so many times about a golden family, we actually found one ourselves. Incredible! I was beginning to think golden families were a myth, something they told us about in the MTC to keep us going. But I was wrong. By the time you get this letter, they will have been baptized—a dad, a mom, three boys, and a grandmother! There's one more, little Sofia, but she's too little to get baptized yet. But I'll tell you, even though they are golden, it has been a rough seven weeks. Pedro lost his job, their car broke down, and Sofia had to have an emergency appendectomy. Instead of these trials having weakened their faith, they have only caused the Leandros to grow closer to the ward members and to the Lord. When we were at the hospital giving Sofia a blessing, Pedro said to me, "You know, even if the whole world were destroyed and there was no branch of the Church in France, I would keep studying the Book of Mormon in my home with my family." Can you believe that? I can't even tell you how much it meant to me and how much I love them. The Lord has blessed me by letting me be part of their conversion.

If there is to be any credit to us for finding this family, it should go to my junior companion, who's a spiritual giant, so to speak. Elder Fields is incredible, and I'll be sorry when we're separated. (It should be soon, because he is more than ready to be a trainer himself.)

Well, I don't have anything else to say, except behave yourselves. Oh yeah, my companion is glad you're teaching his sister French. He got a letter one of you must have helped her write, and it was all in French. He says he's going to start writing to her in French, too. By the way, she writes him every week (a lot more faithfully than two sisters I know).

*Take care. I love you both. I'll try to write at
Christmas.*

Love, Marc

After she finished the letter, Marie-Thérèse found herself looking forward to her own mission with a fervor she hadn't felt since Mathieu's kiss. How wonderful it would be to help people find the truth! To make an eternal difference in someone's life! A lifetime of yearning filled her soul.

"Tomorrow I'm going to turn in my mission papers," she said, deciding suddenly. What had she been waiting for? This letter was certainly the answer to her prayers.

What about Mathieu? a voice asked.

What about him? she answered. *He knows I've always planned to go on a mission. He understands. It's not as if we're in love or anything. We're just friends.*

She forced thoughts of Mathieu aside. "Just think! By January I could be serving a real mission. I need to make an appointment with the bishop. Maybe I'll even be called to the same mission as Marc, and get to serve a few months with him before he finishes in April!"

"That's great." Josette sounded bored. "Mom and Dad will be proud of you both." She arose and wandered into the kitchen.

Marie-Thérèse thought of her birth parents, and knew they would also be proud of her decision. Her father had faithfully filled two years of missionary service, setting the example for his younger brother and sister who later served missions of their own. As a convert, her mother hadn't had a chance to go on a mission, but after her marriage she had helped many people join the Church. Marie-Thérèse could almost feel her presence near, as she had at many times during her life; she had no doubt who her guardian angel was.

"Marie-Thérèse," Josette called from the kitchen. "Marie-Thérèse, how many times do I have to call you? Marc's letter isn't good enough to sit and stare at all day. Hurry up! Mathieu's on the phone. He wants to borrow some flour or something. He says he's in the middle of a project and wants to know if you'll run it over. I can't because I've got to wait for Brionney."

Marie-Thérèse jumped to her feet and ran to the kitchen, vaguely recalling something Mathieu had said last week about a project. "What's this I hear?" she asked. "You want to borrow something, and you want me to bring it over as well?"

"Please," Mathieu said, amusement thick in his voice. "I'm right in the middle of a project, and I can't leave."

"Okay, lazybones, I'll be right there. But you owe me."

Suddenly his voice was gruff, devoid of any lightheartedness. "Anything you want," he said.

Marie-Thérèse didn't know what to say. "Uh, g'bye."

"Wait! Got any salt?"

"How much do you need?"

"All of it. I'll replace it. Now hurry!"

"Aye, aye, captain." Marie-Thérèse hung up the phone and gathered the items in a plastic bag.

"What about your papers?" Josette asked.

"Would you call the executive secretary for me? Please? Just this once?"

"He's the one with the cute new haircut, isn't he?"

"Yes, so will you call him? I want an appointment for any time tomorrow if the bishop has time."

"Sure, I'll do it."

"Thanks."

Marie-Thérèse met Brionney at the door. "Bonjour," she said cheerily.

"Bonjour," Brionney replied, her round face dimpling. She twirled a set of car keys on her hand, announcing to the world that she was finally a driver. Her sixteenth birthday had been the month before and she had been given a learner's license, but today must be the first time driving to her lesson alone since receiving her real license.

Marie-Thérèse hid a smile, remembering when she had received her own driver's license at eighteen. She had been excited—until she realized that Paris wasn't exactly the easiest place to drive a car. Now she preferred using the metro.

An incredible disaster confronted Marie-Thérèse when she arrived at Mathieu's apartment. Flour sprinkled the floor, and bits of a doughy mixture were ground into the linoleum by Mathieu's bare feet, which were also covered with flour. Behind him, the sink was full of dirty pans and bowls containing remnants of different colored doughs.

"I thought I had enough stuff," Mathieu said sheepishly. "But I spilled a little flour . . ."

"A little?"

"And it's taking more dough than I thought it would. Come and see." He shut the door and ushered her in. Now she saw the "project," which sat on the floor in the place of the oblong table that usually graced that part of the kitchen. The foot-high structure was three feet long and two feet wide. He stared at it with reverence.

"What is it?" she asked.

"What do you mean?" he said, feigning hurt. "Can't you see that this is one land mass here, and this is another? The plates they're on are colliding, and this land mass is being pushed under and turned into a liquid because of the intense heat. And these new mountains are forming because of the pressure. See? Well, you will. As soon as I get some more dough cooked up. Meanwhile, see what you can do with those mountains before they dry." He pushed at the lopsided mountains with his dough-caked fingers.

"Here, let me do it." Marie-Thérèse sat on the floor and began to shape the mountains, using as a model a picture from a book Mathieu had propped up against the wall. Now that she studied it, she could see that Mathieu's project was very detailed. He had painstakingly portrayed layer upon layer of geologic time, and in different colors to show the contrast. All that was really missing was the landscaping on the top layer and the budding mountains.

"So much dough," she muttered.

"Not really," he said. "The middle has a Styrofoam base." He stared at her oddly, but Marie-Thérèse didn't understand why. She turned back to the mountains. There was something strange about the one closest to her. It was as if it had something hard inside—perhaps dried-up clay. She squeezed hard and felt it break away.

"You've got someth—" She stared at the shape, her heart nearly stopping. It was thick and round with a hole through the middle and a large, dough-covered gem sticking out from one side. Joy burst through her like a firecracker exploding in the dark. Mathieu loved her. *Her*!

Marie-Thérèse remembered to breathe. Involuntarily, she twisted toward Mathieu who stood at the stove, his clothes dusted white, an enigmatic expression on his face. Neither said anything for a long moment, and then Mathieu approached and sat beside her on the floor.

"I know you want to go on a mission," he said. "But I want you to know there's another option. Like you said last week in relation to your parents and Pauline, I think it's long past time that I stop fooling myself and tell things like they really are."

With his words, reality set in. "But—"

He put a gentle finger to her mouth, and she smelled the dough on his hand before he pulled it away. "I've tried to distance myself," he said. "I've tried to date other women. But I love you, Marie-Thérèse. Only you. I think we could make something of our relationship. Won't you think about it? Pray about it?" His face was earnest, and so utterly loving that Marie-Thérèse would have given almost anything to fall into his arms and accept his proposal.

Almost anything.

"I care about you," she said, "but I need to go on a mission. All my life I've dreamed about going, about making an eternal difference in someone's life."

"You'd be making that kind of a difference in my life," Mathieu said.

"You know what I mean. You've been on a mission. You've seen people's lives change."

"I have," he said, "and I had never felt more joy in my life—until I fell in love with you."

Marie-Thérèse's mind was a mass of confusion. His love exhilarated her, but . . . there was that little word between them. She cared about Mathieu—she wouldn't admit even to herself that it might be love, because then she would commit herself—*but* all her plans pulled her in another direction.

"I could wait for you, if that's what you want."

Marie-Thérèse was tempted, but was that fair to Mathieu? He talked many times of having a family, and she knew he was ready to move on with his life. She had no right to encourage him unless she could pledge her love and forego her mission. "That's not fair to you."

He inclined his head, showing that he understood and even agreed. She believed he loved her, but without time to develop that love, another could take her place. In fact, it was all too likely; she'd seen it over and over with the members of her stake. If she went on a mission, there was no guarantee Mathieu would be available when she returned. He would find another woman, and she would have to find another man. She had always believed that there were many good companions to choose from with whom she could find equal happiness—but then why did her heart hunger so for Mathieu? What if what they had was the once-in-a-lifetime kind of love?

Love? Was that what it really was? The kind her parents shared? Why did she feel like crying and singing at once?

"You don't have to answer now," he said, seeing her indecision. "Talk to the bishop, if you want. Pray about it."

Her tongue ran over her lips, tasting the trace of salt his finger had left. His eyes followed the movement, and for a moment she thought he might kiss her. When he didn't, she offered him the ring.

"Keep it," he said, coming to his feet, "until you decide for sure. It was my grandmother's diamond. I had it set in a new band after my mission. I felt I came to BYU to find my wife, but I have to admit I was a little reluctant because I didn't want to end up staying here." He chuckled softly. "Little did I know I'd meet a French woman. I guess I should have asked you four years ago at my cousin's baptism. Did you know I had a crush on you even then?" She shook her head wordlessly. "Well, it's true." He watched her for a silent moment before sauntering back to the stove where the water boiled madly.

Marie-Thérèse turned back to work on the mountains, clutching the ring between the palm and the two smallest fingers of her right hand. She had been completely taken with Mathieu when she was sixteen. If she had known he had felt the same way, things between them now would have been different. She would have had the last four years to write to him, to get to know him, and to become accustomed to the idea of being a wife instead of serving a mission.

But I want to serve a mission! she insisted. *I won't give that up.*

A short time later, Mathieu returned to her side with a batch of the salty dough. He divided it into two colors, green and brown, and began to landscape the hillside. "I have some little trees I bought," he said, waving at the counter top. "You want to put them on?" His voice sounded normal, as if nothing had occurred between them, but his brow furrowed every time he glanced her way.

"Okay." First she went to the sink and washed the ring he had given her. It was beautiful, catching the light from the kitchen window and reflecting it in every direction. Without thinking, she slipped the thick band of gold onto her ring finger. It was slightly large, but its beauty made her reluctant to take it off.

"There's a box for the ring inside the cupboard," Mathieu said without turning from his project.

Firmly, she put the ring in the box and snapped it shut. Placing it on the counter, she picked up the package of trees.

They worked for another hour before Mathieu was satisfied. He sat back on his heels and sighed. "Thanks, I couldn't have done it without you," he said. "Those chocolate shavings really look like fallen bark, and the green coconut for grass works better than the clay. Where do you learn those things?"

She shrugged. "Around. Your mountain looks great. I like the cave you added."

"Well, I hope this gets a good grade." He glanced at his watch. "Oh, how time flies! I'm sorry I kept you so long."

"That's okay. I had nothing else to do." She remembered his proposal and felt her face color. With all her freckles, her cheeks must look like brown and red splotches. Whatever did he see in her?

"If you'll give me a chance to change, I'll take you out to lunch."

She glanced down at her own flour-spotted jeans. "I need to change too. How about I meet you in fifteen minutes?"

"No," he said quickly. "It'll only take me five. Wait for me, okay? And I need to talk with Josette anyway."

Marie-Thérèse wanted to ask why. Was he preparing to court her sister if she didn't accept his proposal? Or was he going to tell Josette about their relationship?

What relationship? her mind said.

Mathieu darted into his bedroom. Marie-Thérèse scarcely had time to put the ring box in her pocket before he returned. She forced a smile. "You have dough in your hair," she said.

"You do too." They began to remove the clay, but abruptly stopped, letting their hands fall to their sides. They stood close together, but without moving. Marie-Thérèse's breath quickened and all sorts of crazy ideas raced through her head. She turned away and said lightly, "I'll race you." She was out the door before she had finished, with Mathieu not far behind.

They arrived laughing at the apartment door, their chests heaving. Mathieu bowed. "I concede the tie to you," he said, motioning for her to open the door.

"Concede, nothing! I beat you fair and square," she said. She turned the knob and pushed into the apartment.

"Surprise!" Shouts echoed through the room, which was full of her friends.

Josette beamed. "Happy birthday, my dear sister." She glared at Mathieu. "You took long enough! We are just about to start thinking that you—how do you Americans say it?—yes, eloped or something!" Her expression showed she was joking, but her guess was too close for comfort.

Josette put one of her arms through Marie-Thérèse's and the other through Mathieu's. "Come on, your cake is in here. And sandwiches, too. Brionney and I had a busy morning."

It was a wonderful surprise and the best birthday party in a long time. Only one thing marred Marie-Thérèse's enjoyment. As she opened Josette's gift, the triple combination she'd been wanting, her sister cocked her head and announced in awkward English, "These are for Marie-Thérèse to use when she goes to her mission. I got some for my brother before his mission and now for her. Guess what? She is going to hand in some papers tomorrow. Only this morning, I made appointment with the bishop. For her!"

Everyone clapped and gave their congratulations, but Marie-Thérèse saw the misery in Mathieu's eyes. She wished she could strangle Josette. Too bad she spoke English well enough to be understood at all!

"There's one more present," Mathieu said, pulling something out of his pocket.

"But—"

"This is your birthday present." He thrust the little oblong box in her hand.

Of course! The engagement ring wasn't her present, but something else altogether. She tore off the wrapper. Inside the box was a thick herringbone bracelet in 14-karat gold. "But Mathieu, you can't afford this!"

"Don't worry about it," he said. "My credit is good and I'm working. I wanted to get it for you."

"Yeah, Mathieu is almost graduated," Josette added. "Then he will make lots of money. Say thank you and be happy."

"Thank you," Marie-Thérèse echoed. "It really is beautiful. I'll keep it always."

"It's for you to remember me by," he said in French, so low that only Marie-Thérèse heard the words.

Josette fingered the bracelet. "I like it much, Mathieu," she said. "You come to mine birthday next year in France, no?"

Everyone laughed again, and Josette swaggered with the attention. The cake and other goodies were nearly gone, but Josette had an idea. "What if we go swimming? The pool is fixed, I think."

"Yes, I went yesterday," said Rosellen.

"And after we can get videos to watch," Noni suggested. "Let's make a whole day of it."

"Good idea!" shouted Josette. "Everybody go to the pool. And tonight we have more party."

"And bring your favorite snack for tonight!" Noni added as the guests filed out the door.

"I'll go get the videos now," Mathieu said. "That way we'll have a better choice. Any suggestions?" Almost everyone had some. Two of the guys decided to go with him to the video store to make sure they hadn't already seen the movie.

Marie-Thérèse watched everyone leave. "Aren't you coming?" Josette asked.

"I'll be down in a minute," she replied. "I just want to put my things away."

Josette nodded and was gone. Marie-Thérèse laid her head on the kitchen table and shut her eyes, uncertain how she should feel. "Are you all right?" asked a voice from the doorway.

She lifted her head. "Brionney. I thought you'd gone with the others."

The younger girl made a face. "I don't like to swim much. I feel too awkward. Fat, I guess."

"You're very pretty," Marie-Thérèse said.

Brionney shrugged and said nothing.

Marie-Thérèse stood, feeling uncomfortable under her stare.

"It's Mathieu, isn't it?" Brionney said.

Marie-Thérèse sat down again. "How did you know?" Mathieu's feelings hadn't been apparent to her until today.

Brionney sat down at the table. "I see the way he looks at you. What I wouldn't give to have somebody look at me like that! I've known for a long time how he feels about you going on a mission. He gets all upset every time anyone mentions it."

"He never said anything."

"So? Lots of things don't have to be said."

Marie-Thérèse retrieved the ring box from her pocket. "He asked me to marry him."

Brionney opened the box and exclaimed. "Oh, how beautiful! And big. I didn't think college students could afford stuff like this."

"The diamond was his grandmother's."

The girl squealed. "How romantic! Why don't you wear it?"

"I have not accepted." Marie-Thérèse felt her face droop. "I want to go on a mission. I have wanted to go since I was very small. How can I give that up?"

"But your first duty is to get married." Brionney's face clearly showed she didn't understand Marie-Thérèse's priorities.

"Yes, I know, but I have felt it so strongly." *And planned for it,* she added silently. Was rigidly adhering to a lifetime plan a sin?

"What if you don't marry him?" Brionney asked, looking glum.

"Then he'll marry someone else." Marie-Thérèse's heart ached at the thought. "I can't ask him to wait for me. It wouldn't be right."

"I'd ask," Brionney said, trying on the ring.

Marie-Thérèse sighed. Brionney was young; she didn't understand. "There are many worthy people to choose from," she said.

"Yes, but Mathieu's special. I wish I were older and skinnier. Maybe he'd like me."

"He likes you now."

"As a friend," groaned Brionney. "The story of my life."

Marie-Thérèse took the ring from her, avoiding the temptation to put it on her finger. She placed it gently in the box and snapped the cover shut. "I'm going to change into my suit," she said, pushing her chair back from the table.

The rest of the evening, she and Mathieu had no time for private talk. Marie-Thérèse felt torn between relief and agony.

"What's up?" Josette asked after they kicked everyone out just before midnight.

"I'm nervous, I guess," she said, surprised that her sister had noticed her anxiety.

Josette pulled her nightshirt over her head and fished her hair out of the back. It had grown longer than Marie-Thérèse had ever seen it, clear to her bottom. "About your mission? Well, don't worry. I know you'll be great at it. You're good at anything you set your mind to. And I'm proud of you."

Josette's display of faith only made Marie-Thérèse feel worse. She felt that she was on a seesaw, constantly wavering back and forth between her planned future and the enticing surprise she had found in Mathieu.

"Do I love him?" She asked the question of herself and the Lord many times that night, falling asleep on her knees as she prayed against the side of her bed.

* * * * *

The next afternoon, Bishop Denney awaited Marie-Thérèse with a warm smile. "I expected you before this," he said. "You were so anxious to serve a mission."

"Well, I cannot go until January," she said, taking the seat he indicated.

"That only leaves a little over a month. Let me see the papers."

Marie-Thérèse thought he seemed too jovial for the turmoil inside her. She reluctantly set the papers on his desk. The bishop pulled them toward him, but he didn't read them. "What's wrong?"

Marie-Thérèse said nothing. Bishop Denney waited, but when she volunteered no information, he spoke again. "Is it these papers? Are you sure about wanting to go on a mission? Has something changed?"

She lifted her eyes from the gray marbled carpet and met his probing gaze. "I want to go on a mission," she said, choosing her next words carefully. "It is just that . . . a man I care about wants to marry me. His name is Mathieu, and he is from my country."

The bishop chuckled, though she could see no amusement in the situation. "Is he a member? Can he take you through the temple? Do you love him?" She nodded at the first two questions, but hesitated at the last.

"I don't know!" She stood and began to pace. "How can one decide to be married for the rest of eternity? That is so . . . so scary! What if things don't work out?"

Bishop Denney's eyebrows knit in concern. "As long as two people who care about each other put the Lord first and then each other above all else, any marriage can be successful. Most of it is give and take . . . and talking problems out before they become unsurmountable. I feel you're a person who could make any marriage work. Is Mathieu?"

He was . . . or at least Marie-Thérèse thought so.

"But this is the only opportunity I have to serve a mission while I am young. My whole life I have dreamed of it." She paused before rushing on, knowing that in her distress, her French accent made her English difficult to understand. "You said I could make any marriage work. It does not have to be with Mathieu, no? I could wait."

The bishop inclined his head gravely, but a small smile played on his lips. "I think the question here is what does the Lord want you to do? Are you willing to accept his counsel?"

"Oh, yes. But I do not get an answer. At least one that I understand." She sat back in her seat. "What do you think? Should I send in my papers? Or . . . or what?"

"Only you can decide that."

Marie-Thérèse looked up at the ceiling. "Oh, if only I didn't want to marry Mathieu so much. Or if I didn't feel I should go on a mission. I don't know what to choose. I wish there was some way to know for sure. I wish I could go somewhere special and ask the Lord."

"You can go anywhere to ask him those questions. As a daughter of our Heavenly Father, you deserve to receive revelation from him in any quiet place you seek it. You can know for sure."

Marie-Thérèse felt tears coursing down her cheeks. "I know that, but I'm not feeling anything. All night I have prayed in my room. I have walked outside alone, asking him over and over. Today, I have stayed in church and prayed. For more than a month I have been struggling with sending in these papers. I haven't sent them in because of Mathieu, though I didn't want to admit it even to myself. I just don't know what to do! This decision will affect the rest of my life.

And Mathieu's, as well. Can't you help me? Please?" Marie-Thérèse could barely form the words through her sobs. In a rush, she continued, "Last night when I was praying, I kept thinking that if only I could go to the temple, I would be able to hear the Lord there."

"You can hear the Lord anywhere," the bishop said gently, handing her a tissue from the box on his desk.

"I know that, but . . . the temple is so sacred. Maybe there I could separate my carnal feelings and listen only to the Spirit. Please, isn't there any way I could go through the temple?"

Bishop Denney thought for a long time. "Maybe," he said slowly, "there is a possibility. I'll have to talk it over with the stake president. You see, normally we don't give recommends to people unless they are definitely planning to get married or go on a mission—"

"But I am planning to get married or go on a mission. I just do not know which."

"I realize that. And since you are serious about doing one or the other, I think perhaps we can make an exception in your case and let you go through. I mean, if you did hand your papers in today, you would get your call next month and be able to go through the temple anyway. Regardless, going even a month early is not something to be taken lightly. Once you make covenants in the temple with the Lord, there is that much more danger of retribution should you fail to keep the promises made there. There is nothing Satan loves more than to cause someone to break their temple covenants."

Marie-Thérèse's tears had ceased with the hope of attending the temple. "I understand that," she said. "All of my life I have been taught how important the temple is. I would rather die than betray any covenants I will make with the Lord."

The bishop smiled. "Yes. I know that. I wouldn't even be considering letting you go through if I hadn't known you so well these past months. I know that you have prayed as fervently as you say, and perhaps this is the beginning of an answer for you."

After discussing the temple in much more detail, Bishop Denney went with her to see the stake president, who was interviewing down the hall. They eventually issued Marie-Thérèse a temple recommend which she held tightly in her hand, silently thanking the Lord for the opportunity to visit his house.

Darkness had fallen during the hours she had been with the bishop and stake president. She had called from the bishop's office to tell Josette she would be late, so she knew her sister wouldn't be worried or waiting up for her. She certainly didn't expect to find Mathieu pacing outside her apartment building.

"I talked to Josette," he said without preamble. "She told me where you were. Did you . . . I mean . . . the papers . . ." His familiar face showed anxiety mixed with hope.

"I gave them to the bishop, but he's just going to hold on to them for me until I make a decision."

The trepidation in Mathieu's eyes decreased. "Then I guess I'm still in the running."

"Oh, Mathieu, don't say it that way. If I would marry anyone now, it would be you. I just have to be sure." She held up the recommend. "I'm going to the temple to help me decide."

"Can I go with you?" he asked.

She smiled through her tears. "I would like that."

He hugged her briefly before quickly stepping away. "I'll try to behave myself, Marie-Thérèse, but you are so beautiful that I want to kiss you and never stop. But I'm not going to even give you a small one until . . ." He backed away as he spoke. "It's hard enough as it is." With that he turned and faded into the night. Marie-Thérèse watched after him, feeling better than she had felt in months.

* * * * *

Ariana listened on the phone as Marie-Thérèse explained the situation between her and Mathieu Portier. *My little girl's in love!* Ariana thought. She could hear it in her voice and in the way she tried so hard to deny it. But Ariana also knew she needed to encourage her daughter without making her choice for her. The only way Marie-Thérèse could find happiness was to know for herself that what she was doing was right.

"I think going to the temple is a good idea," Ariana said. She hesitated. "I would really like to be there, but I can't leave right now."

"Oh, I didn't expect you to come all this way, but I wanted your blessing."

"You have it, of course," Ariana said. "I just wish I could be there."

The silence lengthened before Marie-Thérèse asked. "Is it Pauline?"

Ariana bit her lip, grateful that Marie-Thérèse couldn't see her expression. "Yes," she said carefully. "She's been sick, but don't worry too much. We've got her on a new program that seems to be working. We'll keep you informed. Meanwhile, you work on making your decision. Your father and I will be fasting and praying for you. Everyone here will."

"I'd actually like this to be kept kind of a secret, if you don't mind," Marie-Thérèse said. "You can tell Dad, of course. But either way I decide, I'd like to break it to the family myself."

Ariana laughed. "We know how to keep a secret. We won't tell."

When she hung up the phone, Ariana recounted the conversation to Jean-Marc. "I can't believe it," he said. "If any of the children served a mission, I would have thought it would be Marie-Thérèse."

"That's exactly what I thought. But you should have heard her voice. She really likes this Mathieu."

"I think I'll call her myself," Jean-Marc reached for the phone. "I still need to ask her the questions I ask all Josette's dates."

Ariana smiled. "Good idea. You do that. But don't talk her out of getting married, if that's what she wants to do."

Jean-Marc summoned a wounded look. "What? Getting married was the best thing I ever did."

She kissed him. "And don't you forget it."

Leaving him to his phone call, Ariana went to check on Louis-Géralde. She found him sleeping in his bed, arms spread out in abandon. She sat beside his inert figure and stroked his soft cheek, loving the feel of healthiness that radiated from him. So different from Pauline.

Should she have told Marie-Thérèse about Pauline's cancer? Maybe it was time. Tomorrow she would try to convince Pauline.

CHAPTER TEN

Zack Fields was proud of the Leandro family and the progress they were making in the Church. Already they had callings, and the children thrived as their spirituality increased, as if their souls had found the place where they belonged. On the other hand, Madame Legrand and her daughters still vacillated.

Brionney's letter came again in French, and Zack wondered about the woman who helped her write it. The letter was friendly, so typically Brionney, and yet there was another flavor to it that he could not exactly describe. A zest for life? A longing? A vulnerability? It was all of these and more. He studied the curve of Josette's face in the picture on Elder Perrault's dresser, reaching out his finger to trace it. Instead of live flesh, it was only the slick feeling of the glossy photograph paper, which was vastly unsatisfying.

A snort behind him showed that his attention had not gone unnoticed. Reluctantly he flipped off the light and went to bed.

When Zack slept, he saw Josette again, but she was far away, almost out of his sight. He felt sadness, though it was only a dream, and when he awoke in the night, the feeling stayed with him. Self-consciously, he prayed. "Please help her, Father. She's going to need it."

The next day he wrote to Brionney, "Please keep an eye on Elder Perrault's sisters." He wrote in English to be sure she understood. "I have an uneasy feeling about something."

* * * * *

"I wish I could go with you!" Josette said late Tuesday afternoon after her last class.

Marie-Thérèse squeezed her arm. "I wish you could, too."

"Don't you feel awkward going without Mom and Dad?"

Her sister nodded. "I always thought I'd go through the temple with them, but this will save us the trip to Switzerland or Germany before my mission or whatever."

Whatever? Josette didn't understand the reference. Of late, her sister had been more reticent than usual.

"Besides, they agreed that I should ask Brionney's parents to take their place," Marie-Thérèse added.

It irritated Josette that Marie-Thérèse had called her parents before telling her. Once they had shared every secret, but now there seemed to be an unbridgeable gulf between them.

Brionney and her mother arrived shortly, and Marie-Thérèse ducked her head in greeting. "Thank you very much for coming, Irene."

Irene gave her a big smile. "I feel very honored to be invited, Marie-Thérèse." The way she said Marie-Thérèse's name showed she had been practicing the pronunciation. "Terrell will be meeting us at the temple."

Brionney sat on the couch. "Well, have fun. I guess I'll hang out with Josette since I can't go to the temple yet either. Is that okay with you, Josette?"

"I don't mind." Josette thought that at least spending time with Brionney would be more fun than being alone.

"Oh, and we saw Mathieu across the way," Brionney added. "He'll be here any minute."

"He's going too?" Josette asked, not sure how she felt about that. Even as she spoke, Mathieu arrived, his gray eyes more intense than usual. He didn't give any greeting to anyone, but looked at Marie-Thérèse silently.

"What is this?" Josette quipped in what she knew was awkward English. "You go not to a funeral, no?" Everyone smiled, but the mood—from Mathieu at least—didn't change.

"Happy bunch," Josette muttered as they left.

"Well, it should be a happy time," Brionney said. "If only your sister would come to her senses."

Josette tensed. "What is it you say?"

"I'm saying that poor Mathieu has a right to be worried. If Marie-

Thérèse goes through the temple and still feels she should go on a mission, he knows he'll have lost her for good."

A sick feeling came to Josette's stomach. *No, no!* she wanted to scream. But with Brionney's words everything fell into place—Marie-Thérèse's strangeness, Mathieu's subtle stares and abrupt silences. He loved Marie-Thérèse, wanted to spend the rest of eternity with her, and once again Josette was just another pretty face.

She struggled valiantly for control, but Brionney gazed up at her anxiously from her seat on the couch. "Is everything okay? Didn't you know?"

"Of course I knew," Josette lied.

"Well, you'd have to be blind not to notice. How did you like the ring? That's really something."

"Yeah," Josette agreed faintly.

"It having belonged to Mathieu's grandmother is so sweet," Brionney added with a long sigh. "I wished it were me."

Josette made an unintelligible noise.

"What's wrong? You look funny," Brionney said.

"It is nothing. I just have ache in my stomach." At least this last was true.

Brionney instantly grew concerned. "I hope you're not getting sick," she said. "You don't need that, with school and all. Maybe you should go to bed."

"Yes, I think so." Anything to get rid of peering eyes, so that she could let down her guard.

"Do you want some juice or something?"

"No, I am fine."

"Okay, then. You get some rest."

When Brionney was gone, Josette went to her room, her steps resembling those of a sleepwalker. In her mind she reviewed the conversation, refusing to believe. Yet in her sister's top drawer, tucked behind her underwear, she found the ring box. The ring fit her hand as if made for her, and she held it out to catch the light. It was large, expensive, and surely something meant for her, not Marie-Thérèse! How she would love to wear this, to show it to her friends!

Then an idea came to her. Maybe Mathieu turned to her sister because he thought Josette wasn't ready for marriage. "But I am," she said aloud. "And I would give up all my other boyfriends for him." She clenched her jaw. "And Marie-Thérèse wants to go on a mission. He has no right to make her give that up."

But I'll show him how I feel, she thought. *Yes! Then he'll leave my sister alone, and he and I will be together.*

She tried to tell herself that her plan was good, that she wasn't only considering it for selfish purposes. *Marie-Thérèse would do the same for me. She did, in fact, when we were testing Marcelin. Well, sort of.*

For a long moment, she stared at the ring on her finger. At last she put it back in the box and tucked it in Marie-Thérèse's drawer, out of sight.

Marie-Thérèse came home much later, her eyes sparkling. "Oh, it was so wonderful!" she said, sitting on the edge of her bed. "I feel like I am fully dressed for the first time in my whole life." She met Josette's eyes. "The Church is true; I know it with all of my heart!"

Josette tried to be happy for her sister, yet she resented the fact that Marie-Thérèse now held even more secrets from her. "Did you get the answer you were looking for?" she asked, as if her sister had confided in her all along. "I mean, regarding Mathieu?"

Marie-Thérèse didn't seem surprised by the question, making Josette wonder fleetingly if her sister had tried to talk with her before about the choice she had to make. "No," Marie-Thérèse said with a sad smile, "but I'll go again. Maybe every day. It's so peaceful there, like heaven. I almost imagined I could see Jesus there. I wish I had."

Her attitude convinced Josette that her plan was sound. Not only did her sister need to go on a mission, she would be a wonderful missionary. She couldn't let her sister marry Mathieu, only to regret it for the rest of her life.

* * * * *

The following Friday turned out to be the perfect day for Josette to enact her plan. Rosellen had gone home for the weekend, and Noni had to work. Even Marie-Thérèse made it easy for her by going to the temple after her last class.

"I'll be doing a couple of sessions this time, but I'll be home by nine or so," she said. "I've got to finish some homework."

Josette felt a twinge of guilt as her sister left the apartment, bundled up against the cold walk to the temple. "What about coming home?" she asked.

Marie-Thérèse waved the concern aside. "I have a ride."

"Mathieu?" Josette asked anxiously.

"No, Irene. She's meeting me there later."

Josette made preparations for an intimate dinner, but waited an hour before calling Mathieu, just to make sure her sister was really gone, and that it wasn't too early to eat. The phone rang three times before he picked it up. "Oh, Mathieu," she said breathlessly, "you're home."

"Sad, isn't it? And on a Friday night, too." His voice sounded unhappy.

"Me too," she said. "Want to have dinner? My treat."

He laughed. "That really would be a treat! Did somebody die and leave you a bundle?"

Josette giggled, though she was too nervous to find it funny. "No, but my test scores are good enough to convince my parents to send my allowance. Besides, you always take us places and pay."

"I'll be there in a few minutes," Mathieu said. He hung up before Josette could tell him what she had in mind.

She changed hurriedly into the black column dress with the spaghetti straps. The sheer material hugged her body, making her feel feminine and alluring. Above her right breast, she fastened the butterfly brooch Alphonse had given her that last night in France. She piled up her long hair on her head, leaving a few strands down to soften her face. With mascara, she lengthened her already long lashes and used blush to enhance her cheekbones. In the mirror, her eyes peered back at her large, dark, and innocent. Mathieu didn't stand a chance!

The doorbell rang and Josette swept to the door, as regally as any noble queen. *If only Mom could see me now,* she thought.

When she opened the door, Mathieu stared around the candlelit room in surprise. "What's up?" he asked cautiously. His eyes focused on her dress and his jaw dropped.

"Like it?" She twirled for his benefit, noticing with disappointment that he wore faded jeans and a sweatshirt.

"Don't you think it's a little cold to be wearing that?" he asked.

"Not if we're staying in to eat," Josette said. "We're alone." Taking his hand, she drew him into the room.

"I thought we'd go out for this," he said, shoving a coupon under her nose. BUILD YOUR OWN SPUD, it read in bold letters.

Irritation flared in Josette's heart. Didn't this idiot know when a girl was trying to have a romantic evening?

"Come on in," she said. "I made dinner."

"Jose, I think you should change and we should go out for something," Mathieu declared with a trace of panic in his voice.

She smiled. He was nervous! He was afraid of letting her know how he felt! Well, she'd put an end to that right now. "Don't worry Mathieu," she said, pushing herself against him and guiding his arms around her back.

Mathieu stiffened. "I think we'd both feel better later if—"

"I love you," she blurted out, letting her arms slide up and around his neck.

"Marie-Thérèse—"

"Is at the temple, praying about becoming a missionary," she interrupted scornfully. "We both know how you feel about me, so leave her out of it. I'm here, and I love you." She kissed him long and deep on the mouth, breaking off when she realized he did not return the kiss. Mathieu reached up and took her arms from around his neck, then pushed her gently but firmly away from him.

Josette felt shock flooding her body. She had been so sure that he would want her over Marie-Thérèse! "I'm more beautiful!" she wailed, not caring how it sounded. She lunged toward him.

He held her back easily. "Stop it right now!" he said through gritted teeth.

"You love me," Josette insisted.

"No I don't," he said harshly. "You are nothing but fluff! Look at you, all made up like a woman in some film. Sure, you're beautiful on the outside, but inside there's . . . nothing. Not like Marie-Thérèse. She's beautiful in here, where it counts." He thumped his chest.

"She wants to serve a mission. She won't marry you!" Josette yelled, wishing the spite in her voice could dig into his heart as his words had pierced into hers.

Mathieu snorted. "That's how little you understand! I want to marry your sister; but even more than that, I want a woman who loves the Lord—before me—whatever choices it leads her to make. I want a woman I can trust to raise my children to be responsible adults, not spoiled children who live only on whims. Grow up, Josette! It's about time that you do."

He turned on his heel and left the apartment, slamming the door after him. Josette threw herself on the sofa and sobbed violently. Mathieu didn't love or respect her! The hurt and humiliation were too deep to bear.

After a long time, her tears slowed and eventually ceased. She sat vacantly, wondering how she could ever face Mathieu again.

A burning smell reached her nose: the dinner she had so carefully planned! Slowly, she stood and went into the kitchen to turn off the stove, not bothering to look inside. Then she moved down the hall to the bathroom, where she washed her face repeatedly with cold water until the redness and swelling eased. The ache in her heart didn't go away.

Before she contemplated her actions, her hand lifted the phone and began dialing. "Hello, Grady?" she asked as a voice answered at the other end.

"Hi, my little cabbage," Grady teased. Josette laughed in spite of herself; somehow the French term of endearment didn't translate well into English.

"Are you doing anything tonight?" she asked, trying to muster her confidence. "I'm all alone, and I thought of you . . ."

"I was thinking of you, too," Grady said. "I was just going to call you." A part of her recognized his lie, but the wounded part of her drank in the glib words. "I'll be right over," he added.

Josette reapplied her makeup while she waited. A few more strands of hair had escaped the pile on her head, but it looked like she had planned it that way. Her eyes showed almost no redness, only a melancholy that she imagined made her more dramatic. The thought brought a trace of a smile.

Grady gave a long, low whistle when she opened the door. "You look wonderful," he said, taking her hands and kissing her cheek. "You smell great, too."

Josette basked in his attention. Now here was a man who appreciated her!

"You look too good for my eyes only," he said. Today those eyes were blue like his dark sweater, but not the clear blue of the sky like

Brionney's and her brother's. Why did she think of them now? She pushed the thoughts away.

"What is spud?" she asked, remembering Mathieu's coupon.

Grady laughed. "That's what I love about you. Everything is so new. A spud is a potato. You can say 'a spud' or 'the spuds,' but not just plain 'spud.' Here we bake 'em, open 'em up, and put stuff on top—whatever you want. Kind of like a salad bar."

"Do you want to eat one?" she asked.

He shook his head, his eyes traveling over her dress. "Not with you looking like that. I know just the place we can go. We'll have to stop by my apartment so I can change, but I'll only be a minute."

He helped Josette on with her good coat. "Wait," she said. "I have to leave a note for my sister." She was tempted not to leave a note to punish her for Mathieu's rejection, but she knew it wasn't Marie-Thérèse's fault. She didn't want her sister to worry. *Went with Grady,* she scrawled on the message board in French. *I'll be back by ten. Call if later.*

Grady shuffled impatiently at the door, and Josette hurried to not keep him waiting. At his apartment building, she waited in the car, its motor running, while he changed. He came out a few minutes later with his shaggy hair slicked back behind his ears, wearing green dress pants and a blazer made in a darker shade. He looked handsome—certainly more the proper companion than Mathieu with his jeans.

He drove past American Fork to a place called The Garden Wall Restaurant at Thanksgiving Point. Josette immediately loved the rich atmosphere, but gasped at the prices. On the budget her parents allowed her, she couldn't afford spending thirty or forty dollars for a complete meal. Grady grinned. "Don't worry about it," he said. "You're worth it."

For a moment, Josette felt she was.

They had an appetizer, then had to wait a long time before the main course was finally brought. Grady chattered easily, and with his attentiveness, Josette all but forgot Mathieu's rejection. When the waiter brought their non-alcoholic drinks, Grady slipped a small bottle from the pocket of his blazer, opened it, and poured something into his cup. "Want some?" he asked.

Josette knew it was some kind of alcohol, and for the first time, twinges of unease stirred in her stomach. "No," she said. "I don't drink."

"Neither did I," he said, "until I realized what I was missing." He stuck the bottle back in his pocket, not forcing the issue.

"Aren't you a member of the Church?" Josette felt stupid that she didn't even know if he was a member. It had never come up in their conversation before now.

He shrugged. "I was baptized, I guess."

Josette felt oddly disturbed by his answer. His drinking also bothered her, but she didn't understand why. Many of her boyfriends in France had liked wine with dinner. Maybe it was because she knew Grady was a Mormon. There were a lot of things she would do, but drinking wasn't on that list—even feeling as depressed as she did over Mathieu's rejection.

They finished the meal, talking about anything that came to mind, and Josette forgot her uneasiness completely. Grady acted like a perfect gentleman.

While they waited for the waiter to bring their check, another waiter behind them dropped a full tray of plates onto the floor, breaking them. When he went down on one knee to begin the cleanup, his shoulder bumped a tray of ice water and glasses balanced on a folding stand. The tall glasses crashed to the ground and shattered. The waiter grimaced and continued his cleanup.

Grady laughed. "A chain of events," he said. "You can't stop it."

On the drive home, Grady was strangely morose. Could it be from the alcohol? Josette watched carefully, but he seemed to drive as well as ever. "How about a video at my apartment?" he asked.

Josette nodded in agreement. Anything was better than facing Marie-Thérèse. What if Mathieu told her what happened? Josette needed more time to come up with a plausible excuse. She glanced at her watch. It was nearly ten; she'd have to call soon so her sister wouldn't worry.

But what could she tell Marie-Thérèse? The more she thought about it, the more worried she became. She would have no choice but to make up a story. Her conscience screamed in protest, and she tried not to listen. She had to do what she had to do. But was it possible that Marie-Thérèse would believe Mathieu over her own sister? "No, she promised a man would never come between us," she mumbled.

"What's that?" Grady turned off the engine and turned to her.

"I said no hunky-punky," Josette said sweetly.

"That's hanky-panky. You're so cute, Josette." Grady leaned over and kissed her briefly on the mouth. He smelled like musk.

He opened her car door and led her into his apartment. By the darkness, Josette could tell no one else was home. The disquiet in her heart returned. "Maybe we should just call it a night."

"Oh, it's too early. Come on, just a little longer." He crossed to the VCR and put in a tape before settling himself on the couch.

"I'd better call my sister," Josette said, "and tell her I'll be late." But she sat beside Grady, not knowing how to explain to Marie-Thérèse what had happened between her and Mathieu.

They watched the video in comfortable silence. Josette began to feel sleepy, and she didn't mind it when Grady cuddled up to her. She settled into the circle of his arm and laid her head on his shoulder. The video went on, but she was unaware of what was on the screen.

Grady was kissing her before she had a chance to object. "You're so beautiful," he murmured. "I love the way you always look."

Josette enjoyed the compliment. At first she responded to Grady's kisses until he pushed too far. "Stop," she said, trying to get up. Everything seemed to be happening in fast-forward, and she needed time to think.

"No," Grady said, pushing her back onto the couch.

Fear came through now, giving Josette the power to escape his grasp. "Take me home," she said, jumping up from the couch. "Please. I'm tired."

He took her in his arms again. "No," he hissed gruffly. "It's too early, and it's about time you stopped playing with me."

Josette raked her nails against his cheek in an effort to escape, but the act only inflamed him further. She struggled desperately for freedom. He backhanded her, sending her reeling to the floor with the stinging pain.

She felt his weight on top of her and she kicked, punched, and bit him, fighting for all she was worth. *If only Mom could see me now.* The bitter thought was as tormenting as Grady's punches.

She freed herself again and ran blindly away from him, down the hall and into a bedroom. It had a lock, but Grady pushed open the door before she could turn it. In a moment he was on her. She heard the ripping of her dress.

Please, dear Father, she prayed. *Help me!*

CHAPTER ELEVEN

Marie-Thérèse enjoyed her time at the temple, her fourth session since Tuesday. The first time she had gone through the temple, she had been nervous and everything had been too new for her to even concentrate on her problem. "Don't rush it," Irene Fields had said to her. "Give yourself time."

Since then, she had been able to ponder the possibilities of her future and the choices she had to make. In the temple, the things of the world were of little importance; for the first time she could glimpse the real meaning of life. Amidst all the white clothes, friendly smiles, and hushed voices, she felt she could envision what heaven would be like. An indescribable joy flooded her soul.

Irene squeezed her hand. Today, Marie-Thérèse had attended her first session alone, but Irene had met her for the second. It helped to have someone more experienced to talk to about her choices.

"I love Mathieu," she admitted to Irene as they talked after the session. She whispered to maintain the reverent atmosphere. "But when I think about how much the Savior has done for me, I want to do my part and serve a mission. Why can't Heavenly Father just tell me what to do?"

Irene laughed. "That would be too easy. We have to do at least some of the work. How did you feel when you prayed about marrying Mathieu?"

Marie-Thérèse felt a flush spread over her cheeks. "I felt good." More than good, tingly even, but she had also felt good about going on a mission.

Irene must have read some of her feelings in her face. "Maybe in your case, either choice is acceptable to the Lord. Maybe you have to decide what you want most."

"I want both," Marie-Thérèse said, staring down at her hands, clenched in her lap. Except for the dark freckles, they were almost as white as her temple dress. "I . . . it would be easier to marry Mathieu, I think."

A wide smile covered Irene's face. "And you're afraid of taking what appears to be the easy way out, aren't you?"

"I guess so."

"Well, I can tell you that a mission can be hard, but it can't begin to compare to a life of marriage and raising children. I know, because I've done both. And what you might be forgetting is that as a mother you *are* doing missionary work. Each child you raise up to believe in the Lord is every bit as important as someone you find and baptize. Ours is a continual mission."

"They say women are supposed to get married, if they have the chance."

It seemed to Marie-Thérèse that Irene was trying hard not to smile again. "That they do," the older woman said. "I guess what it boils down to is if you can chance losing Mathieu." She held up her hand to prevent Marie-Thérèse's reply. "Oh, I'm not saying there won't be another man. But when there is, it won't be Mathieu. Will you be happier with one, or with the other? That I can't say. And you can't know, either. What you have to determine is what is in your heart right now."

Deep down, Marie-Thérèse had known this all along. She pictured Mathieu—his tall, lean frame, his dark hair, the way his dancing gray eyes stared at her. Her heart was full of tenderness and a kind of ache. Could she afford to lose him?

"He said I would be making a difference in his eternity," she said, almost to herself.

"And in your children's. But you have to do it willingly. I mean, he could find someone else, just as you could. Or he could wait for you."

That wasn't an option Marie-Thérèse was willing to consider. How could she give her whole effort to the Lord on a mission if her heart was with Mathieu, continually worrying that she might lose him to another woman? How could she bear to be apart from him at all?

Irene pulled up her sleeve and glanced at her watch. "I think they'll be closing up soon. Are you ready to leave?"

They drove in silence to the apartment complex. "Thanks, Irene," Marie-Thérèse said. "You will never know how much I appreciate your coming with me."

"I'm glad to be here for you," she said. "I hope that if my daughters are ever away from me, someone will be able to help them. I only wish I could see into the future for you."

Marie-Thérèse gave a short laugh. "Me too. I wish I could have two of me for a while."

Irene put her hand on Marie-Thérèse's shoulder. "There isn't a woman alive who hasn't wished that at one time or another. Think of all the housework I could get done—with plenty of time to do what I really enjoy!"

They continued to talk until the cold forced Irene to restart the car. Marie-Thérèse waved good-bye and walked stiffly to her apartment. The sky was clear and black, and the stars winked down on her benevolently. She stopped at the base of the stairs and lifted her face to soak up the beauty, feeling again the peace that had filled her being at the temple. She felt she was close to an answer.

Reluctantly, she climbed the four flights of stairs. Noni lay on the couch facing the television. "Hi," she said without taking her eyes from the screen.

"Hi," said Marie-Thérèse.

She went to her room, shedding her coat as the heat in the small apartment seeped into her flesh. The room was empty, but the jeans Josette had borrowed from her earlier lay in a heap in the middle of the floor. That meant her sister had gone out.

Marie-Thérèse retraced her steps down the hall and into the kitchen. On the message board she saw Josette's scrawled message. Instinctively, she glanced at the clock. It read fifteen to eleven. *Did Irene and I talk that long? Where is Josette? Her message said she'd be home at ten.* Marie-Thérèse hoped her sister hadn't become worried about her and gone looking. She chided herself for being so preoccupied with her own problem that she hadn't thought to call.

"Noni, have you see Josette?" Marie-Thérèse asked, going into the front room. "Her note says she should be home by now."

The girl dragged her eyes from the television. "I haven't seen her. I've been here since ten or so."

"Were there any messages on the machine?"

"Yeah. Mathieu called. He wanted you to call him as soon as you got in."

Where was Josette? Marie-Thérèse found it suddenly hard to breathe past the growing consternation in her chest. She dialed Mathieu's number quickly; maybe he knew something.

"Have you seen Josette?" she asked when he answered.

"What? No 'Hi, how are you?' Just 'Where's Josette?'"

Marie-Thérèse wasn't in the mood for games. "She's missing," she said. "It's not like her to be late without calling. Since we had that first fight about it, she's been more regular than the clock. I'm worried. Her note says she's with Grady."

"I don't like that guy. We'd better go look for her." His voice was grim, stoking Marie-Thérèse's fear. "Something happened earlier," Mathieu added. "Something you should know. With Josette . . . but we'd better find her first. She might need us."

The warning in her heart told Marie-Thérèse her sister did need her, and quickly.

She met Mathieu in front of her apartment. They checked the pool and the common areas of the apartment complex. "I know where Grady lives," Marie-Thérèse said. "We'd better check there."

In the car, Mathieu put his hand over hers. "Everything's going to be all right."

"Then why do I feel so awful?" Marie-Thérèse stared intently ahead, as if doing so would make them arrive more swiftly. "Hurry, Mathieu."

At Grady's apartment building, they jumped out of the car and ran up a flight of outside stairs. Marie-Thérèse banged on the door, and after a long time a sleepy-looking man opened the door. "Whatcha want?" he asked.

"Is Grady here?" Marie-Thérèse asked.

"No," the man said with obvious irritation. "He lives upstairs. Darn idiot makes too much noise. Tell him to shut up." The door slammed, but Marie-Thérèse was already bounding up the second flight, with Mathieu close behind. A dark cloud floated across the moon's surface, blotting out the dim light. Marie-Thérèse pushed on, a sudden urgency filling her entire body.

Once again she banged on a door. There was no answer, but she heard a scream, abruptly muffled. Marie-Thérèse tried to peek in the lighted window, but blinds blocked her view. She turned helplessly to Mathieu, who beat on the door with his fist. Behind the door, everything was still.

"She's in there, I know it!" Marie-Thérèse said.

Mathieu removed his coat and wrapped it around his hand. He punched his fist through the window, breaking the glass. Then he laid the coat over the sill and wiggled through. Marie-Thérèse followed close behind.

"There's no one here," Mathieu said.

"Look." Marie-Thérèse pointed to Josette's coat, which lay crumpled on the floor by the couch. The coffee table was overturned and magazines were strewn everywhere.

"Her shoe!" Mathieu pointed down the hall. Marie-Thérèse tried to push past him, but Mathieu held her back. "Follow me," he whispered.

In a few seconds they were down the hall, flinging the doors open. One was locked. Mathieu held his breath and threw his shoulder against the door. On the second thrust, Marie-Thérèse heard the door splinter and silently blessed whoever had made it so flimsy.

Inside the room, Josette lay on the floor struggling wildly. Grady was on top of her. Fury engulfed Marie-Thérèse. "Get off her!" she screamed.

Mathieu grabbed Grady by the neck and hauled him to his feet. Josette sobbed in relief, holding her arms across her chest. Marie-Thérèse knelt by her sister, gathering the trembling body into her arms. The spaghetti straps on her dress were missing and the silk was ripped under Josette's arm to her waist, revealing her skin. Bruises and scratches covered her face, neck, and arms.

"It's okay now," Marie-Thérèse murmured, pulling her sister's dress down over her legs, bare except for ruined nylons.

Josette pointed an accusing finger at Grady. "He—he tried to . . ." She turned her face into Marie-Thérèse's dress and sobbed.

Grady struggled, but Mathieu kept a firm grasp on him. "She asked for it!" Grady protested. At that Josette lunged for him, but Marie-Thérèse held her back, fearing for her safety. Grady laughed and stuck out his chin. "She's a tease."

"She asked for it, did she?" Mathieu muttered. "Just like you asked for this." He whirled Grady around and slugged him in the stomach. Grady doubled over, whimpering. Mathieu snorted in disgust as he fell to the ground.

Josette pulled away from Marie-Thérèse and hovered over Grady's body. She kicked him. "I hate you!" she muttered. Grady's eyes showed red, but with Mathieu standing above him, he didn't dare attack.

Josette crumpled again, and Mathieu wrapped her in Marie-Thérèse's coat and swept her up in his arms. "Let's get her home," he said, making his way down the hall.

"It's my word against hers," Grady called after them. "And everyone knows she's a tease!"

They ignored him.

"We have to call the police," Marie-Thérèse said in the car. She sat in the backseat with her arm around Josette. "We have to."

Josette had her eyes closed tight and didn't answer.

"Of course we do," Mathieu said. "But we're only three minutes from home. We'll do it there."

Josette had both Marie-Thérèse's coat and Mathieu's wrapped around her, but she continued to shiver. Marie-Thérèse rubbed her back and arms until her hands ached.

Mathieu carried Josette toward the apartment. "I can walk," she protested, momentarily rousing from the apathy she had lapsed into.

"You don't have your shoes," he said.

There was something odd between them that Marie-Thérèse couldn't pinpoint. Mathieu's words of earlier returned to her. What was it he wanted to tell her? Was it about them? Had he decided he didn't want to marry her after all? And how did Josette work into the equation?

In a star-bright flash, Marie-Thérèse knew she loved Mathieu and wanted to be with him forever. A mission was important, but not as important as marrying the right man at the right time. It took the possibility of having lost him to help her understand how vital Mathieu was to her happiness.

It was interesting to her that the revelation about Mathieu hadn't come in the temple as she had expected, but near her own apartment while talking with Mathieu and Josette. The bishop had been right all along. The temple experience had helped her understand so much about life, but personal revelation did come to those who needed it—no matter where they were.

The apartment appeared deserted, and Marie-Thérèse thought Noni must have retired.

"This is partly my fault," Mathieu said as he laid Josette on her bed.

"What?" Marie-Thérèse asked, cradling Josette's head in her lap. An ugly bruise had formed on her left cheekbone, in the shape of a man's fingers. Blood dripped from a deep scratch near the bruise. Josette touched it gingerly, and Marie-Thérèse saw that three of her sister's beautiful fingernails were broken.

"Your sister and I had a talk," Mathieu continued, "and I'm afraid I wasn't very nice to her."

Josette lifted her head. "You tried to kiss me!" she accused.

Mathieu looked taken aback. "What? No way!" He looked at Marie-Thérèse. "She came on to me, and I refused to play her little game, whatever it was."

A deep flush stained the unbruised part of Josette's face, and Marie-Thérèse knew Mathieu told the truth. Relief rushed through her—relief that it was Josette who had tried to betray her and not Mathieu. There was a time when she would have wished it to be the other way around. With anyone else, she still would, but not with Mathieu.

"It's not true!" Josette cried, sitting up. "You can't believe him over me!"

"Can I talk to my sister alone?" Marie-Thérèse said to Mathieu. She smiled to show her belief in him, and he nodded once, sharply, but the concern didn't leave his face.

"Okay, but don't clean off any more blood. The police will want pictures for the report. I'll go downstairs and wait for them." Mathieu leaned down and kissed Marie-Thérèse's forehead, and an unfamiliar warmth spread through her, subduing her anger at Josette.

"Why did you do it?" Marie-Thérèse asked when he was gone.

Josette froze. For a long moment she didn't say anything, just stared at Marie-Thérèse with her brown eyes wide and sad, her bruised face crying out for help.

"I was testing him," she said finally. "Like the way you tested Marcelin in France."

"You agreed to that," Marie-Thérèse said. "And there was a reason."

"There was a reason here, too." Josette stared at the quilt on her bed, plucking at the yarn ties. Her fingers were red and scratched. "I—I liked him. I just wanted to know if he had any feelings for me."

Marie-Thérèse felt her anger build. "So you tried to steal my boyfriend because you liked him? For heaven's sake, you have so many men interested in you, why him? Why the only man who cares about me?"

"He's different," Josette said. Marie-Thérèse understood what she meant, but was surprised that her sister had noticed at all. "And he's not the only man interested in you," Josette continued. "A lot are, you just don't know it. And they're all like Mathieu." She held her palms to the sides of her head as if it ached. "Oh, why can't a man like that want me?" She collapsed onto the bed and sobbed as if her heart were breaking.

Marie-Thérèse gathered her sister in her arms. "I love you, Josette. And you will find someone as good as Mathieu one day. But first you have to be a woman they can admire."

Josette pulled away. "I can't change who I am!" she declared passionately. "I like me. I like me!" Her head dropped once again into Marie-Thérèse's lap as she dully repeated the phrase over and over, as if trying to convince both of them.

Marie-Thérèse stroked her sister's hair. "Shh," she said softly.

Josette's sobs gradually subsided. When she had been quiet for several minutes, she twisted her head to gaze into her sister's eyes. "You're not giving him up for me, are you? Mathieu's coming between us. Or is he?"

Marie-Thérèse knew what Josette was asking. Her thoughts went back to when they had been sixteen and the same boy had asked them out. At first they had fought, but little Pauline had made them understand that sisters were more important than any transitory boyfriend. They had both dumped the American boy, Kenny, and made the vow to never let a man come between them again. Both had kept that pledge—until now.

"He's not just a man," Marie-Thérèse said slowly as her mind searched for words to voice the feelings she hadn't fully understood until now. "He's far more than that. He—he represents eternity. In the back of my mind, I think I always knew this day would come, only I thought it would be you first. But here we are. I love Mathieu, and I want to marry him . . . forever. That bond is stronger than ours, whether we like it or not." Tears slipped down her cheeks now, dribbling off her chin and mingling with the tears on her sister's face. "I'll always be here for you," she added. "But please don't make me choose. I don't want to lose you."

Josette sat up and hugged Marie-Thérèse, pressing her cheek against her sister's, wincing slightly but otherwise seeming to ignore the pain her wounded face must feel. "I won't," she whispered. "And I'm happy for you. I really am." The desolation in her voice ripped at Marie-Thérèse's heart, but there was nothing she could do to change it. Her course was clear; she loved Mathieu!

Rapid footsteps sounded in the hallway, and the door burst open to reveal Brionney and Irene. "Josette! We just heard what happened!" Brionney said, her blue eyes wide. Her head shook back and forth, making the light reflect off her white tresses. "Mathieu called us."

"You poor thing," Irene said, settling herself on the bed and taking Josette's hand. "The police are downstairs now. A couple of them are going to hunt Grady down."

"I hope they smash him like the bug he is," Josette hissed.

Irene's face didn't show shock, only compassion. She looked at Marie-Thérèse. "The other officers are on their way up. They feel it would be best to question you separately. But don't worry, Josette, they said Brionney and I could stay with you."

Josette sighed in relief and let Irene put an arm around her. "Thank you," she murmured.

Marie-Thérèse gave a last squeeze to her sister's arm and left the room. She met a woman police officer in the hallway. "Be gentle," Marie-Thérèse said to her.

The woman flashed her a smile. "I will. Don't you worry. But will she need any translating?"

"No, she speaks very well." In fact, since coming to the U.S., Josette's English had improved immensely. English verbs weren't as difficult as French verbs, and the biggest problem for both of them remained in spelling and pronunciation.

Marie-Thérèse answered the policeman's questions quickly as he wrote on a pad. "So you definitely can identify the suspect," he said.

"There's no doubt at all," she said. "We had to pull him off of her."

The officer smiled grimly, flipping his book shut. "Then we'll get him. It's just a matter of time." He touched a black rectangular object at his waist. "He hasn't returned to his apartment yet, but we have it staked out. We think he may be connected to several on-campus rapes. Your sister was very lucky."

Marie-Thérèse thought luck had little to do with why Josette had been saved. Faith did. And perhaps her sister had learned something, or at least had started down the right path.

Noni stuck her frizzy head out of the kitchen. She wore long pajamas and thick, fuzzy slippers. "I'm sorry," she said, hesitantly. "I feel it's my fault. I introduced Grady to her."

"You know him well?" the policeman asked.

"Yes."

"Did he ever attack you?"

Noni colored. "Not like that. But one night, we'd been drinking and we . . . that was a long time ago. I knew what I was getting into." She shook her head. "Josette didn't. She's basically innocent."

"Do you know where he might go?" the policeman asked.

Before Noni could answer, Marie-Thérèse made a clearing noise in her throat. "Do you know where Mathieu Portier is—the man who called you?"

"Oh, that's right," the policemen said. "He asked me to send you down when we were finished."

"Will you let me know when you're done with my sister?"

"It'll probably be a little while. Then we'll have to go down to the precinct to file a formal complaint. We'll need pictures, too."

"I'll go with her."

"Of course." The man's eyes twinkled his approval. "But right now there's a passionate young Frenchman downstairs waiting for you."

Marie-Thérèse smiled to herself as she sprinted down the steps, slowing as she reached the bottom. Mathieu sat on the cold cement sidewalk with his back against the red brick of the apartment building. He stood, shivering in the cold, his breath billowing in warm clouds.

"Marie-Thérèse." He said nothing more, but opened his arms in a silent plea.

She went into them, feeling the coldness of his clothes through her own. She lifted her lips to his. He leaned forward, but at the last minute pulled back with a groan. "But I love you," she said.

A grin spread hesitantly over his handsome features. "Does that mean . . .?"

"I want to marry you," she said.

"No regrets?"

She met his earnest gray eyes, loving the way he was willing to be sure. "The only regret I think I would have is if I let you go."

He hugged and kissed her until she gasped for breath. They both laughed, and a few tears of happiness escaped as well.

"Besides," Marie-Thérèse added, "we can do missionary work together in France."

"And when we're older, we'll go on a mission full-time."

For a moment they said nothing as they drank in the newness of their love. Marie-Thérèse rubbed her cheek against his, feeling the prickling of his beginning beard. It did feel like sandpaper, as Josette had once said, but she loved it!

Mathieu whispered in her ear, "Oh, Marie-Thérèse, my love, you've made me the happiest man in the whole world. I promise to make you just as happy—if it takes the rest of my life."

"The rest of eternity, you mean."

"That too." He kissed her again.

CHAPTER TWELVE

Pauline and Emeri walked hand-in-hand down the cobblestone sidewalk of the busy street. They moved slowly, stopping whenever they needed to rest. For Pauline, the frequent stops were a necessity. If it hadn't been for Emeri, she wouldn't have left the apartment at all. But she had to see him.

Her head was mostly bald now, after the hair had dropped out in bunches. She had at first tried to wear a wig, but both André and Emeri had laughed at the result, and the wig itself had been so hot and itchy that Pauline had given it away. She cut her few remaining hairs very short and constantly wore a hat.

"Look! Some Christmas cards," Pauline said, stopping at an outdoor display. "I need to get a few." She thumbed through the cards, picking out the ones with the brightest colors. "Don't you want to get some?"

"No," Emeri said. "I don't have anyone to send them to, and my friends and I don't exchange anything."

Pauline placed a card in his hands. "What about this one? For your parents."

Emeri glared at her. "Pauline, that's ridiculous. I'm not sending them a card."

"Why not? It'll be Christmas soon. And you said yourself that they don't know where you are. Wouldn't that be a nice gift for them? To know their son is okay?"

"What'll I say? 'Hi, Merry Christmas. I'm dying of AIDS. Hope you're happy for kicking me out in the cold.' Is that what you want me to say?" He shook his head. "No, Pauline, don't go there."

Pauline would have laughed if not for the seriousness in Emeri's voice and expression. She had suggested sending the card without any real hope, but now she knew he needed to send it as much as his parents might need to receive it. Whatever had gone on between Emeri and his parents was far from over, and she became determined to help all of them open a channel of communication. One way or the other, Emeri needed closure.

"Well, that's not exactly the sort of information you should send in a Christmas card," she said lightly. "But we could call them or visit. I'll go with you."

"No way! Get that out of your head right now. I'm never going back there. Never! And I'm not writing them."

Pauline knew he meant what he said. "Very well, then, *I'll* write the card. You just give me the address." Before Emeri could object, she grabbed the card from him, dug in her purse for a pen, and began writing.

"There. It says, 'Just wanted you to know that I am fine. Hope you have a good Christmas. Emeri.'" She had debated writing "Love, Emeri" but felt that might be going too far.

"Pauline, I'm not sending that card."

"You're not, but I am," Pauline insisted. "Look here, Emeri. I've been cutting you a lot of slack in your refusal to meet my parents, even though I don't agree. And that's because I really care for you. But if you don't let me send this card, I won't go out with you anymore. And I mean it! Your parents may not be wonderful people, but they deserve to know you're okay."

"I'm not okay," he said sullenly.

Pauline frowned at him. "I'm waiting." She hoped he wouldn't call her bluff. The truth was, she didn't think she could go more than a day or two without seeing him. When he wasn't with her, she felt part of herself missing.

He scowled, and Pauline impulsively leaned forward and kissed him. It took a few seconds before she felt his face relax enough to kiss her back. Pauline giggled and drew away. "So what's the address? Or at least the last place you know they were living."

Shaking his head in disbelief, he told her. When she was finished writing, she bought the card and some stamps and slipped it into the nearest mailbox before he could change his mind.

Emeri stared silently at the mailbox for an entire minute. Then he put his arms around her and pulled her close. "Would you have really refused to go out with me?" he asked softly.

"No."

"What! I never knew you could be so sneaky."

"I learned a few things from Josette."

"Well, sending a card is one thing. Just so you don't get it into your head to call them or something."

Pauline winked at him. "I'm making no promises."

"Huh! You'd better not."

She gave him an enigmatic smile and took his hand. They strolled once more down the sidewalk, comfortable in their companionship, the argument forgotten.

"Oh, look at that!" Pauline pointed to a small musical merry-go-round with tiny unicorns moving up and down as they circled. She laughed. "How adorable!"

Emeri stared at it. "Unicorns are supposed to be magical, you know."

"Then let's make a wish."

He grinned. "I don't know if it's that kind of magic. I think it has something to do with healing properties. If you touch them, or something."

"All the better," she said. "We could both use some of that magic. Come on!"

She tugged on him and he followed her into the store. There was a long line and only one clerk. Pauline leaned against Emeri and he looked at her worriedly. "Maybe we should come back later," he said. "You're looking a little pale. Do you want to sit down?"

"Emeri, I'm always pale," Pauline objected. But then the room flickered and she grabbed onto him. "Maybe I'm not feeling so well. Emeri, I think I'd better go home."

He caught her as she fell. From far away she heard him call a taxi and give the driver the address to the clinic. In a short time Pauline lay in the examining room, listening as Dr. Medard assured them that this sort of fatigue was a normal symptom of the cancer. "I think you've overexerted yourself today," he said. "Why don't you rest right here, and I'll go call your parents."

"Thank you," Pauline said.

When the doctor left, Emeri paced the room, his anger showing through the mocking exterior he had put in place for Dr. Medard. "Dang it, Pauline! I'm the one who's supposed to die first, not you!" She knew the fact that his cancer had responded better to chemotherapy than hers ate at him constantly.

"That's not for us to say," she said, trying to keep her voice steady. More than anything, she had to help him face what would happen. "It could be worse. One of us could have been hit by a car, and then we'd have *no* time."

Emeri crossed to the bed and grabbed her hands. "Marry me, Sunshine. Please! I love you, and I want to spend what time we have left together. I want to be with you every second of the day and night. To see your smile. I want to go to the mountains with you, and to the beach. Everywhere. I want to hold your hand when you're scared or sick. I want to take care of you."

A part of Pauline almost laughed. For so long she had dreamed of such a day as this, but without any real hope, considering her illness. She knew that she loved Emeri, more than she had ever thought it was possible to love another human being.

"Only in the temple," she said. "I love you, but I'll marry you only in the temple."

Anger flashed on his face but was gone again just as quickly. "I can't go there," he said.

"Not yet," she agreed gently, "but there's still time. Why don't you come and meet my parents and the missionaries?"

Emeri's mouth drew tight. "I love you so much. Ever since that day at the Eiffel Tower, I've known that I love you. But that doesn't change the way I feel about God. I won't listen to your missionaries."

Sadness threatened to overwhelm Pauline, but she pushed it away and smiled. "One day you'll realize how much Heavenly Father loves you," she said. "And when you do, you'll understand that we can be together forever."

He said nothing, but his dark eyes brooded. She tightened her grasp on his hands and pulled him down to kiss him on the cheek. "I love you," she whispered. "And that will never, ever change."

"Dear God in heaven," he said. "I don't want to lose you." He kissed her tenderly on the mouth.

"Am I interrupting something?" said a voice at the door.

Emeri straightened, his mocking smile back in place. "It's about time you got here, André," he said. "Some brother you are, coming after the crisis is averted."

"I only just heard," he said. "Mom's here too, but she's with Dr. Medard. Dad's on his way."

Emeri looked uncomfortable. "I'd better get to work anyway, now that your family is here to take care of you," he said to Pauline. "Dr. Medard has a whole room of files he's making me go through. When I finish, I'll call you later."

"Or come by?" It was a question she always asked, but he had never taken her up on it.

"Maybe." With a wink he was gone.

André walked over to the bed and kissed her cheeks in greeting. "How're you feeling, Dolly?"

She pointed to the hat near her pillow. "A little bald, if you know what I mean."

"You look cute," he said, running his hand over her bare head.

She laughed. "You are such a bad liar."

He kept his face serious. "I like to be good at everything I do."

She curled her fist and punched his shoulder, though there was barely enough force behind the blow to make itself felt. The effort sent pain rippling throughout her body. She let her arm drop to the bed.

As usual, André pretended not to see her weakness. They fell into an easy conversation, but Pauline found it hard to concentrate.

"What's wrong?" André asked finally.

"Emeri asked me to marry him." It felt good to tell someone.

André held perfectly still. "And?"

"I told him I would—in the temple."

André frowned. "That means he would have to be baptized and wait a year. Maybe if you really love him . . ." His eyes didn't meet hers, and she knew he referred to the obvious fact that neither of them might have that long to wait. "I mean, I wouldn't suggest it under other circumstances. And . . . well . . . I really like Emeri."

Pauline sighed. "I can't do that—even if Mom and Dad agreed. Don't you see? I really love him, André. I need him to find the truth so that we can be together forever. I don't want him just for this little bit of time." She struggled to sit up. "Promise me you'll keep working on him, no matter what. Please!"

André was silent for a long time. Then he slowly nodded in acquiescence. "I will," he promised solemnly. "If it's the last thing I do."

Pauline knew from experience that André's promises were never given lightly. She smiled at him, feeling happiness return. "Thanks. But don't say anything about Emeri asking me to marry him," she added. "Mom's worried enough about what happened to Josette in Provo. I don't want to add to her worries any more than I already have."

André saluted. "Yes, Madame! Whatever you say."

Pauline giggled. "Then go find the doctor, so you can take me home. I'm feeling much better now."

"I've already talked to the doctor," Ariana said from the doorway, her expression somber.

Pauline's smile faded. "I can go home, can't I?"

Ariana came to sit on Pauline's bed. "Yes. But you have to promise to take it easier."

"I will, Mom."

Ariana hesitated a moment before adding, "Perhaps we should call the girls home from college."

André looked away from them, his face pained. Pauline felt her own fear twisting inside. "The treatments aren't working, are they?" she said softly. It wasn't the first time her mother had made the suggestion.

Ariana's eyes brimmed with unshed tears. "Not as well as we'd hoped. The tumor still hasn't grown since we started the new treatments, but it hasn't become smaller either."

"But I'm feeling fine," Pauline said. "Please, Mom. They only have two weeks left or something like that. I'm not . . . I'll be here. Please, Mom. I just don't want them to hover over me. I don't want them to be sad. And in her last letter, Marie-Thérèse said Josette was doing so well in school. Give them just a few more weeks."

Ariana studied her for a long moment without speaking. Then she appeared to make a sudden decision. "All right. I'll have to talk to your father about it, of course, and see how he feels. And we'll need to pray. But one more episode like this, and I'm calling them to come home. It isn't right to keep it from them anymore."

"Okay." Pauline answered steadily, but in her heart she rebelled. She wasn't going anywhere—yet. She would fight for every second to be with Emeri.

* * * * *

A few days later, Pauline felt well enough to go to the group meeting at the clinic; at least that was what she told everyone. To herself she admitted that she should stay in bed, but nothing could keep her from Emeri. André had brought him to the house the day before when her mother was out shopping, but lying in bed all today without him had been much too long. She had to take every chance she could to see him. When he was with her, she felt . . . well, if not good then at least better than before.

Emeri waited at the door for her. He grabbed her in a bear hug. "I've missed you, Pauline!"

"You just saw me yesterday," she said, but she knew exactly how he felt. An entire night was too many hours to be separated from each other. She almost began to doubt the wisdom of her insistence on a temple marriage. But something inside wouldn't let her give up the blessings of eternity for a fleeting joy on earth—in the doubtful event that her parents even agreed to her marrying so young. Pauline felt convinced that Emeri would never accept the gospel if she gave in. *This is a sacrifice we both must make, even if you don't realize it,* she thought.

He kissed her briefly before pulling off her hat and holding it out of her reach.

"Emeri, stop that!"

"Okay," he said, plopping the hat onto her head. "But you look cute bald."

"Shining, you mean," she retorted, adjusting the brim so she could see him better. "It's any wonder you want to be seen in public with me now."

"This is public," he said. "And if you haven't looked around, a good third of those here are missing hair."

The members of the group began to gravitate toward the chairs. Beside her, Pauline felt Emeri stiffen. She looked up and saw a man coming through the door. "He shouldn't be here," Emeri grated. "That's why I joined this group instead of the adult one. I couldn't stand being with him and his kind." Emeri's hands clenched at his sides.

"That's Renard," Pauline says. "He comes here sometimes. He's okay."

"No, he's not. He's gay, and I don't like him. No, that's not strong enough. I detest him!"

"Emeri!" Pauline didn't in the least condone homosexuality, but she didn't share Emeri's hatred toward those who practiced the lifestyle.

"Oh, come on, Pauline," Emeri said. "They're to blame for what is happening to you, and to me as well, and for all the others who have AIDS. Don't you see it? They are the perfect political machine, with no children and all their money. They get publicity for kids and women who've contracted AIDS to try and win the sympathy of the general public. Tell me, how many times have you been set up as a poster child for AIDS? You or some other child who was born with it. All to get a few more dollars for research." She tried to speak but he ran over the words. "Oh, I know you got it from your mom and she from using drugs, but the bare truth is that those gays with their free lifestyle of bar-hopping and their filthy orgies caused the disease in the first place, and they're still spreading it. They don't want the freedom to be with one person of the same sex; they want to be immoral, to fall in the sack with anyone who's willing. If they would just stay with a single partner, the epidemic would be over. Everyone who had it would die out, and no more people would be infected."

Emeri hadn't kept his voice down, and the others were gathering around where they stood. Pauline sensed resentment in almost everyone present, but more exuded from Emeri than from everyone else combined. Renard stood alone by the door, a devastated expression on his face.

"He's right," said the mother of the youngest boy in the group. Pauline knew the child had contracted HIV from a blood transfusion. "They keep asking for money—billions of dollars for research—when if they'd just be moral, none of this would continue."

"Any way we look at it, the gays are to blame for the spreading of AIDS to women and drug users," someone said bitterly. "If they could be stopped, the epidemic would eventually die out. But they've sure been successful convincing people it's a women's and innocents' disease. According to them, they have no responsibility for it at all."

"I read in the paper that they tried to make it a law forcing a person to disclose the fact that they have AIDS to anyone they might sleep with," Emeri said, "like you have to with any venereal disease. But they struck it down as not fair; can you believe that? Where is the fairness to the other person? It's like legal murder."

"The gays want the lifestyle," someone added, "but then they cry because they get AIDS. What do they expect?"

"Then they give it to us," a bitter voice said. Murmurs of assent rippled through the group.

Pauline worried what might happen next. The crowd stared angrily at Renard, urged on by their fear and helplessness. Pauline knew that Emeri and the others told the truth, that the horror of AIDS would never be conquered unless anonymous promiscuity in the gay community ceased. But she also believed that hatred would not solve the problem.

"Emeri," she said, fighting the weariness in both her body and soul.

"Don't tell me you condone their actions." His voice was full of revulsion she knew was not directed toward her. "Even your religion doesn't do that."

"I don't condone it," she said. "But . . ." She waited until she had everyone's attention. "But there is a difference between compassion and condoning." She crossed to Renard's side. "I know Renard here, and I know he suffers with his sickness as much as we do."

Renard bowed his head in agreement. To her surprise, he spoke. "But Emeri is right. For many years I've believed the lies they told me, that I was born this way and that I needed to fulfill all my desires to be complete. But they were wrong. I've never been happy, not really, and I know that giving in to ugly desires is not the life that will ever give me the relationship I want. Before I die, I want to change. That's why I'm here. I want to find out what a normal life is like. I want to face God with a clear conscience." He turned to Pauline. "Can I be forgiven, do you think? Can I become whole again?"

She blinked back the tears. "We have to forsake our sins to know God. If you do that, yes, I believe he'll forgive you."

The mood of the crowd had suddenly changed, and the people wandered back to their seats, the conversation turning to less volatile matters. Emeri drew Pauline aside. "I still hate them," he said.

"I think you hate their actions."

He glanced at Renard. "I didn't know any could change. I thought they really were born that way."

"I think Satan wants them to believe that," she said. "That way he puts a barrier between them and God. But the fact is, we all have our struggles, and those who have weird urges need to get over them just like the rest of us have to get over our problems . . . like hate and anger."

"I will never condone homosexuality. Not ever."

"Neither will I. It's wrong, there's no doubt about that. But I won't waste my life hating them or anyone else. Life's too short as it is."

He watched her for a moment and then said slowly, "I love you, Pauline. And I would do anything if I could save you."

He touched Pauline's cheek, and she placed her hand over his. "Just loving me is enough, Emeri. Love can solve just about everything." She motioned to where Renard was talking with the mother of the youngest HIV victim. "Even with him."

Emeri didn't seem convinced, but in her short life Pauline had seen people make drastic changes because of love. Renard was proof of that. And loving Emeri was all she could do for him. That and pray. Someday he would find the truth for himself.

She knew now, without any reservations, that she was right not to marry Emeri. He still had a long journey ahead of him before he found happiness. But at least as long as she and André were alive, he wouldn't be alone.

Chapter Thirteen

She felt the swing of Grady's fist, and then he was on top of her again. "Tease!" he screamed as she tried futilely to escape. She heard the rip of her dress and felt the cool air against her bare skin.

Josette sat up in bed, breathing heavily as the dream faded from reality. She had pushed the blankets from the bed, and goose bumps covered her flesh in the cold morning air. She crossed her hands and rubbed them on the opposite arms to bring the warmth back into her body. An old T-shirt was all she wore, though her discarded jeans lay on the floor. She didn't remember taking them off after her late night of study, but she must have.

Pulling them on again, Josette glanced at the clock. It was ten already, and Brionney would soon be here for her Saturday lesson. She had asked Josette if they could study an hour earlier today.

The mirror on the desk captured her attention. Her face looked thinner than she remembered it from two weeks earlier, before that fatal date with Grady. Her eye no longer hurt, but the bruises still left traces of green. She knew that emotionally, the hurt would take longer to heal. Through the counseling Marie-Thérèse insisted she take, she was beginning to understand that while she could have done a great deal to prevent the attack, she was not responsible for it.

Am I a tease?

The question haunted her. She refused to go out on any more dates—no matter how good-looking or rich the guy happened to be—and threw herself into her studies with a renewed determination.

"Not all men are like Grady," Marie-Thérèse had said after the sixth night she had stayed home to study. Logically, Josette knew that;

but she wasn't ready to take any more risks. Grady's attack had frightened her beyond words, and there was no way she would place herself in a position to repeat that dreadful night.

Something's wrong with me, she concluded. One thing was certain: no one wanted her for herself, and she was sick of men liking her for how she looked. She played down her makeup—if she wore it at all—and her long hair that people so admired was worn in a severe ponytail down her back. As her hair was now long enough to sit on, her head often ached with the concentrated weight. Josette considered the pain part of her sentence.

Now, she put on a sweater and checked the heat. The dial read seventy-four degrees Fahrenheit; she shouldn't be cold. Did it come from her heart?

Her stomach growled and she went into the kitchen. There she found the note Marie-Thérèse had left on the message board: *Went shopping with Mathieu. Be back by two.*

Mathieu had been good to her after that night, and in fact had apologized. "I shouldn't have been so abrupt," he'd told her last week.

"It's nothing," she had insisted. But she felt two blotches of telltale red come to her cheeks as they did every time she thought of what had happened between her and Mathieu.

"It is not," he said. "When someone says they love you, you shouldn't act the way I did."

Josette shut her eyes against the pain. "Fluff doesn't have feelings," she said bitterly.

Mathieu grimaced and sat down beside her on the couch. She pulled her knees up to her chin and laid her head down on them, facing away from him.

"I'm really sorry about that, Josette. What I meant was that you haven't decided what is important in life yet. You're kind of in limbo, waiting for something to happen. I don't know what. But I know what I want in life, and so does Marie-Thérèse. And I love her. That's all there is to it. I wish I could be more to you, but I can't. But that won't stop me from being here for you if you need me."

"Am I even worth that?" Josette retorted, blinking back the tears that seemed to always be just behind her eyes.

Mathieu made a noise in his throat. "If I could take back those words, I would. Josette, no matter what you feel right now, you're a daughter of God and he loves you. He has a great future planned for you. You just need to figure out what it is."

Mathieu's words made Josette feel marginally better. Even if she was fluff, being tossed to and fro by the wind, she could change. She turned her face toward him. "Let's just never mention this again, okay?"

"Okay," he agreed emphatically. The relief on his face was almost amusing.

Marie-Thérèse had also been very kind and had never referred to Josette's attempted betrayal. All irritation seemed swallowed up in her newfound love. Josette had never seen her sister so content, and she loved her enough to be happy for her. She felt sure Marie-Thérèse had made the right choice. On the other hand, Mathieu and Marie-Thérèse were so caught up in each other that it was easy to feel left out.

Like today.

Now, Josette's hunger vanished with the memories, and she went into the front room to wait for Brionney. On the coffee table, she spied the butterfly brooch Alphonse had given her in Paris. The police had found it in Grady's apartment and brought it back to her in a plastic sack. She picked up the plastic and let the pin slide into her hand. The diamond dust glittered in the weak sunlight coming through the window panes. One of the wings was bent, and she straightened it with a tug. It looked as good as new. Not at all as ruined as she felt.

When Brionney arrived, Josette was still staring at the pin. "Thanks for letting me come early," Brionney said. "I just know if I don't supervise the decorations for our school Christmas dance, it won't get done right."

"Didn't you just have a dance a month ago?" Josette asked.

Brionney shrugged. "Homecoming, like you guys had here. But that's a formal date thing, and I didn't go."

Josette had gone to the Homecoming at BYU, though she could barely remember the face of the student she had gone with. It hadn't been as fun as she expected, and she almost wished she had stayed home with Marie-Thérèse and Mathieu. Was that the night they had begun to fall in love? Did it matter?

"Whatcha got there?"

Josette handed her the brooch.

"It's beautiful," Brionney said, her voice a trifle envious.

"Keep it," Josette said. Even to her ears, her voice sounded distant.

"Oh, but I couldn't! It looks so expensive."

"If you don't, I'm just going to throw it away." As she had the silky black column dress. She had cut it into tiny pieces before dumping it in the trash.

"But—"

"I wore it that night. It reminds me."

"Oh." Brionney pushed up her sweater and pinned the brooch on the shirt she wore underneath, then pulled it down, hiding the pin completely.

Josette gave a sigh of relief. "Besides," she said in a lighter tone, "it'll give you something to remember me by."

Her friend frowned. "You're not coming back then. Next semester."

Josette met her gaze. "No, I don't think so. I was going to; I even registered for classes. I really liked it here, but now . . ."

"I'm going to miss you," Brionney said in an odd voice. "You're my best friend, you know."

Josette smiled—her first real smile in two weeks. She put her arm around the younger girl. "Getting to know you has been the best part of coming to America," she said impulsively. "I don't know what I would have done without you these past few weeks." Brionney had taken to visiting her almost nightly, and since Marie-Thérèse and her roommates had their own busy schedules, it was these visits that kept Josette sane.

Brionney reached up and removed the thin rope chain she wore around her neck. A yellow-gold charm fell off into her hand. It was half of an inch-high heart, cut in a precise zig zag on one side where it had been separated from its other half. She handed the charm to Josette.

"What is this?" she asked.

"It's half of a heart," Brionney said. "When put together it says, 'The Lord watch between me and thee while we are absent one from another,' or something to that effect. My brother Zack has the other side, so I haven't read it for a while. I gave it to him before he left on his mission. I want you to have this half."

"But it is special to you!"

"Which is why I want you to have it."

"What will your brother say?"

"He'll understand. And it'll make me feel good knowing that the two people I love most have something from me. Besides, I could always go and buy another pair and have a side to match both of you!"

Josette hugged Brionney. "Thank you," she whispered. The sundered heart was exactly right for how she felt. It would remind her to never let another man hurt her. She unfastened her own necklace—a fine byzantine chain her parents had given her when she graduated from high school. The thickness barely allowed for the charm to slip on.

"So, how are the two lovebirds coming along?" Brionney asked as she brought out her French book.

"Lovebirds? Oh, you mean Marie-Thérèse and Mathieu."

"They are so cute together. I can't wait until I fall in love. Do they still stare at each other with goo-goo eyes?"

Josette laughed, though she wasn't sure what goo-goo eyes meant. "They are very funny," she said. "I never saw Marie-Thérèse act this way." She raised her voice in imitation. "Oh, how did I ever breathe before I met him?"

"And how did the world rotate before I met her?" Brionney lowered her voice to sound like a man, speaking with an exaggerated French accent. She giggled. "Maybe they both should see a shrink."

"Why? They are not too tall."

They fell onto the floor, laughing so hard they almost missed hearing the phone ring.

"Hello?" Josette asked a bit breathlessly.

"May I speak with Josette Perrault?"

"This is she."

"This is Officer Blaine Ewell, and I'm calling to inform you that yesterday we picked up Grady Ladd. I thought you'd want to know. Also, we've had several charges added to yours by some women in his apartment building. He's planning to plead guilty, so there'll be no need for a trial."

"Thank you for calling," Josette said, her knees suddenly weak. She was glad she didn't have to face Grady again. She replaced the receiver and sat down on a chair, the realization coming that it could have been a lot worse. In the end, she had been lucky that Mathieu and Marie-Thérèse had come looking for her.

Instead of cheering her, an ominous feeling seemed to hang over her, like the dense fog that occasionally shrouded Utah Valley.

If only Marc were here, she thought. *I miss him.*

* * * * *

"I just don't get it," Elder Fields said. "Why don't you want me to write your sister? It must be me, because she's absolutely beautiful. I can't imagine her not being perfect. From the way you talk about her, I think I'd like her. After all, I like you."

"She's not like me, really," Marc said.

"How can she not be? You're twins, and raised in the same family."

Marc hesitated, torn between his friendship with Elder Fields and the love and loyalty he felt for his twin sister. Josette won out; there was no way he would tell his companion that the sister he adored wasn't worthy of him. "It just wouldn't work," he said. "Trust me. I know her and I know you, and it wouldn't work."

Elder Fields must have heard the sincerity in his voice, because he didn't persist. "If you say so, Elder. Well, I guess you'd better get going; the cab's outside." He stuck out his hand and the young men shook solemnly. "It's been good serving with you," Elder Fields continued. "I'll come visit you before I leave France. My parents are coming to pick me up, so we're going to stay a week or so."

Marc grinned. "Seventeen months is a long time away," he said. "But I might still remember you." He laughed. "I'll show you around. And you're going to love my family."

Elder Fields didn't speak for a long time, then a slow smile spread over his face. "Elder, that's what I've been trying to tell you. I'll love all your family, *including Josette.*"

"You never give up," Marc said with a snort.

"If we gave up, we'd never have baptized anyone."

"Madame Legrand is taking her time." It was Marc's one regret in being transferred from the area.

"I'll keep working on her," his companion said confidently. "She's almost there. And with her daughters being baptized next week, that should help."

Marc clapped him on the back. "If it were anyone else, I think

I'd be a lot more reluctant to leave this area," he said "But I have faith in you."

"Even if I'm not good enough to be family." Elder Fields' voice was light, and his tone told Marc he was teasing.

"I'd better get going."

"Hey, maybe you should forget about being an engineer and go into real estate with me. My dad'll make an opening for you."

"And leave France? I don't think so. Besides, my brother's counting on me. We're going to open an engineering firm together one of these days."

"Well, if you change your mind . . ."

Marc left, feeling sad to bid his favorite companion farewell, but also feeling anticipation for the new area the president was sending him to open. With a greenie from America, no less! It would be hard work, but Marc felt up to it. Already it was nearly Christmas, and he had only until the end of April do the work he adored—at least full time. After his mission there would be school, work, and eventually a family.

When he arrived at the mission home to collect his new companion, the mission president called him into his office for a private interview. He was a tall man, big without being fat, and full of suppressed energy. In the place of his usual kind smile, he wore a frown and his face was drawn with concern. "I'm afraid I have some bad news about your family."

Marc listened in numbed silence as the president explained. "I'm so sorry, Elder."

Marc felt the president put his arms around him, and gradually the shock subsided, released by a clean flood of tears.

* * * * *

They had been in the library, studying, for nearly two hours. Marie-Thérèse glanced over at Mathieu, whose face was buried in his book. Her face felt raw. She loved it when Mathieu left his beard for a few days, but it played havoc with her sensitive skin when he kissed her. They seemed to do a lot of that nowadays—kissing. She gave a short laugh. Never in her life had she been tempted to break or even stretch the law of chastity—until now. It was one thing to be morally clean when you were waiting to find the right person to marry, but quite another thing when you had finally met someone you wanted to spend the rest of eternity with. Suddenly, staying morally clean took on a whole new light. A difficult one.

It was Monday, and in a week classes would be over. The end of this week and part of next would be full of exams, and then they would go home—together. Marie-Thérèse pictured the surprise on her parents' faces. After going through the temple, she had talked to her parents a few times, but hadn't told them about their engagement. Since they hadn't pressed, giving her space to make her decision, she and Mathieu had agreed it would be fun to surprise them.

May would be the best time for the wedding because Marc would be home, but Marie-Thérèse wished she didn't have to wait. Four and a half months had never seemed so long.

Mathieu looked up and caught her gaze. "I love you," he mouthed. Marie-Thérèse giggled, then glanced around to see if she had disturbed anyone. Mathieu stroked the back of her hair and she held onto his other hand, watching him. At this rate, she'd never get any studying done!

"Let's go back to your apartment," he said. "Maybe a walk in the cold will clear our minds."

"I'd like to check on Josette," she said, gathering her books. "I feel bad leaving her alone so much. She seems better, though, since you had that talk with her."

Mathieu shook his head. "She's not the same. I miss the old Josette. Parts of her, anyway."

Marie-Thérèse understood what he was saying. She didn't miss Josette's flightiness, her questionable boyfriends, or her selfishness, but she did miss the bright laughter and her sister's exuberance for life. Somehow the vitality had left Josette, leaving an empty shell.

"We'll give her time. I think she'll come back, now that Grady's been caught. She and Brionney were laughing at church yesterday."

"That girl is good for Josette," Mathieu said. "I like her. She's got her head on straight. You can tell her parents raised her right."

"I like Brionney, too."

They buttoned their coats against the cold and hefted their backpacks. Mathieu tried to take hers, but Marie-Thérèse glared at him.

"Just because we're getting married doesn't mean I'm suddenly weak."

He pulled her close. "Just practicing for when you're expecting our baby," he murmured against her ear.

She punched him, feeling her face turned red. "I'll be pregnant, not an invalid," she said.

"Well—"

"Race ya!" She took off in a fast walk, weaving in and out of the crowd of students in the library.

Outside, snow fell in large, puffy-looking flakes. Marie-Thérèse stopped and stared. It rarely snowed in Paris, and since she had been in Utah the snow hadn't stayed long on the streets and had been rather slushy. She scooped some up in her hand, and it felt like powder . . . tingly powder that burned her hand with its icy sharpness. Instinctively she brought it to her mouth, tasting the coolness with delight. How fun! And how cold! She dropped the snow and stuck her hand in her coat pocket for warmth. Mathieu put his hand inside with hers.

They stared at the blanket of snow that had layered the walks and grass while they were inside. Students made footprints in the snow, but they were quickly filling up again. The trees and bushes held inches of the snow, as did the rooftops. Everywhere she looked there was white.

"It's beautiful," she murmured. "I'm glad I got to see it this way."

"Now you know what the people here mean by a white Christmas," Mathieu said. "I never understood that before I came to Provo." They walked hand-in-hand along the snow-covered path, saying nothing but enjoying the atmosphere and the company.

When they arrived at the apartment, Marie-Thérèse noticed immediately that all was not well. Brionney sat on the couch, comforting Josette, while Irene hovered nervously nearby. Marie-Thérèse twisted the engagement ring on her finger. Mathieu had sent it to be sized so it fit properly, but she still had not grown accustomed to wearing the thick band.

"Marie-Thérèse," Josette wailed, jumping up. "It's Pauline! She's sick! She has cancer! We have to go home. We might even be too late."

Marie-Thérèse hugged her sister, her breath coming faster as the shock set in.

"We've arranged with your professors to have your tests done today or early tomorrow morning," Irene said. "It's not common practice, but in this case they've made an exception. Your mother called me and asked me to take care of it. She didn't want you to be alone when you heard."

"My mother?" Marie-Thérèse asked dully.

"Well, one of the missionaries in your home ward, actually. They translated for her." That made more sense, since Ariana spoke little English.

"I've booked you on a flight tomorrow," Irene continued. "Right after you finish your tests."

Marie-Thérèse wanted to jump on a plane that instant, but the logical part of her knew that they shouldn't give up nearly four months of hard work.

Irene wrung her hands. "Your mother wanted to wait until you went home for Christmas, but she was worried that you might not have the chance to say good-bye."

"But Pauline was doing so well!" Josette had stopped crying, but her face was streaked with tears.

"Are you ready for your tests?" Marie-Thérèse asked her calmly. Her insides churned with emotion she wouldn't let herself feel. How could she have been so wrapped up in her own new love that she hadn't recognized that her sister was gravely ill?

"I don't care about the stupid tests. I just want to go home."

"The flight isn't until tomorrow; we might as well get the tests over with," Marie-Thérèse said. With all the studying Josette had done recently, taking the tests early shouldn't be a problem for her.

She felt Mathieu's arm around her shoulder. "I'll be there as soon as I can," he said. She nodded but said nothing, fearing the tears would come seeping through. There was no time for that—not yet.

The next twenty-four hours went by like a bad dream—slow and torturous in some parts, surrealistically swift in others. They went to the testing center to take the tests available there, and later that night they each took an exam with separate professors. Marie-Thérèse slept little as she packed and studied for her one remaining test, to be taken at six the next morning. She called her parents to find out about Pauline's condition, but there was no answer at their apartment.

On Tuesday morning, Mathieu took them to the airport at nine, after their tests and in plenty of time to catch the plane home. Brionney and Irene accompanied them. "Let us know," Irene said.

"We will." Marie-Thérèse accepted her hug.

Brionney threw her arms around Josette. "Write to me," she said.

Marie-Thérèse didn't hear Josette's response because Mathieu took her in his arms. Desolation at leaving him overwhelmed her, hurting almost as much as the fear of losing Pauline.

How could I have ever thought of not marrying him? she thought.

"Take care of yourself," he said.

"I'll call you when we get there."

Much later on the flight, after the flight attendants had served lunch and Josette snored softly in the seat next to her, Marie-Thérèse put her head under the tiny flight pillow and cried.

CHAPTER FOURTEEN

When Jean-Marc brought the girls home from the airport Wednesday morning, Ariana rushed to meet them at the door. Both Marie-Thérèse and Josette looked tired, and their faces were red and splotchy. Josette's hair was rigidly drawn back in a long French braid, making the new sharp planes in her face jut out unbecomingly. She had become as slender as Marie-Thérèse, but the thinness didn't complement her as it did her sister. Ariana made a mental note to talk with her daughter and make sure she was all right. Josette had seemed to recover from the attack in Provo, but obviously she was still suffering.

"Where is Pauline?" Marie-Thérèse demanded. "Why isn't she in the hospital?"

"She's in her room," Ariana said. "Resting. There isn't anything more the doctor can do for her. She wanted to come home, and we agreed."

"How—how long does she have?" Marie-Thérèse's voice was less resentful now.

"The doctor doesn't know," Jean-Marc said. "It depends on a lot of things. We thought having you here would help. Marc's here, too."

Tears slipped down Josette's cheeks. "Why didn't you tell us sooner? I—I'm so furious with you for not telling me!"

Silence filled the entryway as Josette glared at Ariana. Instead of the customary fire in her eyes, there was an icy sadness.

"We thought it important that you finish your semester, if you could," Ariana said. She had expected a little anger or resentment from both her daughters, but Josette's coldness took her by surprise.

Josette tossed her head. "I don't care about school—and I hate Provo. Pauline's more important!"

Ariana tried to reach out to her, but she stepped away. Jean-Marc pushed past Ariana and firmly put his arms around their daughter. "Pauline wanted it this way," he said. "And we had to respect her wishes as well as do what we thought was best for you. We told her the last time she collapsed that if it happened again, we would need to call you home. She agreed."

"She collapsed?"

"Yes, from exhaustion," Ariana explained. "The first time last week it wasn't bad. She was out with a friend and he took her to the clinic. She was up and walking again in a few days. This last time it wasn't a collapse exactly; she simply woke up without the energy to get out of bed. So we took her to the doctor, but there's nothing more he can do except give her medication if the pain gets too bad." She put her hand on her upper stomach, beneath her breasts, in the same place where the tumor grew inside Pauline's body. "Mostly, she tries not to take the medication because she wants to be aware of what's going on."

"I want to see her," Marie-Thérèse said.

Josette nodded in agreement. "Me too."

Ariana smiled. "Well, she's been waiting for you." She held up her hand. "But try to be positive, okay? Pauline may be the bravest person we know, but she's still afraid."

Josette started to cry again. Ariana held out her arms and to her relief, Josette accepted her comfort. "What should I say?" Josette asked. "What if I say the wrong thing?"

"Just tell her how much you love her. That will be enough."

They went to Pauline's room, and Ariana saw the girls' expressions lighten when they heard Pauline's tinkling laughter. Inside the room, André was on the floor, lumbering around on hands and knees with Louis-Géralde on his back saying, "On horsey, get going! Oops, I'm gonna fall off!" The two fell to the floor. Marc, sitting on a chair next to the bed, leaned over and tickled the small boy.

Louis-Géralde noticed them first. "They're here!" He jumped off the floor and launched himself first at Marie-Thérèse and then at Josette, chattering as fast as his four-year-old mouth would allow.

Pauline's eyes brightened. "You look so different, Josette! You're skinnier than Olive Oyl! Marie-Thérèse, I love your hair." The sisters hugged and tears flowed down their cheeks. "It's so good to see you!" Pauline added.

Marc and André hovered near the bed, awaiting their turn to greet their sisters. Josette hugged Marc tightly, and Ariana saw her whisper something in his ear. Her twin smiled and pressed his cheek against hers.

Ariana felt Jean-Marc's hand in hers. She looked over at him and read her own thoughts in his green-brown eyes. All of their children together again—full of smiles and joy. For this peaceful moment, at least, the realities of life were set at bay and Ariana was happy.

* * * * *

Marie-Thérèse stayed with Pauline that night when everyone else had retired to their rooms. "Marie-Thérèse," Pauline said, waving a thin hand in front of her sister's eyes. "Hey, Marie-Thérèse, you're about a million worlds away. What is it?"

Marie-Thérèse started guiltily. "Oh, I'm sorry, Pauline. I guess I just was thinking."

"You looked like you were dreaming. Your face was all soft and . . . Marie-Thérèse, I can't believe it! You're in love!" Pauline pushed herself farther up on her pillows. "Goodness, you can't hide information like that, you have to tell me! Who is it? Not an American, it can't be an American! Mom couldn't take losing you right now, not when . . . Spill everything, right now!"

Marie-Thérèse found herself telling Pauline all about Mathieu. "I knew going to America was going to be good for you," Pauline gushed. "Oh, I can't believe it. I'm so excited!" But she started to cry.

"What's wrong, Pauline?" Marie-Thérèse stared at her sister, hardly knowing how to comfort her.

"I'm not going to see the wedding. I won't be there to see your babies. I—" Pauline stopped and swallowed hard. She closed her mouth and pinched her lips together as though to keep herself from sobbing.

Marie-Thérèse held her sister as she had when she was small and had skinned her knees or had been teased by the other children for having HIV. "I'm so sorry," she mumbled, hating the inadequate words.

"I know you're sorry. Everybody is sorry."

"But it doesn't change things," said Marie-Thérèse. This was a side of her sister she had never seen. "What can I do? How can I help you not be afraid?"

"I'm not afraid," Pauline whispered. "I was once, but I'm not anymore. I just think that when I'm in heaven, sometimes I'm going to look down and wish I could be with you. I know they say this life is but a blink in the eternity of time, but right now it seems like an awful big blink."

"To me, too," Marie-Thérèse said. "Oh, Pauline, I love you so much."

Pauline wiped the tears from Marie-Thérèse's face. "Then don't be sad. I want more than anything for you to be happy."

She pulled away and reached under her bed for a battered bundle that Marie-Thérèse recognized immediately. "That's the baby blanket Mom made you before she died, the one you keep Dolly in," she said.

Pauline nodded. "I don't think I ever thanked you for giving Dolly to me."

"You were just a baby when I did."

"I know, but she's always been my favorite. I should have told you."

Marie-Thérèse fingered the worn blanket, still covering the doll. "You didn't need to. I knew. You never went anywhere without her."

"It was the only real connection I had with our mother," Pauline said. "Dolly and the blanket. I remember lying in my room sometimes at night, wondering where Mother was and how she'd felt when she made Dolly in homemaking." She paused and added softly, "I used to talk to her."

"So did I," Marie-Thérèse admitted. "And I think she heard. Dad too." She tried to unwrap the doll, but Pauline put her hand over hers.

"Do you think they'll look just like they did in the video tapes?" Pauline asked. "Will they come to meet me? Will I know them?"

Marie-Thérèse began to cry again at her sister's earnest questions. "Oh, yes, Pauline! They loved us so much. They will be so glad to see you!"

"Then maybe I won't miss you as much as I think," Pauline said with a watery smile. "Now stop that crying. I'm trying to give you a present. Remember how Dolly used to look? With only one embroidered eye gone and her stuffing coming out? Well, look at her now!" Pauline opened the blanket and revealed the treasure. The rag doll had been carefully patched and wore a new set of clothes. She had two eyes and new yarn for hair.

"I fixed her these last few days, lying here," Pauline said. "Mom helped me. I want you to have her back and keep her for your first daughter. I know she'll treasure her as much as I do."

Marie-Thérèse hugged the doll to her chest. "Thank you. It's the best present in the whole world."

Pauline grinned happily, but her face showed the effort their exchange had exacted. Marie-Thérèse touched her sister's arm. "Look at me," she said, "keeping you up so late. I'm afraid I'm still running on American time, and they haven't even eaten dinner yet. Come to think of it, I'm hungry."

"No, don't leave," Pauline said. "Just stay with me a little longer, until I fall asleep."

"Okay, if you don't mind."

Pauline smiled and held her hand, her eyes drooping. With her free hand, Marie-Thérèse turned down the three-intensity light in the lamp. "Sing me a song," Pauline said. "Daddy's song."

Marie-Thérèse knew immediately what song she meant. It was the one their father had sung to them each night before he died. Pauline had been too young to remember, but Ariana and Jean-Marc had captured the song on film. Marie-Thérèse didn't know where the song had originally come from or even if her father had used the right words. But for years after his death, she had insisted on singing parts of the song to baby Pauline so she wouldn't forget.

Tell me why life is so beautiful.
Tell me why life is so gay.
Tell me why, dear Mademoiselle.
Is it because you love me?

Four times through, and Pauline was asleep. Marie-Thérèse watched her sister's face, its contours sharpened by the shadows. So thin. So fragile. So guileless. Marie-Thérèse recognized the look, though it had been years since her parents had died. For a brief second, the pain in her heart was too terrible to bear.

She kissed Pauline's cheek and left the room, still clutching Dolly, and found Ariana waiting for her in the hall. Without speaking, Ariana held out her arms. Marie-Thérèse went into them and the pain in her heart lightened—just as it had when Ariana had opened her heart and home to her as a child.

"Thank you. Thank you so much," Marie-Thérèse whispered. "Thank you for loving Pauline—and me."

"I have received more from you two than I have ever given," Ariana said. "And I have never regretted having either of you in our family."

"Not even during the hard times?"

"No. Not ever." Ariana paused. "But I was worried you were still angry at me. I sensed you were this morning."

Marie-Thérèse sighed. "I was angry. I thought you should have told me about the cancer before. But when I was unpacking this afternoon, I found all the letters Pauline wrote me while I was in Utah. I'm so grateful for them now. And seeing her this way . . ." Marie-Thérèse brought a hand to her heart. "It hurts so much. But it's strange, Mom. Sometimes when I think about her going to see our parents and all that, I almost feel a happy hurt. I know she'll be so content to see them. And then I feel sad again, because I don't know if I want her to be happy without me." Marie-Thérèse started to cry. "I mean, I want her to be happy, but I'll miss her so much!"

"I understand. I feel the same way," Ariana said.

For the first time, Marie-Thérèse noticed the worry lines in her adopted mother's forehead. Ariana had buried her first child at eight months old—how must she be feeling now to watch a second daughter die? How could she be so strong? Surely Pauline's death would be harder on her than anyone else.

Marie-Thérèse gently said good night and went to her room, silently vowing to do everything she could to help her mother. Only then did she realize that Ariana hadn't questioned her about her decision regarding Mathieu. *Well*, she thought, *that information can wait.*

She lay on her bed and thought about Mathieu.

* * * * *

The next morning, Josette crept into Pauline's room to make sure she was all right. Her sister had the phone in her hand and looked up, guilt written on her face.

"I'll call you later," Pauline said. With effort, she leaned over and hung up the phone.

"Who was it?" Josette asked. *Pauline with something to hide?* What an amazing thought!

Pauline shrugged a thin shoulder. "A friend, that's all."

"Come, tell me." Josette sat on the bed.

"It's Emeri."

"You mean the boy you wrote us about? Well, is he coming over? I can't wait to meet him!"

Pauline shook her head miserably. "He won't come—not while Mom and Dad are here. And they won't leave me now."

"But why won't he come? That's so strange."

"It's something to do with his own parents," Pauline said. "He's had a falling out with them. He won't tell me exactly, but I think they kicked him out of the house. It was right when he found out about his AIDS."

"Did his parents know?"

"That he was sick? No. I don't think so. Before I got so tired, I bought a Christmas card and made him send it to his parents. I memorized the address. I keep hoping they'll come looking for him, that whatever happened can be worked out." Pauline looked at Josette with pleading eyes. "Oh, Josette, I need to see him! Can't you figure some way to get Mom and Dad out of the apartment for just a little while so that André can bring Emeri over? Please? If I ever wanted anything from you, it's this. Can't you figure something out?"

"You really care about him this much?"

"Yes, I do," Pauline answered softly, but the look on her face told Josette more than any words ever could.

Josette straightened, her mind already working out the possibilities. "I may not be able to get them out of the house, but I'll bet a nice little outing in the fresh air would do you some good."

Pauline frowned. "I can't walk now, I'm too weak. I've tried, but it's no use."

"A chair! You should have a wheelchair!"

Pauline brightened. "Of course!"

"I'll be right back!" Josette ran from the room, feeling more useful than she had in weeks. She found her parents in the kitchen and blurted out her idea.

Jean-Marc shook his head. "I don't think you realize how sick your sister is, Josette. She can barely sit up."

"But she's horribly bored!" Josette exclaimed. "We can't let her stare at the wall until she dies. Don't you see how much she hates that? This way she could just lie back in the chair, and I could take her for a walk down the street or to the swing sets to watch the children play."

"It's winter," Ariana said. "She shouldn't be out in the cold."

"The sun's out and it's almost warm," Josette countered. "She can wear a jacket and a mound of blankets. Please! She really wants to go!"

Ariana and Jean-Marc discussed the options. "It may make her weaker," Jean-Marc said.

Ariana glanced at Josette. "But it may make her happy."

In the end, Josette won, and she drove with her father to pick out a wheelchair. They arrived at home shortly before lunch with the coveted chair.

"Dad wanted to buy you a better one," Josette told Pauline, "but I insisted on this one because they had it in stock."

"I'm so glad!" Pauline said. Two rosy spots appeared on her pale cheeks.

Ariana went to the bed and checked her forehead for fever. "You had better eat something first, Pauline," she said.

"But I'm not . . . okay, I'll eat."

When Ariana left to make lunch, Josette grinned. "So did you call him?"

Pauline smiled weakly. "Yes, I did. But I have to call back and tell him what time. I was so afraid you wouldn't get the chair."

"Well, call him!"

But André and Marc came into the room. "I see Josette got her way, as usual," Marc teased.

"That's right. And Pauline is going outside as soon as she eats."

"So where are we going?" André asked.

Josette looked at Pauline. When Pauline nodded, she explained that Pauline wanted to see Emeri. "I should have known," André said. "Why don't you just leave it to me? I'll have Emeri down at the swings in, say, an hour."

"Thank you, André," Pauline said.

Ariana came in with lunch for Pauline and while she ate, Josette waited in the TV room with Marc. "I can't believe little Pauline's old enough to fall in love," Marc said.

"Well, she isn't," Josette returned. "But she's had to grow up fast." Before she could help herself, tears flooded her eyes and she hid her face in her hands.

"Are you all right?" Marc asked.

"I don't know," Josette said sadly. "I don't know if any of us will ever be all right again without Pauline."

He put an arm around her. "We'll get through this together."

She felt her heart ache. Her problems seemed so insignificant now, in the face of Pauline's impending death. A part of her didn't care if she was ever happy again. "I'm so glad you're here, Marc," she said. "I don't want to be without you now. I've missed you so much."

"I know," he said. "I've missed you, too. It must be that shared amniotic fluid or something."

Despite her mood, Josette smiled. She was about to reply when their mother came into the room. "Pauline's ready for you."

As her father placed Pauline's limp body into the wheelchair, Josette had second thoughts. Pauline was more frail than she had imagined. Would this outing do more harm than good? But she couldn't bring herself to take away Pauline's happy smile.

As promised, André waited for them near the swings. With him stood a thin, angry-looking boy about André's age. His dark-blond hair wasn't long but not as short as Josette expected. He wore faded jeans and a long-sleeved T-shirt.

"This is Emeri," André said.

"Of course it is." Josette put out her hand. "Nice to meet you."

But Emeri was already kneeling next to Pauline's chair, ignoring Josette completely.

"Be nice to him," André murmured in her ear. "He doesn't mean to be rude. He's anxious to see Pauline, that's all. And he can't help what he's wearing. None of your snobby college boyfriends will see you with him anyway, so don't make fun."

Josette glared at him. "I don't care what he's wearing," she mouthed. André looked surprised, but before she could think why, Emeri spoke to them harshly. "Please, could you leave us alone for a minute?"

They stood some distance away, watching but not close enough to hear. "He's trying to talk her into marrying him," André said.

Marc frowned and took a step forward. "I don't know if I like that."

André put a hand out. "He's all right, Marc. Please, just give them another moment. Pauline's a smart girl. She knows what she is doing."

* * * * *

"Pauline, come with me now," Emeri begged. He knelt on the cement in front of her, grasping her hand. "There's still time."

Pauline traced the lines of his face with her eyes. How she wanted to hold him! But her arms were too weak to respond. "Emeri, I've come to say good-bye," she said. "The rest is up to you."

"No, Pauline, no," Emeri moaned. "I can't live without you! I don't want to."

Pauline forced herself to be strong. "I don't want to be without you either," she said simply. She leaned her head down until it met his. For a long moment they stayed that way, touching and yearning. Pauline wished this moment would last forever. Neither spoke, for there was nothing left to say.

* * * * *

When they took Pauline back to the house, she seemed more content. Emeri, however, appeared miserable. André tried to talk with him, but Emeri shrugged him off and darted down the street.

"What did you talk about?" Josette asked Pauline when they were once more in her room alone.

Pauline didn't act as though she had heard. "Will you help him, Josette? He's a good person, he's just had a hard life."

"Of course. But he didn't even notice me."

"I know. He's a little preoccupied right now, but you can forgive him that, can't you? For me?"

Josette blinked back the tears. "For you I'll do anything. I'm just sorry I haven't been the kind of sister I should have been all these years. I haven't exactly given you a good example."

"What happened to you, Josette? You're different now."

Josette gulped. She had refused to talk about what had happened with anyone except the counselor she had been forced to see after the attack. But Pauline had always been special; it wouldn't be so bad to tell her. "That boy, when he tried to rape me. It's just, well, one part of me thinks . . . I feel I deserved it."

"No way!" Pauline said. "You must never think that!"

"Well, I've been doing a lot of things I shouldn't have. But all that's going to change. I'm going to be good, like you and Marie-Thérèse. And I'm never going to trust a dumb man again."

"But you'll find someone good, I know you will."

"I don't want to, Pauline. It just hurts too much. I'm tired of the effort. I could never be sure that he loved me for me, and not just my looks. Oh, that sounds so conceited, doesn't it?"

Pauline smiled. "Kind of. But Josette, I know you'll find someone when it's time. Until then, you could focus on something else. You could reach out and help a lot of people, maybe teach them the gospel. In fact, you could start with Emeri! I'll bet you could charm him into listening better than I could. If he could just feel the Spirit, I know he'd change."

"I'll do anything to help you or Emeri. But I'm through trying to charm anyone. Every time I've done so, it's only made things worse. Look at what happened the last time."

Pauline looked at her gravely. "If there's one thing I've learned in my life, it's that everything has a purpose, Josette. It's how we look at it that makes the difference."

Grady's attack had a purpose? It was a new idea for Josette, but one that bore consideration. *Maybe this is how the Lord intended things to be.* If she and Marie-Thérèse hadn't gone to BYU, Marie-Thérèse might not have met Mathieu, and Grady's attack would never have happened. And whether she liked to admit it or not, both Mathieu and Grady had made an impact on her life, urging her to reevaluate her priorities.

"Thank you, Pauline," Josette said. But her sister was already asleep. Josette tucked the covers around Pauline and settled back in her chair to think.

CHAPTER FIFTEEN

During the days that followed Pauline's outing, the weather was too stormy for her to go out again, but she didn't seem to mind. She lay in bed listening to music or watching her siblings who stayed with her almost constantly, even during the long hours she slept. There was a resigned contentment in her manner that Josette had never seen before. Only when they talked of Emeri did Pauline look unhappy.

Three days after seeing Emeri, the home care nurse who visited Pauline began to come twice daily. She explained that the end was near. Pauline ate and drank little as her body prepared to shut down. They asked about an IV to prevent dehydration, but the nurse explained that the IV would only prolong Pauline's pain.

On Sunday, Josette found her mother in the kitchen sobbing as though her heart was breaking. Fear cut into Josette's stomach, making her feel ill. Jean-Marc, Marc, and Marie-Thérèse had gone to church, and André and Louis-Géralde were with Pauline. Josette wanted to run away from her mother's pain, but she knew she should try to help.

Josette patted her shoulder. "Don't cry, Mom."

To her relief, André galloped down the hall with a grinning Louis-Géralde on his back. She motioned quickly. Louis-Géralde jumped down from André and climbed onto Ariana's lap, laying his head against her chest and patting her cheek with his chubby hand. Ariana's sobs stopped, but the tears still leaked out of her eyes. Josette had never seen her mother so upset, not even when Marc had nearly died in the bomb explosion that had damaged his kidneys.

"I saw her getting married," Ariana said, drawing a deep breath. "I never told anyone except your father this, but years ago I had a dream. I saw Pauline smiling like she always does, as bright as the sun. She was dressed in white and kneeling at an altar in the temple. Across from her, I saw a man with blond hair. They were both so happy." She wiped a hand over her eyes, clearing them of tears. "I guess I started to believe that it would really happen. I mean now, not in heaven." Her voice broke. "I wanted to believe. I'm sorry, children, forgive me. I just don't want to lose her. She has always reminded me of little Nette."

Nette was the daughter Ariana had lost when she was in her first marriage, before she had met their father. Josette had seen pictures, and the baby didn't look much like Pauline, except for the dark eyes and ready smile; but there was no logic to feelings. She hugged her mother, wishing she could take her pain away.

"But it will still happen," André said. "Pauline *will* get married."

"I know that," Ariana replied. "And I am so grateful for that knowledge. How blessed we are to have the gospel—to know that she will live on, and that we will get to be with her again! I don't know how we would cope if we didn't have that assurance. But . . ." Her voice drained away. "I just wanted to meet him, I guess. I wanted to go pick out the wedding dress."

"But, Mom, I know who he is," André said.

She looked up at him with remorse. "Oh, I'm so very sorry," she murmured, wiping her face with both hands. "I'll be all right. You don't have to try and make me feel better."

André laughed, and the sound shocked Josette. André and Pauline had always been inseparable, and she had thought that he would be the most affected by her decline. "I mean it," he said. "There's a guy at the clinic. The one Pauline has been dating. He asked her to marry him."

Ariana stared at him. "Emeri," she said. "It has to be him."

"That's right," Josette said excitedly. "She wrote us about him. She said she was in love. Marie-Thérèse can show you the letters."

"She really loves him?" Ariana looked more concerned than happy at the prospect. "It's not like Pauline to keep such a secret from me. I thought they were just friends. I've never even met him. I kept asking, but she kept avoiding me."

"She wanted to tell you, but Emeri has refused to meet you." André's face was earnest. "I think he's afraid you'll send him away or something. Maybe not let him see Pauline. But I was with them during most of their dates. Pauline never did anything for you not to be proud of."

"When she talks about him, she glows," Josette said. "And she misses him now."

André shot a thankful nod in her direction. He added nervously, "I wanted her to marry him right now, but she said she would only do it in the temple. He's a great guy, Mom."

Ariana smiled, and Josette felt her insides relax. "I want to meet him," Ariana said. "He should be here."

André headed for the door. "I'll go and tell him." He hesitated. "He has no family of his own. I'm afraid he might do something to himself when—if—Pauline . . . well . . . I'll be back as soon as I can."

Josette's eyes met her mother's. The tiny wrinkles surrounding them seemed lighter now. "Everything is going to be all right, Josette," she said. "The Lord has his plans; sometimes we're just too stubborn or wrapped up in our own feelings to understand them. Now, let's get back to Pauline. We've left her alone too long."

* * * * *

When André arrived at the clinic where Emeri was working on Dr. Medard's files, Emeri was sure he had come to tell him that Pauline was dead. The feeling he had inside was an all-encompassing emptiness. He couldn't speak or move or do anything.

Instead, André smiled at him gently. "Pauline needs you to come to the house."

"I can't."

André snorted. "Garbage. I won't take that excuse anymore. My parents aren't your parents. I don't know what happened in your family, but that has nothing to do with Pauline. Either you're coming or I'm carrying you."

"But your parents—"

"Want you to come. Don't you see? They need you."

"They don't even know me."

"And whose fault is that? Pauline may forgive you for not being with her, but I won't. My parents aren't going to forbid you to see her—and what difference would it make if they did? At least you would have tried for Pauline!"

Emeri watched André's face deepen to a dark shade of red. "You are a coward, Emeri! A coward, I tell you! Now, are you coming, or do I go home to my sister and watch her die without the man she loves?"

André stared at him for a full minute before turning on his heel, shaking his head in disgust. Emeri couldn't let him go. The last three days without Pauline had been the worst hell he could imagine. "Wait," he said. "I thought you were going to carry me." No matter the risk, he knew he had to see her. She had captured him, mind, body, and soul; he was nothing without her.

André smiled. "Come on, then."

They were silent all the way to the apartment. Emeri felt a mixture of anticipation and dread. He had been to the Perrault apartment building each day, yearning for the courage to knock on her door. Why was he such a coward? An ache grew in his heart that had nothing to do with Pauline. Had his parents received his Christmas card? Did they even care, or had they thrown it away?

His heart pounded furiously as André opened the door and led him into the entryway and down the empty hall. Inside a room, he saw Pauline lying in bed with her eyes closed. There were others around her, but Emeri couldn't take his eyes from the beautiful older woman who sat next to Pauline.

Pauline's mother, he thought.

He stiffened, steeling himself against the anger and rejection he knew he would read in her eyes. She wouldn't want him here; he didn't belong. He was dirty both physically and spiritually, well-deserving of the ultimate punishment God had bestowed upon him.

"Emeri." Ariana's eyes held his. "Thank you for coming. I needed you here." Emeri didn't understand why she should need him when she had so many of her own children around her, but he knew she spoke the truth.

"Emeri?" Pauline's eyes opened.

"Yes, Sunshine," he managed.

She held out her hand. "I knew you'd come."

* * * * *

All that day and the next, Emeri stayed by Pauline's bedside. Often she would open her eyes and watch him, and he could see the gratitude she felt for his presence. Sometimes she would smile and talk to him or to her family, but occasionally the pain would be too great and the nurse would give her medication to help her rest.

Emeri was never alone more than once or twice with Pauline. Ariana and Jean-Marc rarely left their daughter's bedside, and when they did, there was always one of her siblings present. As they sat around the bed, the family relived past adventures, and though he felt apart from them, Emeri enjoyed the stories and the feeling in the room. There was a spirit of comfort he had felt before only when alone with Pauline.

Jean-Marc and Marc gave Pauline several blessings to deal with the pain. Once, Emeri prayed with them in his heart, wishing God really lived and that he had the power to heal her. But the blessing gave no such promise. *A fantasy. A crutch. A lie*, he thought. But sensing the family's serenity, he wished he could believe.

On Monday evening, Pauline opened her eyes. She tried to move, but grimaced with pain. "Would you like something?" Ariana asked.

"Marie-Thérèse," Pauline said.

Marie-Thérèse came to the bed, her eyes anxious. "I'm here, Pauline."

"Your little boy is going to be just fine. I'll help look after him until he gets to you."

Marie-Thérèse wrinkled her brow in confusion. "Thank you," she said.

Pauline's words made no sense to Emeri. "A dream," he murmured. The nurse had warned that the medication could cause hallucinations.

Pauline smiled at him faintly. "My Emeri, always the critic. But this time I know what I'm saying." She swiveled her head to André. "Remember your promise. It means more to me than anything."

They both glanced at Emeri. "I will," André said. Emeri felt that Pauline was talking about him, but he didn't know what she meant. Did André understand the message, or was he patronizing her as Marie-Thérèse had done?

Early the next morning, Pauline was much weaker. Several times they tried to give her water, but she refused. During breakfast, Emeri was alone in the room except for Ariana.

"Emeri?" Pauline said.

His throat constricted. "Yes?"

"I love you."

He glanced at Ariana's face, but didn't see resentment or hatred as he half expected. "I love you too, Sunshine," he whispered.

Ariana touched his shoulder before moving to the bed to sit next to Pauline. She stroked her daughter's hair, humming a song Emeri didn't recognize. Pauline grinned up at her. "Daddy's song," she said. Then she closed her eyes and slept.

Two hours later Pauline died, surrounded by her family and friends. Emeri was nearest the bed when her breathing shallowed and stopped, almost an imperceptible change. He gave a cry and put his arms around her. "No, Pauline! No!" He shook her gently and then hugged her to his chest.

Ariana was sitting in a rocker with a sleeping Louis-Géralde in her arms. She gave the child to someone and rushed to Pauline's bedside, with Jean-Marc close behind. Soft sobbing began in the room around the bed as the family turned to one another for comfort.

Only Emeri was alone.

He stared at the people around him, mostly strangers he had seen lingering for two days, but whose names he'd never bothered to learn. An older, sliver-haired man said, "She's happy now. I'll bet she's with her parents."

"No!" Emeri roared, jumping to his feet. "No! No! No!" André tried to reach out to him, but Emeri shoved him against the wall. "I curse you all!" he shouted. "And I curse your God! I—I—" He turned and ran from the room.

Torment like he had never felt wracked his thin body. He ran and ran in the cold streets until he had no strength left. He fell and lay on the road, motionless, wishing that he could turn back the clock. He had known Pauline was dying, but had thought that with him holding her it would be easier. It wasn't.

He heard squealing brakes on a car. "Is something wrong?" someone asked. "Are you hurt?"

Emeri ignored the voice and continued to lie on the blacktop, dry-faced and voiceless. There was too much agony in his heart to give in to the release of tears. People continued to talk to him, but he didn't notice them or what was said. All thoughts focused on the brief glimpse of paradise he had shared with the only woman he would ever love. *No one could ever take your place,* he told her. He felt this as strongly as he breathed air.

He recalled her face, her shining smile, her ready laughter, and the few kisses she had given him. His whole being ached with the need he felt. "Oh, Pauline," he groaned. Something inside him broke, and he began sobbing and screaming, pushing away the strange hands that tried to offer comfort.

Someone called the police, and they took him home to an empty apartment. As it was already late in the morning, his roommates were gone to work. "You gonna be okay?" one of the policeman asked. He seemed genuinely concerned.

Probably afraid of having to clean up after another suicide. Emeri managed a grim smile. "I'll be fine," he grunted.

Alone once more, he lay on his bed. The policeman had read his intentions correctly, but Emeri didn't need to take drastic measures; he would simply neglect to take his medication. Given a little luck, he would die within the month.

He knew Pauline wouldn't be pleased, but she would never know. How could he go back to the horror of his life without her to soften his fears? Without her to give him hope? He hit the wall with his fist. And why hadn't she married him? Then he would have had more special memories and the added dignity of mourning a spouse. She had loved him! She had! And now there was nothing.

If only it was true, he thought. *If only I could see her again like she believed.*

Emeri turned his face to the pillow and wished he were dead. When darkness came again, he heard his friends in the next room. They knocked once on his bedroom door, but didn't enter. He waited until their noises ceased before creeping to the kitchen for something to stop the gnawing in his belly, feeling disgust at himself for having to eat at all. How long did it take for someone to starve to death? He threw the bread in the garbage and returned to his room. From under his pillow he drew out the lock of Pauline's hair, the one he had kept since their outing at the Eiffel Tower. Clutching it in his hand, he fell into a fitful sleep.

CHAPTER SIXTEEN

The next two days were not lonely ones for the Perrault family. They had constant visitors and the house filled with fresh flowers, plants, food, and condolence cards as people came to share their grief. After the first day Josette didn't cry anymore, because every time she became sad Marc would find some way to chase away the tears. Sometimes Josette felt that Pauline wasn't gone at all, but just where they couldn't see her—a constant invisible presence.

At the moment of Pauline's death, things became clear in Josette's mind. Mathieu had said that she didn't know where she was going in life, and his words had been true. Now, as she pondered the gospel principles, she understood with a surety she had never felt before that they were true. There was an afterlife! Pauline would be happy! A warm rush of feeling confirmed her realization. But Josette wasn't sure that the life she had been living would bring her to the same place her sister had gone.

I will change, she vowed. She didn't know where to begin, but felt Pauline would lead the way . . . somehow. Her little sister had always been the one to bring perspective to their lives . . . and so much joy.

Marc came up and put his arms around her. Josette clung to him, grateful to have her twin—her other half—at her side. How lucky she was to have him!

For some reason, her thoughts turned to Emeri. She remembered his fevered exclamations on the day Pauline had died, how his brown eyes had stared into space with no apparent will except to die. There had been something so aching and defenseless about him that Josette felt the wall she had built around her heart soften. He was someone who loved her sister as much—perhaps more—than she did. He wouldn't be looking for a good time, or for anything at all from Josette. And yet, maybe she could help him as Pauline had asked.

Yes! Maybe she could finally do some good.

* * * * *

Wednesday passed in a pain-filled haze. Emeri thought he could feel no worse, but Thursday morning brought André and a renewed agony. He wanted to tell his friend to get lost, and yet at the same time he yearned to throw himself into André's arms and cry.

"Come on, get up," André said. His voice was gentle but firm.

"No." Emeri's voice was muffled by the pillow.

His friend sat on the bed. "It's Pauline's funeral this morning. I would think she'd want her fiancé there."

Emeri turned. "Her fiancé?"

"Yes. She told me about you two. She tells me everything. We're almost as close as you were."

Despite his resistance, André's words made Emeri feel better.

"I told her she should marry you right away—even being just sixteen and all," André added. "But she said she was going to do it right. She can be pretty determined."

"Tell me about it." Did that sharp chuckle come from his own mouth? Emeri couldn't be sure.

"My parents know how she felt about you. And my sisters and brothers, too. You need to go to the funeral. Besides, Pauline will want you there."

Emeri pasted on a smile, the sneering kind he had stopped using around André and Pauline. "She's not going to be there."

André's voice was steady. "Yes she will. And more importantly, her family is, and we need you. You're part of us."

"I'll never be a part of your family," Emeri's voice grated. "Pauline's dead!"

"So? Does that mean we all give up on life? Didn't you listen to anything she taught you? Emeri, please come. If not for Pauline, then for me! I need you to come—we all do."

Emeri felt the naked pain in his voice. He knew that André

suffered as much as he did. Perhaps there was some way he could help his friend before he died. "Okay, I'll go."

André helped him out of bed and pushed him toward the bathroom. "Hurry and shower," he said. "There's not much time."

The funeral was held at a church house because there wasn't enough room to hold all the guests at the mortuary. Emeri felt out of place, but he knew it had nothing to do with the poor way he was dressed. How different he would feel if Pauline were with him! Nothing else mattered but her love.

The chapel was filled to overflowing with friends and relatives. The immediate family kept together near the front, holding tightly to one another. But as Emeri and André entered, a beautiful girl with incredibly long hair separated herself from the family and swooped down on him. He knew he had met her before, but until now he hadn't paid attention to her beauty. Josette was whole and vital, much like he imagined Pauline would have been without the sickness.

"Thank you for coming," she said, leading him up the aisle. He almost believed she meant it.

"Glad you're here, Emeri," Marc said to him as they approached. His eyes were red, but his manner calm. This was the one Pauline had called a missionary; he looked much like André.

Pauline's father, Jean-Marc, held out his hand and shook Emeri's firmly, nodding in greeting. Ariana turned from a white-haired woman, and without a word of reproach for the way he had acted at the house, she put her arms around him and pulled him close. She was shorter than he was, but he felt the comfort in her arms as though he were an infant. For the first time since Pauline's death, he cried. Ariana continued to hold him until the tempest calmed, her own tears joining his.

When he drew away, she smiled and spoke. "Come and sit by me."

Throughout the service, Emeri was aware of Pauline's family. They mourned her, but each talked about Pauline as though she was among them, listening in. He almost expected to see her, and several times caught himself searching the chapel for her bright face. An unusual calm came over his heart. Could there be something to Pauline's claims? Could it be that he had not lost her forever?

The thought was almost too good to be true.

* * * * *

Marc sat next to Josette during the service. Despite the circumstances, he thought how good it was to be back with his family. His appreciation for them had grown on his mission; and now, with Pauline's absence, everyone felt a renewed determination to be worthy to see her again. Marc felt even more gratitude toward the Savior and the sacrifice that made eternal families possible. This helped stem the ache of missing his sister.

Josette surprised him. She was different somehow, but he couldn't pinpoint exactly what it was that had changed. Her laugh rarely came, but that was to be expected during this time of mourning. She smiled and talked to him as usual, but . . .

He gave up wondering and followed his family from the chapel, nodding at friends who had come to comfort them.

"Marc!" A little body followed the words, coming at him like a missile.

"Rebekka!"

Danielle's ten-year-old daughter hugged him as tightly as her slender arms allowed. "Oh, I missed you! I tried to come and see you before, but Mom wouldn't let me. I'm so glad you came back."

"She's been talking about nothing else since she heard you were here," Danielle said, coming up beside them. Marc felt a leap inside him as he always did when he saw the beautiful Danielle, the woman he had risked his life to save when he was fifteen. Not once had he regretted the act. He admitted to himself that he cared deeply for her, though he knew nothing more than friendship would ever come of it; even if she hadn't been fourteen years older than he was, she was completely dedicated to her husband.

"How great to see you," he said. "Mom told me you came by the house yesterday, but I wasn't home."

The little girl in front of him hugged him again. "You did miss me, didn't you, Marc?" Rebekka had gray eyes, high cheekbones, and auburn hair like her mother. From her father she had her firm jaw and her height. The little girl had been his faithful admirer since she was five. Two years ago, she'd asked him to baptize her. "You're not going back to Nice, are you?" she continued. "I can't bear to lose both you and Pauline!"

Her eyes glistened with tears, and her utter sincerity made Marc take notice. She was too big for him to kneel down and scoop her into his arms like he once had, but he leaned down and met her tearful gaze. "I am going back, but I'll write you like always. And at the end of April, I'll be back. It'll go fast, you'll see."

Rebekka held his hand. "Promise?"

"I promise."

"Hey, I thought missionaries weren't supposed to hold hands," André said. He tweaked Rebekka's ponytail.

"Sisters don't count," Marc said, straightening. "Rebekka's practically a sister. Besides, she's too young to worry about."

That must not have set well with Rebekka, because she promptly dropped his hand and drew herself to her full height. "Well!" she huffed and stalked away.

After the interment, most of the people left to go about their lives, but family and close friends returned to the church where the Relief Society sisters had prepared a luncheon. Little Rebekka sat next to Marc on one side; Josette sat on the other. Next to her was Emeri, looking slightly more happy than when he had first come— if that mocking smile on the hard face could be called happy. Rebekka chattered endlessly, forgetting Marc's earlier comment, and he tried to give her his full attention. Danielle sat opposite them with her husband, Philippe, and Marc didn't like to watch them together. The way they sat comfortably close, with their shoulders touching, and the way their eyes occasionally met and held showed their obvious love. It bothered Marc that Philippe wasn't baptized, and that Danielle still could love him so completely. What did she see in that guy?

Grandfather Géralde had just offered the prayer when a young man Marc didn't recognize burst in the door, his head bobbing back and forth as he searched the small crowd. Marie-Thérèse gasped and jumped to her feet. It took her only a few seconds to throw herself into the man's arms and begin kissing him with a passion previously unseen in his reserved sister.

Marc felt his mouth open, and he tore his gaze away from the spectacle to see shock and surprise on all the faces around him. Only Josette and Emeri weren't interested and talked together in low voices.

"It's Mathieu, my cousin," Danielle said in her velvet-soft voice. "The one I sent the package to."

"That must have been some package," Marc muttered. Rebekka laughed, her tinkling voice seeming to break the spell.

Marc followed his parents to where Marie-Thérèse stood with the stranger. "Marie-Thérèse, is there something you'd like to explain?" Jean-Marc asked. Marc saw that his father was trying very hard not to smile.

Marie-Thérèse's face and neck turned a bright red, but the man with her laughed confidently. Marc saw he had the same color eyes as Danielle and Rebekka.

"This is Mathieu, my fiancé," Marie-Thérèse said. Her flush deepened, but she didn't let go of Mathieu's hand. "I meant to tell you before, but there hasn't been time."

"I'm glad to see you again," Mathieu said, proffering his hand to Ariana and Jean-Marc. "We met at Danielle's baptism."

"Yes, I remember you," Ariana said. Marc saw that she was pleased.

"I hope you're not disappointed," Marie-Thérèse said. "I know you thought I was going on a mission. It's just that"—she glanced at Mathieu–"the Lord called me on a different one."

"Of course we're not disappointed," Ariana said, hugging her daughter. "We told you that when you called us from Provo before you went through the temple. As long as you do it right, I'm happy for you."

"We'll be married in the temple," Mathieu said. "And I'm going to spend the rest of my life making her happy."

"See that you do," Jean-Marc said with a wink. "And welcome to the family."

"Oh yeah, the ring." Marie-Thérèse fumbled in her purse and drew out a dark box. She opened it, and Mathieu took the ring and slipped it on her finger.

"There, it's official," he said.

A contented smile graced Ariana's face. "I guess I'm going wedding dress shopping with one of my daughters after all."

Until Rebekka giggled, Marc hadn't known she'd followed him. Somehow it reminded him of Pauline and how happy she had always been. Only a short time before they had all said good-bye to Pauline, yet already their family had increased by two—if they included

Emeri. Marie-Thérèse's face shone with happiness, and she and Mathieu could hardly tear their eyes away from each other. Marc was fiercely glad that she had become engaged now; it was just what his mother needed. What they all needed. How like Marie-Thérèse to change the tone of the day!

Marc almost laughed aloud. *Only Mormons could celebrate a funeral and an engagement on the same day,* he thought, shaking his head.

Rebekka tugged on his hand, her feet dancing excitedly on the shining wood floor, her eyes happy. "I wish it was our turn, Marc," she said, winking at him.

This time Marc did laugh aloud. "I told you before," he said to her as they returned to their table. "By the time you're old enough to marry, I'll be an old man and you won't have anything to do with me." He had told her that repeatedly since she was five years old, and he had thought she had finally given up the idea.

"No way," she said. "I'll always love you."

Marc sighed.

CHAPTER SEVENTEEN

"Are you taking your medication?" Josette asked Emeri early the next morning. One of his roommates had let her in, but Emeri was still in bed. She walked farther into his room and opened the blinds.

"Oh, go bug someone else," Emeri moaned. But he let her bring his pills and a cup of water.

Josette worried that there wouldn't be enough time to save Emeri. Marc would only be staying until after Christmas, which would come in four days. Could they teach him everything in that short time? As an ordained missionary, Josette felt sure that Marc could help Emeri better than she could. Not that she wouldn't give it her best try. Why else would she wake up so early on a Friday morning, when normally Marie-Thérèse had to drag her out of bed?

She knew her self-appointed role as Emeri's savior helped her not to dwell on her own loss, but there was something else involved. He exuded a helpless desperation she found appealing.

"You are invited to lunch at the house," she said. "We all want you there—will you come? Please?"

He groaned. "I guess. If you promise to let me sleep in tomorrow."

"Maybe," she said.

Josette was afraid to leave him alone for a minute, and she was glad André felt the same. In fact, the whole family, except Marie-Thérèse, who was in a sphere of her own with Mathieu, made Emeri their family project. Each person went out of their way to make Emeri feel more comfortable. Lunch consisted of a variety of foods brought by the Relief Society. There was plenty for even the pickiest eater to choose from. But Josette noticed that Emeri ate little.

Afterwards, he slipped out of the house while Josette was in the bathroom. "Why did you let him go?" she demanded from André.

"I couldn't tie him down," André said. But seeing her frustration, he added. "Don't worry, he promised to meet me at the clinic in an hour. We're going to play basketball."

While André was gone, Josette studied the discussions Marc had brought with him from the mission field. Marc showed her how he would conduct a real first discussion, and Josette marveled at its simplicity. She was still at it when André returned home late that evening.

"Did he seem all right?" she asked anxiously.

André's face was serious. "Yes, for right now. But I'm scared he won't make it. He doesn't want to try."

"The gospel's the answer!" Josette cried. "It has to be. Let's go teach him now."

André shook his head. "Tomorrow. I left him in his underwear. He's going to bed."

"All right then," she agreed reluctantly.

That night Josette prayed harder than she had prayed in a long time. "Please, dear Father, let him feel the truth."

Early the next morning, she insisted on going to Emeri's apartment. "He may need us," she told André. "Come with me or I'll go myself."

"I promised Pauline I'd take care of Emeri, and I will," André said. "Even if it means protecting him from *you*."

Josette heard the laughter in his voice and didn't take offense as she usually did.

Marc rubbed the sleep from his eyes. "I'd better come too then."

The drive to Emeri's was silent. One of his roommates answered the door sleepily and motioned them to go on in to Emeri's room. "I thought I got to sleep in today," Emeri groaned when they knocked and entered.

"Ha!" Josette said. "From the dark circles under your eyes, I doubt you are doing any sleeping. Here, take your pills. Here's water, too."

"Thanks," Emeri said dryly. But he accepted the medication and the water. After gulping them down, he asked, "Now can I go back to bed?"

"I thought we could talk a little," Marc said.

Emeri's face darkened. "I'm not listening to your discussions. I've told André before."

"We're just going to talk," Josette said.

"Fine, let's talk." Emeri sat Indian-style on his bed and folded his arms loosely on his lap. The others settled themselves around the room, Josette on a low table, Marc on a chair, and André on the floor.

Josette used every opportunity to slip the principles of the missionary discussion into the conversation. She became impatient when Emeri didn't understand or didn't agree with her perceptions, and she had to continually make an effort to curb her sharp tongue. She wished she possessed Marc's control and ability to express himself.

A few hours later, she and Marc left Emeri with André.

"Sometimes I feel like I want to put my hands around his throat and choke him," Josette said to Marc in exasperation as they drove home. "Then he'd know I was telling the truth because he'd die and see heaven. How can you be so patient with him?"

He laughed. "It's the mission. You learn very quickly that unconditional love gets you a lot farther than force. If you can just get the investigator to feel and recognize the Spirit, most of your work is done."

"So how can we get Emeri to feel the Spirit?" Josette asked.

Marc looked at her strangely. "I didn't think you'd want to learn this," he said. "You're . . . different somehow."

Josette snorted, but she knew he spoke the truth. Emeri's salvation had abruptly become the most important thing to her, more important than anything money could buy. She had honestly grown to love Emeri in the days she had known him. Not as she had loved Mathieu, but more like the love she might have for a sibling . . . like she felt for Pauline, or perhaps Louis-Géralde. Already she felt as though Emeri had been her friend for a long time, and thoughts of him rejecting the gospel made her want to cry. The hard exterior he showed was nothing more to her than a transparent mask.

"I have to make him see how important it is," she said to herself.

Marc's eyebrows knitted as he concentrated on his driving. "You can't *make* him do anything."

"Then how can I help?"

"Pray, fast, bear testimony, and pray some more. And just be his friend."

Josette had begun to do all that. It had been a long time since she had completed an honest fast, but tomorrow she would succeed.

Silently she vowed to fast again each Sunday until Emeri accepted the gospel. At every opportunity, she would pray long and hard.

*   *   *   *   *

Being friends with Emeri proved to be the most difficult of Marc's suggestions. But Josette wasn't going to take no for an answer. On Sunday morning she awoke early and headed for the metro, this time leaving her brothers behind.

"What do you want from me?" Emeri asked irritably when she arrived at his apartment. He threw himself on his bed, stomach upward, and put his thin arms under his head.

"I want you to come to church with me today."

He shook his head. "No, really. What do you want?" His smile mocked her.

Josette thought for a moment. "I want you to be happy."

"I can never be happy without Pauline," he said flatly.

"That's also why I'm here," Josette said. She sat across from him on the hard-backed chair. "Because I love Pauline." The insinuation that he cared more for Pauline than she did infuriated her, but she stifled the stinging retort that first came to mind. "My sister loves you. And she wants to marry you."

Emeri stood, his face glaring. "Then why didn't she? I'm so sick and tired of you and André talking like Pauline's just gone to the store to buy some bread. She's dead, gone, kaput . . . a drop in the cup of milk that is the universe, so to speak. I hate you trying to make me feel better. I *want* to feel bad. If you loved her as much as I did, you'd feel the same way."

He shook his fist in the air, and instinctively Josette recoiled. As in her dreams, she saw Grady's face and felt the terror of the night of his attack. She must have cried out, because Emeri dropped his fist and came to her side. "I wouldn't hurt you," he said. "Heck, you're probably stronger than I am. Don't cry. Please, I'll behave."

Josette took a shuddering breath and took full advantage of his remorse. "It's Christmas Eve tomorrow. Mom's expecting you for Christmas dinner at midnight. Will you come?"

His cheeks rippled as he clenched and unclenched the muscles in his jaw. "I'll be there," he said without inflection.

Josette let her smile cover her face. "Oh, thank you, Emeri."

"I—I don't have presents." The slight stutter told Josette of his insecurity as he could not.

"You won't need them. Just yourself is enough." She hesitated. "Besides, you know what we want—all of us."

"I can't believe something just because you want me to."

"No, but you could ask the Lord."

"When I know he doesn't exist? That's pretty silly."

"Maybe. Then again, think of it this way. Was Pauline an idiot?"

"No, of course not," he said hotly.

"Well neither am I, and neither is André or my parents, and we believe."

Emeri mumbled something about mass delusion, but Josette thought he sounded less certain than before. "I'll come for dinner tomorrow night," he said. "But don't expect presents—of any kind!"

Josette arose hastily. "Just come—that'll be enough."

"And tell André he doesn't need to come see me tonight," Emeri said. "I won't be here."

"He won't listen to me." Josette knew André would come, and Emeri would be waiting. The boys shared a bond forged by Pauline in life and made stronger by her death.

As she left the metro and neared her apartment on foot, shivering in her leather coat, she saw André waiting for her in the street. "Come on," he said jubilantly. "I've found it! It was in my drawer—one of the places you thought she might put it. I've been waiting for you so we could go."

"Tell me about it on the way. Oh, but first I'd better tell Mom where we're going. I don't want her to worry."

"I already told her." His nose was red from the cold, and his warm breath made a cloud in the cold air.

"You're freezing," she said. "How long have you been out here?"

He shrugged. "Not long."

They retraced her steps to the metro. "Dad said we could take his car, but we have to go get it at the church."

A honking horn drew their attention. "It's Alphonse," Josette said, her heart beating more rapidly than before.

The car pulled up to the curb in front of the entrance to the underground train. "Josette, it *is* you."

"Hi, Alphonse," she said faintly, staring at her old boyfriend. She pulled her foot back from the stairs that led down into the metro. Embarrassment spread through her to be caught using public transport like an average working person. She should have begged her mother to take her in the van instead of braving the discomfort of the hard-seated train—especially in such cold weather. She could usually get her way if she tried—and that would have prevented the humiliation of this meeting.

"Do you want a ride?" Alphonse asked. His black eyes stared at her lazily, making Josette suddenly aware that she wasn't wearing any makeup. And he had never seen her with her hair tied back so severely. Why hadn't she at least worn her hat?

"We could go out to dinner tonight," Alphonse suggested.

Josette felt an urge to jump into the warmth of Alphonse's car, to tell him to take her home and wait for her to get ready. She rubbed her gloved hands together. Being with him would be like old times. Fun. Not to mention warm.

"I can't. I'm going somewhere important." *And it's Sunday*, she added silently.

"You don't sound too sure," drawled Alphonse. "Besides, what can be more important than having fun with me?"

Josette glanced at her brother and saw that he watched her with guarded eyes. Regardless of what she chose, he would go on and their mission would be accomplished. He didn't need her.

Something inside her rebelled. This outing had been *her* idea, and it was much more important than spending time with a playboy like Alphonse. She stared at him with new eyes. What had she ever seen in him anyway? Sure, he was good-looking, wealthy, and knew all the latest fads, but would that help her get to heaven where Pauline waited? Would he be able to take her to the temple? No; more than likely, he would lead her to more heartache than Grady had ever wreaked upon her. The things Alphonse craved meant so little—why hadn't she understood that before? This realization forced an embarrassing thought into her mind: *What have people seen when they've looked at me?*

"I can't go," she said. "I'm sorry."

Irritation flashed over his features. "Okay then. See ya around."

"Yeah, see ya around." Her last words went unnoticed in the squealing of his tires on the cold blacktop.

"Thank you," André said quietly. "I didn't want to go alone. You're better at meeting strangers."

"I need to go," she replied. Then she grinned. "Besides, when Emeri gets his surprise, I can't let you take all the credit."

André sighed. "I just hope it works out. And that he doesn't hate us."

"Me too." Josette was all too aware that their plan could be a horrible mistake.

They rode the metro to near the chapel where their father was attending meetings. "Are you sure about doing this?" Jean-Marc asked them.

Josette nodded in assent, though she wasn't really sure. "We have to try, don't we?"

"Yes, I guess you do."

"Besides, it was Pauline's idea," André added. "She was the one who really found them."

"Good luck, then." Jean-Marc flipped Josette the keys to the car. "Try not to be too late. Your mother will be worried if you don't show up for church."

"We'll try to make it back in time."

As he slid into the passenger seat, André asked, "What if they really don't want to see him?"

Josette chewed her lip thoughtfully. "Then we'll never tell him. I wish Marc was with us; with his missionary training, it would be easy for him."

"Somebody has to go to church with Mom and Louis-Géralde. Besides, he promised to go invite Emeri."

That brought a smile to Josette's face. "I already did, and he didn't seem too anxious. He said for you not to bother coming tonight."

"He always says that."

Their conversation drifted to other things—mostly to memories of Pauline. Josette was surprised to find she could laugh again.

The hour drive went all too quickly. They found themselves in the countryside far away from the bustle of Paris, and here they could see small groups of houses instead of towering, closely packed apartment buildings.

André peered at the map. "Turn here," he said. "Go straight until we get to the end of the road, then turn right. The house number should be easy to find."

It was. Josette brought the car to a full stop and killed the engine. She met André's nervous gaze. "Okay," she said. "Let's go."

They opened the freshly painted white iron gate and walked up the cobbled path. The stones were bigger than Josette was accustomed to seeing in most places in Paris, but she thought them pretty. Everything looked immaculate and well cared-for. How could people like these throw away their son?

Footsteps responded almost immediately to their knock at the door. Josette's heartbeat quickened. *Is this how Marc feels when he knocks on doors as a missionary?*

A woman about her mother's age answered the door without peeping through the spy hole or asking who was there. She had blonde hair swept into a roll at the base of her neck. Strands of a lighter gray streaked through the hair, but it fit naturally with the thin-skinned cheeks and kind eyes. "May I help you?" she asked.

André looked at her and said nothing; Josette wished she had brought Marc. "Are you Madame Fauré?"

"Yes." The woman's brow wrinkled. "Why do you want to know?"

Josette took a deep breath. "It's about Emeri."

Madame Fauré paled. "Oh," she said, bringing an open hand to her heart.

"Who is it, dear?" a man's voice came from somewhere behind the lady. She turned to answer, the light catching her face and emphasizing the fine lines around her blue eyes.

"They know Emeri."

A tall man came into view in the hall behind Madame Fauré. Josette could see from the wide set of his brown eyes and the square face that he was Emeri's father. Unlike his wife, who was thick in the waist and legs, he tended toward leanness.

"Is this true?" he demanded. "You know my son?"

Josette nodded, afraid to trust her voice.

"He's our friend," André said. "He dated our sister."

Monsieur Fauré looked them over, as if searching for visible flaws. What he saw must have pleased him because his face relaxed.

"Come on in then. Leave your coats and come into the sitting room." He gestured to a coat tree behind the door. Josette would have preferred to keep her coat, as she felt it insulated her nervousness; but she obeyed.

The couple led the way to the sitting room. Its furnishings were simple: couch, rocking chair, coffee table, bookcase, and the typical family pictures. A younger Emeri smiled out at her, but with none of the mocking that was so prevalent in his manner now. He looked confident and in control.

Josette and André sat on the couch, while Emeri's mother settled into the rocking chair. Only Emeri's father stood, with his hands plunged into the worn pockets of his rough pants.

"Where is he?" Madame Fauré asked.

"He's in Paris," Josette said. "Didn't you know?"

The older woman shook her head. "We haven't heard from him since he left two years ago. We weren't sure where he was. Except for this." She picked up a Christmas card on the coffee table. It had a nativity scene on the front—a glittering-robed Mary cradled a tiny Jesus to her breast. "This came in the mail a few weeks ago." Madame Fauré handed Josette the card, opened so she could read what was inside.

"Just wanted you to know that I am fine," Josette read. "Hope you have a good Christmas." She looked up from the card. "That's my sister's writing."

"Pauline bought the card," André explained. "She made Emeri give her the address, and they mailed it together."

"Then it wasn't from him." Monsieur Fauré's voice was bitter.

"But it was," André said earnestly. "At least as much as it could be. Emeri gave Pauline the address, didn't he? He wanted you to know he was all right."

"Two years without contacting us." Monsieur Fauré began to pace. Josette could feel the power and frustration in the tight strides. "Two years of worry, of wondering if he was even alive." He stopped abruptly. "Tell me, would you do that to your parents?"

Josette shook her head and opened her mouth to speak. Madame Fauré beat her to it. "I tried to find him at first," she said. Her husband's stare focused angrily on her, but she shrugged it aside. "I did, but he wasn't anywhere. I think he knew I would look." She swallowed hard. "Then I just prayed that he'd come home and we could work things out. He's a good boy at heart. Really."

Josette glanced at André for explanation, but he shrugged.

Monsieur Fauré saw their confusion. "Emeri was a smart little boy," he said. "He knew all the answers in school, and we had real hopes that he'd grow up to be something, not just to lay cobblestone like his old man." He gave a short, mirthless laugh. "Then when he got older, things changed. Suddenly he didn't like to show how smart he was. I see now that we probably pushed him too hard. He's our only child; we just wanted him to be happy." Monsieur Fauré's eyes begged for understanding.

"He started running with a crowd of misfits," Monsieur Fauré continued, "and they did things we didn't approve of. Finally, we told him he had to change . . . or leave. The next morning he was gone. He didn't even leave a note."

"But do you love him?" Josette felt stupid even as she asked the question. Emeri's mother clearly had love in her eyes, and his father's love was there too, if buried deeply beneath the hurt.

"We love him," Monsieur Fauré said, "but I still meant what I said that day. I won't have him turning this house upside down with his selfishness, or let him hurt his mother again. If he wants to come back, it'll have to be on our terms."

Emeri's mother was crying. "Is that what he wants?" she asked. "To come home?" Josette wanted to weep at the hope in her face.

"Emeri doesn't know we're here," she said. "We came because he needs you, but he won't come himself."

"I think he's changed," André put in.

"How?" the couple said together.

Josette closed her eyes, praying silently that the couple would open their hearts to Emeri and his situation. Pauline had known Emeri would have to face them one day; that was why she had paved the way for this visit. For all their sakes, he needed to make peace.

CHAPTER EIGHTEEN

Josette is so pushy. Yet even as Emeri thought the words, he knew she and André were the only things standing between him and death. They brought him food, friendship, money, and made him take his medication. And why was it that when they were near he could feel Pauline?

He went to the dresser where he kept his few clothes, most of them given to him by friends or bought with the paltry sum he made at the clinic. The top of the dresser was completely bare, except for the box he kept there. Inside this was the musical merry-go-round he and Pauline had seen in the shop that day, complete with the mythical unicorns. He had intended to give it to Pauline for Christmas to remind her of their hopes and dreams. At first he wanted to buy her a ring, but she had been adamant. "When we're ready," she had said with a beautiful smile. For some reason, the memory didn't seem so painful now.

Emeri wound the base on the merry-go-round and set it turning. Music filled the room, and Emeri was amazed to find he was smiling. "Can it be true, Pauline?" he asked.

The music told him anything was possible, but Emeri was long used to disappointments. The AIDS, cancer, other opportunistic illness, and even his parents. Once he had believed they would find him and say they loved him despite the illness he knew he'd brought upon himself—perhaps even deserved. But never once in two years had he heard from them. Pauline had wanted him to call them, but he wouldn't, just as he refused to meet her parents.

Ariana is so nice. He would have gone with Pauline to meet them much earlier if he had known how the family would treat him. The way Ariana had put her arms around him reminded him of his own mother when he was small.

Emeri sat down on his bed, still watching the white unicorns bob up and down on their gold posts. He had been wrong about not meeting Pauline's parents. Was he wrong about other things as well? He had tried so hard to keep his perspective, to reject anything that could let him down or cause him pain. Until he met Pauline. She had changed him, and now he was afraid; there was nothing to hide him from the truth—whatever it was.

The unicorns continued in their circle and the music urged them on. Emeri stood and turned it off.

* * * * *

The package was still in Pauline's top drawer, where she had left it before taking to her bed. It was addressed to Emeri. Ariana put it beneath the tree with the other presents awaiting midnight on Christmas Eve.

She and Marie-Thérèse had gone through Pauline's belongings, storing some things for keepsakes and giving the rest away. There was only one special item Ariana couldn't find, but perhaps Pauline had given it to Josette or André for safekeeping. She would remember to ask them later.

"Is it time yet?" Louis-Géralde danced from foot to foot. "Is Father Christmas coming?"

She smiled. Christmas was so much more exciting through the eyes of a small child. Her youngest son brought back memories of other Christmases with other little children.

The guests began to arrive, and a subtle energy filled the air. The large apartment had been created from two smaller ones joined together, making the kitchen twice its former size and a perfect setting for a special Christmas dinner. Jean-Marc had put the leaves in the table and Marie-Thérèse set it with the best china. Louis-Géralde laid out the silverware that had once been Ariana's grandmother's.

"We're back," Josette said from the entryway. She came into the kitchen with the outside cold clinging to her coat. Her nose and face beneath the large brown cap were rosy and her eyes bright with suppressed excitement. "We brought Emeri."

André and Emeri came in behind her. Louis-Géralde ran up to them. "I'm glad you got here before Father Christmas," he said. "He might not know where to leave your presents!"

"So are we eating yet?" asked Grandma Simone.

"We have to sing first," Marc protested, "or it won't be Christmas."

They gathered in the sitting room before the small tree that nestled in a corner of the room. Ariana scanned the beloved faces of her children, her parents, Jean-Marc's mother, Lu-Lu and her family, and Grandma Simone. Everyone she loved gathered in one place, plus the two new additions, Mathieu and Emeri.

"I never imagined it would be Marie-Thérèse to get married first," Jean-Marc said in her ear.

Ariana smiled, snuggling closer to her husband on the couch. Marie-Thérèse and Mathieu were so wrapped up in each other that little seemed to penetrate their world. She knew the Lord had timed Marie-Thérèse's romance perfectly to offset the loss of her sister.

"Poor kid." Jean-Marc's voice was full of sympathy. Ariana turned her head to see him watching Emeri. The boy's eyes were wide, taking in the atmosphere around him. How long had it been since he'd had a proper Christmas? How long since he had been included in a family?

"Pauline always did have a soft heart," she whispered.

"He's a good boy," Jean-Marc said.

The buzzer rang and Josette, who had been hovering by the door, darted into the entryway. "I'll get it!" she called over her shoulder.

"But everyone's already here." Louis-Géralde jumped up from his place by the presents under the tree. "Maybe it's Father Christmas!"

Josette reappeared in the doorway a short time later. The family was singing and Emeri sang with them, his eyes glued to the sheet music in front of him as though he'd never learned the simple words. When the strains died away, he looked up and saw the newcomers with Josette. The color drained from his face.

"We went to see them," Josette said quickly. The anticipation was gone from her manner, replaced by trepidation.

Emeri shot her an angry glance. "You shouldn't have interfered!"

"They wanted to see you."

"It's none of your business!"

"I care about you!" Josette's voice wobbled, but she held her chin high, her eyes flashing with a hint of her own anger. She swallowed hard, then added more calmly, "And Pauline left André their address."

"Son," said Emeri's father.

Emeri's attention snapped away from Josette. He stood up slowly, not taking his eyes off the couple in the doorway. Ariana felt her heart go out to him. The fake smile he usually wore had faded to no expression at all. Only his watery eyes showed how much the outcome of the next few minutes meant to him.

"Why are you here?" he demanded.

"We've missed you, Emeri," his mother said.

His father took a step into the room. "Can we talk?"

"These are my friends," Emeri said. "We can talk here."

Monsieur Fauré hesitated. "We'd like you to come home."

"You didn't want me before."

"Yes, we did," his father said. "There was more to it than that."

Emeri's voice became sullen. "But you didn't come for me."

Madame Fauré took a step forward, her hand outstretched. "I wanted to. God in heaven only knows how much. Only he heard my prayers. Dear, dear Emeri, my little boy." Her voice broke and tears ran down her cheeks in rivulets. "Please hear us out. Please, please, if you ever cared even a little, give us a second chance."

Emeri tore his gaze away from them and stared at the carpet. In the abrupt silence, the grandfather clock in the corner chimed nine-thirty. Ariana wished she could put her arms around Emeri, but she knew she shouldn't interfere—not yet.

"I did look for you," Emeri's mother said. "I love you."

Emeri glanced at his father, whose face wrinkled with worry. "I love you, too." The words were heartfelt but obviously difficult for Monsieur Fauré.

"I'm sick," Emeri said.

"We know."

Emeri's expression again showed no emotion. "And you still want me?" There was a slight catch in his voice that his immobile face couldn't hide.

His mother was across the room in an instant, gathering him into her arms. Monsieur Fauré was only a step behind. Emeri's broken sobs filled the room. "We're going to be here for you—whatever it takes," his father said.

The tension in the room dissolved, and everyone began their own conversations again, often glancing at the Fauré family with open curiosity. Louis-Géralde resumed his survey of the presents under the tree, his interest in Emeri's parents completely erased.

Ariana stood and put her hand on Emeri's arm. "We'd like your parents to stay, if they will. I know you have a lot to talk about, but perhaps it could wait just a little while? Remember there's still dinner, and you have presents to open after." She wasn't sure if she was over-stepping her bounds, but something told her this reunited family needed to be in a non-threatening atmosphere while they adjusted to each other again.

Emeri smiled—a normal smile this time. "Thank you." She had never heard his voice so sincere.

"We don't want to intrude," said Emeri's father.

"You won't be. We planned on your coming." Ariana gave Emeri's arm a final squeeze and returned to the couch. Jean-Marc had brought in a couple of kitchen chairs for the visitors, squeezing them between the tree and the couch, and soon they blended into the rest of the family.

They sang songs, gradually working from the fun ones to the ones with a deeper, more spiritual meaning. After all the singing, Marc presented the true story of Christmas. He told of the Savior's birth with feeling, and Ariana was amazed to see the spiritual growth he had made on his mission. Was this the same boy who had teased his sisters so mercilessly? It was too bad that Josette couldn't make the same progression. But then she, too, seemed different now—not as changed as Marc, perhaps, but on the right road. It was a beginning.

The Faurés were very touched with this special family evening. "I never knew Christmas could be like this," Emeri's mother murmured to Ariana as they left for the kitchen and the dinner, kept hot in the oven. "Thank you so much for everything—especially for . . . for loving my son."

"I only wish I could have met him earlier. He and my daughter were in love, did you know that?"

"Your children told me. But I have so many questions."

"Then ask Emeri," Ariana said. "I'm so glad you came tonight. He needs you. As much as we care for him, no one can replace his parents."

Madame Fauré looked fearful. "But what can I do? How can I have him back, only to lose him again?"

Ariana understood exactly what Emeri's mother was asking. Hadn't she asked the same question of herself before she accepted responsibility for Pauline? "That I can't tell you," she said. "But I do know that it will be worth every second."

"Thank you. Looking at you and being with your family here tonight, I believe that's true."

Ariana smiled and led her guest into the kitchen that welcomed them with laughter and love. Everyone helped move the food to the table, and in the confusion Ariana made sure Louis-Géralde didn't see his father sneak from the room to help Father Christmas lay out additional presents and Christmas goodies. Other years they had opened presents before eating; but always when the children had been young enough to believe in Father Christmas, they had done it this way. The idea was to build anticipation during dinner, and it was certainly doing that, at least for Louis-Géralde. "I'm so excited," he kept saying.

Emeri looked happier than Ariana had ever seen him. She saw him whisper into Josette's ear and noticed her daughter's quick return smile.

Ariana hardly had time to miss Pauline until much later, when Emeri opened the present Pauline had left. Inside the flat box was a set of scriptures she had sent out to be newly bound in a raised leather cover. A card said in bold letters: *To Emeri—I love you with all my heart—forever.* Taped onto this was a thick gold band that Ariana had been looking for earlier in Pauline's room.

There was silence in the room as Emeri stared at the ring.

"It belonged to Pauline's birth father," Ariana said. Silently, she berated herself for not opening the present to save Emeri the pain the gift must cause him.

Emeri's laugh startled her with its unexpectedness. "Pauline was right about a lot of things," he said in an odd voice. "Who knows? Maybe she was right about this." He slipped the ring onto his finger.

From behind the couch, Emeri retrieved another present Ariana hadn't seen before. She and Jean-Marc had bought Emeri as many gifts as they had for the other children, but she hadn't expected anything in return. "I bought it for Pauline," he explained.

Ariana unwrapped the merry-go-round with an exclamation of delight. "It's beautiful. She would have loved it. *I* love it." She set the unicorns in motion and the tinkling music filled the air, sounding curiously like Pauline's laughter.

Somehow, everything was all right.

Chapter Nineteen

The day after Christmas, Josette took Marc to the airport. "I'm going to miss you." She hugged him as tightly as she could.

"I'll be back at the end of April, Jose," Marc said. "That's only four months away. Then we'll be together again."

Josette didn't reply. She didn't think she would be living at home when he returned, but she wasn't sure enough to tell him.

Marc carried his scriptures in his hands. They had deep puncture marks in the lower corner. "What did you do to the scriptures I gave you?" Josette asked, glad to change the subject.

He lifted them. "What? You haven't heard that story? Where have you been? I must have told it a hundred times in the past week."

"Sorry, I've been preoccupied."

"Well, these saved my life. You can't know how precious they are to me."

Josette suddenly felt like crying. "I'll write you," she promised.

"You've said that before," he said. "You should take lessons from your friend, Brionney. She writes her brother every week!"

"Maybe he's nicer to his sister."

"What! I'm the nicest brother you've got."

"No, Louis-Géralde is the nicest brother I've got. He shares all his sticky suckers with me. Besides, maybe if you were as good-looking as Elder Fields, I'd write you every week."

Marc slapped his open palm on his forehead. "Oh, no! Not you too!"

There was an edge to Marc's voice that Josette hadn't noticed before. "What do you mean?"

"Nothing," Marc said. "But just get him out of your head, Jose. He's not your type, okay? Besides, he's a year younger than us."

"What makes you think I'd even be interested in him? I tell you I'm through with men!"

Marc took a staggering step backward. "What! You?" He laughed so hard that he began to choke. "That's like bread without butter, Christmas without presents, songs without music . . ."

"Get on your plane."

" . . . dogs without cats, babies without pacifiers . . ."

"Good-bye!" Josette started to leave.

" . . . cheese without mold, banks without money . . ." He hesitated. "What about missionaries without missions?"

"That too." Marc cast her a cheerful grin, picked up his carry-on, and was gone.

Josette laughed softly. Marc always knew how to cheer her up. The bleakness of facing the next months without him was swallowed up in her twin's undeniable love.

* * * * *

The two long breads in the cloth bag were warm under Emeri's arm and side where he carried them, fresh from the small neighborhood bakery. Their smell tantalized him, and he reached in and tore off a piece as he had always done as a child. His mother had never minded the missing piece, and it tasted so much better hot and flaky like this.

Pauline's ring flashed in the weak December light. The band on his finger was a constant reminder of Pauline and her love. In fact, all the good changes in his life also were evidences of her love. Having his parents back made up for the long months of suffering alone before meeting Pauline. He wished his parents could have met her.

It was almost impossible to believe he was home again, and had been for two days. He and his parents had driven home from the Perraults' early Christmas morning, and in the silence of the car, the euphoria and peace Emeri had felt with Pauline's family vanished. What would happen now? How could he and his parents make up for the past? But when they arrived home, he found Christmas waiting all over again: presents stacked around the tree, his room cleaned, the bed freshly made.

Emeri stood in the hallway between his room and the living room, speechless. Evidently his parents had planned for his return. "But you didn't know I would come," he said.

His father shook his head. "No, but we hoped."

Emeri swallowed hard. He remembered his father's face the way it had been two years earlier, how his finger had pointed out the door. "Why?" he had to ask.

"Because we want to help you."

A bitterness filled Emeri's throat. They only wanted him now because he was going to die. They wouldn't have to deal with his shady friends or bad habits because there wasn't strength for rebellion in his body. Besides, it was certainly the proper thing to do. The old familiar ache began in his chest. Why couldn't they want him for himself? Emeri wanted to run into the night and scream out his anguish, but his father's next words halted his flight.

"I was wrong to send you away," he said. "I wish we could have talked more. I wish . . ." His wrinkled face crumpled. "Oh, son, I wish we had more time! I'm so sorry. Can you ever forgive me?"

Emeri felt tears flood his vision. "It was my fault," he managed to say. He had known that all along, just as he knew he deserved to have AIDS.

His father snorted. "You were just a child! I shouldn't have been so hard on you. I should have let you know that I still loved you, and that you were welcome to come back once you were ready. I know that I will regret that moment to the end of my life. But I promise you I will do everything I can to make it up to you. Will you let me?"

Emeri said nothing but accepted his father's embrace. As the warm arms closed around him, he realized that his parents loved him. Not only were they willing to accept him back with his illness, risking persecution from uniformed neighbors, but they were willing to try to alleviate his heavy burden of guilt. As Pauline had also done.

Thank you, he said silently. Then he wondered to whom he spoke. Pauline? Himself? His parents? Certainly it wasn't to God . . . or was it?

His mother began shoving presents at him then, and he was caught up in the excitement, despite the early hour and his exhaustion. He felt like a small child again, and found it impossible to maintain his emotions as he normally did. "But I don't have anything for you," he protested.

His mother rubbed her hand on his back. "You are here." In her eyes he saw happiness. Warmth filled his heart until it almost hurt. He had never expected to find a reason to live after Pauline died, but maybe for the look on his mother's face and the comfort of his father's hugs—maybe those would be enough to give him the courage to live a few more days.

Now, as he approached the house with his warm bundle, the memories faded. His mother opened the front door and he handed her the bread. "Here you are."

She must have been watching for him out the window, as she had when he had gone at five years old to fetch the bread alone for the first time. He had felt so proud that day, clutching the francs in his clammy hand and marching to the corner store like one of the big kids. Close on the heels of that memory came others: of him sullenly refusing to do the simple errand, of his choice to leave with his friends rather than taking time to help his mother.

Shame washed over him, and he kissed his mother's cheeks tenderly. How could he have been so blind to the importance of his family? Those so-called friends were gone now, replaced by others who had come and gone over the years. But he was learning that families were special. Hadn't Pauline said that to him a hundred times?

"Thank you, Emeri," his mother said. She peeked inside the cloth bag and laughed. "Some things never change. Will you even be hungry for dinner? It'll be ready in an hour."

"For your cooking, I'll always be hungry," he lied. It wasn't that his mother's cooking was bad, he simply didn't have much of an appetite due to his illness. But for her, he would pretend. "Besides, when you say an hour, I know that means at least two."

She laughed. "Oh, well, but it'll be good." She put her arm around his waist and squeezed briefly before turning into the kitchen. Emeri heard her humming, a sure sign of contentment.

It was still hard to believe his mother loved him after the horrible things he had put her through in his rebellious years. Emeri vowed to make it up to her by being the son she deserved.

Before this last thought was complete, panic filled his heart. What if there wasn't much time? How could he bear to leave them? Now that his parents were beginning to trust in his love, how would they face life without him? How long would his parents mourn his death? For the first time, Emeri understood how Pauline had felt about her family.

He walked into the room he had used since childhood, fighting the torment. How had Pauline faced this fear?

With her faith. It was that simple.

Before he realized what he was doing, Emeri fell to his knees on the throw rug covering the wood floor. "I don't know if you exist, God," he said. "But I want you to. Oh, how I want you to! I can't bear thinking of the pain my parents will have to go through again when I die. Haven't I hurt them enough? Oh, God! Please!"

Tears overcame him and he could no longer voice his thoughts. *I miss Pauline so much. Will I see her again? I love her still; I will always love her. This feeling is so strong—how could it simply end? Do you exist?* He paused, focusing all his attention out to the universe beyond. *Oh, God, if you do exist, do you love me as Pauline said? Is there a plan?* The words came from the depths of his soul, releasing the yearnings he had felt perhaps all of his life. *There has to be more than what I see.*

He knelt in the middle of the room until his knees ached and the cold in the unheated room crept into his body. His face lifted earnestly toward the heavens in silent pleading. Just when he thought he could stand no more, the answer flooded warmth into his body, penetrating each vessel and deep into the part of him that was his soul.

The next thing he knew, his mother was holding him, her cheek pressed tightly against his. "Wake up, Emeri," she was saying frantically. "Are you all right? Do I need to call the doctor? Emeri, please!" He felt her tears on his cheeks.

He opened his eyes and saw the face that was so dear to him, etched with worry. "Oh, Mother," he said. "I'm all right. I've never been better than today. I know that God lives!"

* * * * *

The Sunday after Marc returned to the mission field, Josette met with the bishop privately in his office at the church house. "What can I help you with?" he asked. His warm smile and sincere manner told Josette he cared, and she felt all her reserves dissipate. They talked for a long time, and Josette poured out her heart to him as she never had before. The little sins she had committed, things she had never thought twice about before, came bubbling to the surface like sour blotches on her conscience. Some were embarrassing, but she was determined to free her soul from even the smallest thing that might keep her from being one hundred percent pure—or at least as close as she could come.

"We are a people of obedience," the bishop said. "And that means not stepping on the lines the Lord has drawn. I think you've done that quite regularly, but I can also see that you are repentant. I know it's not easy coming to me like this, but be grateful you have seen the seriousness of your path before it led you to some real heartache."

Josette was beginning to understand that her actions had caused a great deal of her inner loneliness and pain. The way she behaved had attracted a certain kind of boy—completely opposite from Mathieu and others like him whom she respected. Even Grady's attack might never have happened if she had been more careful in her choice of dates or more mindful of her own priorities.

"I guess it's been a game with me to see if I can get all the guys to like me," she said, feeling her face flaming.

The bishop smiled. "That in and of itself is not such a terrible thing, but you need to always keep your standards very high. However, I want to make it very clear that in this situation with Grady, he was definitely in the wrong. While you might have prevented the attack, you weren't responsible for it. There is no excuse for what he did."

Josette knew that, but she was glad he told her all the same. "I'm through with men," she said in a low voice.

"Well, that's all right, for now," he said, his voice kind. "But someday your feelings will change. Until then, you need to make something of your life. Make yourself a worthwhile contributor to those you love and to the Lord's cause. Then you will have something to offer a spouse."

Josette didn't think she'd ever want to have another relationship, much less get married. How could she know if he would be another Grady? Or reject her like Mathieu?—that still stung more than Josette cared to admit. But making something of herself wasn't a bad idea. *I want to be proud of me,* she thought. *I want my mom to be proud of me.*

She looked over at the bishop, sitting easily across from her. "How do I begin?"

"Well, I think I have an idea," he said. He opened the drawer and pulled out a sheaf of papers. "Do you recognize these?"

"Yes," she said. "In fact, I think that's why I'm here."

* * * * *

When Josette arrived home later that afternoon, she found her family waiting anxiously for her. "Emeri's in the sitting room," André said. He had a wide grin on his face.

"Go on, talk to him," her mother urged.

Josette hurried into the sitting room where Emeri stood by the Christmas tree, toying with one of the ornaments. Immediately, she saw that he was different. The hard look in his eyes had softened, and he held himself with a confidence that was real, not faked like before.

"How are you?" she asked. She had talked to him several times on the phone in the four days since Christmas, but he had been too involved with his parents for any more of her awkward discussions.

He turned toward her, smiling. "Thank you for not giving up on me," he said.

"I care about you."

"See?" he said. "That's part of it. Like with Pauline, when I first saw her walk into that room at the clinic. It was like I knew her already. I knew I would love her and that I would never find anyone who would love me more than she did. She felt it too. It was . . . indescribable. I had some of the same feeling when I met your family. I think you all must have promised both Pauline and me up in heaven that you'd help me find the truth when the time came."

Josette felt tears on her cheeks, but she almost laughed. "And did you?"

"I prayed about it." He shook his head. "It seems so stupid, but I got to thinking about how my parents still loved me, and how I felt when I first saw Pauline. That was meant to last. And there was only one way that could happen; it must be true!"

"It is!" Josette said fervently.

"I know!" He hugged her. "I asked André if he would baptize me next Sunday. My parents have agreed."

The whole family came in then, spilling through the entrance to the sitting room in a way that told her they had all been listening at the door. For a long while Josette just watched them, feeling the love in her heart. She would miss them all.

"And we've finally set a wedding date." Marie-Thérèse said. She held onto Mathieu's hand as she always did. Mathieu had begun a new job, but on his days off and every other spare moment, he had become a permanent fixture in their home. Part of Josette would be glad when she didn't have to look at him anymore and remember what had happened between them. She envied his love for Marie-Thérèse. Was there anyone out there so wonderful for her? She seriously doubted it.

"Good, then you two can stop mooning over each other in front of us," Josette said, forcing her voice to be light.

Marie-Thérèse grinned. "Well, it's not until May, right after Marc comes home. We'd wanted it sooner, but this way we can all—"

"If you wait until May I won't be there," Josette said.

Her sister dropped Mathieu's hand. "You're not still mad about . . ." She trailed off, obviously not wanting to bring up the past in front of their parents.

"No, no. It's not that. I just have plans."

"Are you going back to BYU?" her mother asked. "The semester ends in April, doesn't it? That shouldn't be a problem."

Josette laughed, enjoying their puzzlement. This wasn't the way she had envisioned telling her parents of her decision, but since everyone else seemed to have a life-changing announcement, who was she to fight fate? She jumped up onto the couch, trumpeting through a make-believe instrument she made with her hands.

"Hear ye, hear ye! Take your seats or grab something to hold on to, because you are all not going to believe this. I'm going on a mission!"

* * * * *

"Are you sure you want to do this?" Emeri's mother asked him as they arrived at the church.

Emeri smiled gently at her worried expression. "Yes, Mom. I have never been so sure about anything as I am about this."

His father cleared his throat, a sure sign he wanted to say something. Emeri waited. "I think," his father began finally, "that you are really vulnerable right now, with your girlfriend dying and your own illness. We just don't want to see you hurt. That's all."

"This isn't a whim brought on by my illness," Emeri replied. "I've been dealing with my sickness for two long years. I've grown resigned to it. But only now do I know there's hope. And do you know what I want now, more than anything in the world?" His parents shook their heads. "Well, I want you to know as I do that God lives so that we can be a family forever."

His father shook his head sadly. "I don't know, son. I just don't know. I believe God lives, but I don't know about the rest. It all seems so . . . so different from what I believe."

"Well, all I ask is that you try," Emeri said earnestly. "And I pray the Lord will let me live long enough to help you understand the truth."

His mother was crying again. She seemed to have spent much of her time since his return either being incredibly happy or mired in despair. Emeri jumped from the car and helped her out, putting his arms around her. "I love you, Mom."

"You are so changed," she said. "How can it be that your terrible experiences have led you to this happiness? How can bad lead to good?"

"It isn't bad leading to good so much as it is submitting to the Lord's will and becoming strong through the challenges. I think—I had a lot of time to think—and I've decided that maybe I needed all of this to change, to believe. To be humbled. It was the only way for me to recognize the truth."

"That makes a person worried to pray," his father said. "For fear of what God might send. We prayed for you to come back, but perhaps if it could have spared you this horrible disease, it would have been better for you not to return to us."

Emeri smiled. He could see beginning faith in his father's words. Prayers bringing trials were still prayers answered. "I contracted AIDS before I left home," he said. "And I know it might sound pretty stupid, but I wouldn't change knowing Pauline and the gospel for any health in the world."

"She must have been very special."

"She is." He put a hand over his heart. "Oh, yes. She is. And one of these days you'll know just how special." His parents said nothing, but followed him into the chapel.

During the baptismal service, Emeri felt the Spirit strongly. From the reverent expressions on his parents' faces, he knew they felt it too. Gratefully, he noted that Ariana and Josette sat next to them on the front row and appeared to be answering their questions.

When he arose from the water, feeling curiously refreshed and stronger than he had in months, he saw Pauline grinning at him from one of the chairs in a front row of the baptismal font. Happiness radiated from her being, like light from the sun. He waved and blinked the water from his eyes, and Josette replaced the vision of Pauline. She lifted her hand in answer to his wave.

Emeri wasn't sad. He had seen Pauline as whole and beautiful as she was in heaven, waiting for him. He had seen an angel!

His parents met him as he came from the dressing room. Ariana and Jean-Marc stood near to them. "I'm so proud of you," Ariana said, hugging him.

"I saw Pauline," he said. "I really did. She was sitting in the front row." He wondered what Ariana and Jean-Marc would say to that. Aside from Joseph Smith, he had never heard of ordinary mortals having such visions. Why him? But perhaps it had only been the water in his eyes.

Jean-Marc and Ariana shared a glance before turning to Emeri. "I guess it's only right that she would come to you first," Jean-Marc said. "Perhaps our time to see her is coming soon."

"Then you believe me?"

Ariana dabbed a tissue under her eyes. "It's not the first time it's happened. Miracles follow those who love the Lord." Her voice became soft. "Once in the temple we had a similar experience. It gave us much comfort."

Emeri looked at his parents to see how they were taking this information. Would his confession assure them he was having delusions?

His father simply nodded gravely. "My mother always said she had a similar experience as a young girl. I didn't believe her when she told me as a teenager, but now I wonder. I'm still not convinced, mind you, but I'll keep an open mind. It's too bad I didn't see your Pauline for myself."

Josette came out of the room where they would hold the confirmations. "They're about ready to begin," she said. She put her hand on Emeri's father's arm. "And I talked with the missionaries like you asked. They said they were looking forward to teaching you."

"Thank you."

To Emeri, his father appeared confused. Could it be that Josette was forcing the discussions upon them, the way she had tried to force Emeri? But as they entered the room, his father leaned over and whispered to Emeri. "I know this sounds strange, son," he said. "But I could have sworn that girl wasn't the one sitting next to me during the baptism. I thought she looked younger. I guess my memory's getting soft in my old age."

Emeri relaxed. He slapped his father on the back. "I guess it is," he said. Then he added silently, *Or maybe you saw Pauline.*

CHAPTER TWENTY

Portugal? There must be some mistake! The words were to stay with Josette for a long time to come. When the shock faded, she busied herself with preparations. She was to leave for the Missionary Training Center in Provo in early February, shortly before her twenty-first birthday.

"What I don't understand is why you have to go there for training," Emeri said. "And then back to Europe to serve."

"Well that's not usually how they do it. There is an MTC in England where—"

"Then why don't you go there?"

"They don't teach Portuguese. Spanish, yes, and another language, I think. But no Portuguese."

Her friend's head wagged back and forth like the pendulum on her parent's grandfather clock. "Weird, you going to Portugal."

"I know. It does happen, though."

"There must be a reason."

Josette moaned. "Yeah, to torture me with another language. But maybe once I get to the MTC, they'll change it on me, and I'll stay there to serve. That happens sometimes, too."

"Well, at least you'll be able to attend my parents' baptisms before you go," he said. "Funny, them accepting so quickly when it took me so long."

"Some people are simply prepared," Josette said.

Emeri grinned. "So I'm stubborn?"

Josette put an arm around him. "You are. But I wouldn't have you any other way."

The days flew by quickly. Marie-Thérèse opted to move her wedding to the week before Josette left France, and Josette had the opportunity to receive her endowments in the German temple before seeing her sister sealed. Both were touching experiences, but Josette almost cried when she saw how much Mathieu loved Marie-Thérèse. *Why couldn't he have loved her like that?*

She put the thought aside and threw herself into last-minute mission plans. The day before her flight to Provo, she received a package in the mail from Marc. She laughed when she recognized the scriptures she had bought him before his mission—the ones with the deep bite marks. "These'll keep you safe," Marc wrote, "since I won't be there to do it."

The other thing she did before leaving France was to have her long hair cut to shoulder length. There would be no time to take care of it on her mission, and though she missed the feel of it against her back, it felt good to be free of the weight. Her neck no longer ached from the tight, heavy braid, and the frequent headaches disappeared.

Brionney picked her up at the Salt Lake airport. "I missed you. Dang it! I wish I could go with you on your mission." Everything she said, except for the "dang it," was in passable French.

"Me too. But wow! Your French is getting better. You must have been practicing."

"Not much else to do," Brionney admitted.

"Well, that's a relief, because I haven't practised English at all. If you don't mind, I'd like to continue in French."

Brionney appeared pleased. "Okay." She hefted one of Josette's suitcases. "I can't wait to tell my brother you're going on a mission."

The thought of Brionney discussing her life with Elder Fields bothered Josette. She didn't want anything to do with men, and that included him. Besides, from what Brionney told her, Zachary Fields was a lot like Mathieu, "except he jokes around a lot more." What would he say about her?

"Don't tell him about me, Brionney. Please."

Brionney looked surprised. "But he likes it when I write about you. He asks how you're doing all the time."

"It's probably because I'm Marc's twin," Josette said. "But please, just don't say anything to him. Or to anyone we know. I just want to go on a mission without everyone talking about it."

Brionney shrugged. "All right, I guess. But Zack is hardly just anyone. He's my brother."

Josette put her arm around Brionney. "I'm sorry," she said. "I don't mean anything bad by it—I guess I'm just not quite ready to face what I'm about to do."

Brionney giggled. "I remember you once saying that the only sisters who went on missions were ones who couldn't catch a man. I never thought you'd be in that category!"

Josette hid a grimace. She was *not* running away. "I want to go on a mission," she said a little too fiercely. "You should have seen it when Emeri was baptized last month. I want to see that joy again, Brionney. It was incredible!"

"Do you think he and Pauline will get together in the next life?" Her voice was wistful.

Josette was only too glad to change the topic. "Oh, yes!" That strong feeling was something she would hold on to for the rest of her life.

* * * * *

At the MTC, Josette was plunged into learning the language and the discussions. She had little time to miss her family. The busy, reclusive life of the MTC was just what she needed to keep her mind away from her personal insecurities. As the weeks passed, only the language remained a problem. The sisters were friendly, and the elders reminded her of her little brother, André, so at least there were no problems with romantic attachments. While many were admiring, they were too young to be taken seriously. Josette simply wasn't interested.

"Will you write to me?" asked an elder in her district. He was going to Brazil, so it wouldn't be against the rules to keep in touch.

"Maybe," she said, not wanting to hurt his feelings. He was the second elder who had asked. Should she tell him she simply wasn't interested? "I have problems writing my own brother," she added. The missionary looked disappointed, but Josette felt sure he should be concentrating on his missionary commitment instead of paving the way for future romance.

Brionney came to the airport to see her off. "You've changed," she said when Josette explained about the elders. "Once you would have laughed them out of the room."

"I would?" The information shocked Josette. *Could I have been so cruel?* She vowed to be more careful in the future.

* * * * *

For the first two months, Josette hated everything about Portugal. While the people were kind, there were many cultural differences—much greater than she had noticed in the States. Three things bothered her in particular. There was visible poverty in the country—a life that before had only been real on the TV or in books. Not that poverty didn't exist in France or America; it simply hadn't been a substantial part of her world.

She later found that many places in Portugal were very similar to her homeland, but her first few months in Portugal were spent in Chelas, which included large stretches of cement or wooden shacks. The people who lived in these hovels were very poor, though perfectly willing to share anything they had with the missionaries. Many had no running water, but used a communal water spigot in the center of the dwellings. These poor people readily accepted the gospel, though many did not have the stamina to stay active after the missionaries moved on.

"They just don't have the membership here yet to fellowship them," said Sister Jackson, her American trainer. "But one day they will come back. I just know it."

The first few times they taught these impoverished souls, Josette tried to give her part of the discussion in her meager Portuguese, but faltered as she saw fleas hopping onto her body. A few hours later her skin was raw with the bites.

Nothing in these poor houses was very clean, and she shuddered to think what some of the children ate before they went to bed. Her companion often rolled up her sleeves and cleaned with the mother, while Josette tried to entertain the grubby children. It was a part of life she would have preferred not to see.

Even worse for Josette was the language barrier. Accustomed to being the center of attention, she was abruptly plunged into silence.

The language they spoke didn't seem to be the same one they learned in the MTC. It was all "sh" sounds and endless empty vocabulary. At least the nasal vowels came easily because of her French.

The third thing that Josette had difficulty getting used to was the incessant walking. In France she had walked a great deal, but it was nothing compared to her mission. Nearly everywhere they went they walked, because using the bus wasn't always practical. Many of their investigators lived on opposite sides of the city, and a few of the tallest apartments didn't have working elevators. The backs of her calves burned with the effort, and even when that faded, a constant physical weariness ate at her. She felt as though her companion was determined to single-handedly teach each of the twelve thousand people in their area before she was released.

"I just love Portugal," Sister Jackson said when Josette had been in the country less than a month. "I don't want to go home—ever."

Josette hid a grimace. Sister Jackson had only three months before she left; Josette had five times that.

To make matters worse, the room they rented in the unheated apartment of an inactive sister had broken glass in the window, and the green carpet was so dirty that it made her shudder to walk on it without her shoes.

"Think of it as camping," Sister Jackson said brightly. "That's what I do. I've never cooked on a gas stove before."

Josette groaned. "The stove's not the problem. I use the same kind at home—well, ours lights automatically. It's the carpet I'm worried about. We could grow beans in it."

"At least we wouldn't starve."

"No, but we might freeze to death." Josette knew she was whining, but she couldn't help herself. "If I have to take one more cold shower, I'll die!"

"Fernanda bought a bottle of natural gas today," said Sister Jackson. "I saw her hooking it up." Fernanda was the member lady who rented them their room. She had no husband, but lived alone with her son, a small boy with a vision impairment.

That night Josette huddled in her bed, feeling the bitter breeze from the broken window. She wore her flannel pajamas, and on top of the blankets Fernanda had given them she had thrown her heavy coat. *Camping,* she thought bitterly. She was beginning to have second thoughts about serving a mission. Why was she so impulsive? She could be at home right now in her own warm bed. What she would give for a week of uninterrupted sleep!

I'll just do my time and never look back, she said silently. *I'll never be sorry to leave this miserable country.*

* * * * *

Two months later found Sister Jackson in bed with a severe cough and fever, and there was no way she could work in the April rain. "You don't have to worry about anything," she said to Paula Muxana, the young member girl who would be going on a division with Josette. "My companion will do all the talking."

"But we have five second discussions scheduled for today!" Josette felt overwhelmed. The second discussion was the one where they committed their investigators to baptism.

"You can do it," Sister Jackson said. She coughed violently for a few minutes before adding, "It's not like you have a problem with the language anymore. I could never have done it with only a few months in the country."

"You are good," said Paula. "Much better than I am at French. It must come easily for you since the verbs are similar."

"And the backward way you Europeans arrange your sentences," Sister Jackson put in. "That's the same too, isn't it? It's enough to drive me nuts."

Josette blinked. It was true! After all that study and prayer, the language had stopped being a problem. It was certainly a lot easier than English. She closed her mouth, unable to voice the grumbling protest on her lips. The Lord had blessed her!

She still didn't understand why she had been sent here. Would she break all the baptizing records in the mission? Become a media figure in Portugal and bring millions to the truth? What could it be? Something great, she supposed. Maybe she would find out soon. Maybe even today.

* * * * *

"You left your towel on the bathroom floor again this morning," Marie-Thérèse said as Mathieu kissed her lightly on the mouth.

"What, are you a member of the towel police?" He lifted her head from the armrest of the sofa and sat on the couch, cuddling her head on his lap. The sofa, coffee table, and floor lamp were the only pieces of new furniture they had been able to afford for their rented apartment, and they were still paying on those.

"No, it's just that I seem to spend a lot of time there now." She lifted her arms and let them slide to the back of his neck, but she didn't repeat their kiss for fear of losing her last snack.

The six months since she and Mathieu married had been the most amazing of her life. Oh, there had been disagreements, especially about money, but nothing overly serious. As for day-to-day living, Mathieu was as easy to live with as he was to love.

Except that now she couldn't seem to get off the couch unless she crawled, brush her teeth without gagging, or even give her husband more than a peck for a kiss. She'd much rather be tracting with Josette.

"What's for dinner?" Mathieu asked.

Marie-Thérèse groaned. "I was afraid you'd ask that."

He laughed, but it sounded sympathetic. "I'm kidding. I stopped for something on the way home." He smoothed her forehead.

"Oh, good. Because I'm getting hungry—and you know what that means." Mathieu had already cleaned up after her several times when she hadn't made it to the bathroom.

He planted a hasty kiss on her forehead. "I'll be right back then."

She held onto his hand a while longer. "Are you sure we have money to keep getting take-out food like this? Oh, if only I weren't so sick!"

"They say it eases up after three or four months." He said the words often, as if trying to convince both of them. The thought gave her some comfort in a world where all her days blended together with the soggy, rolling feeling that encompassed her every waking moment.

"It must be a boy," she said, remembering what Pauline had said before she died.

"Or a girl with fire like Josette."

He had a point.

"I'll never forget her face when she got her call," Mathieu said.

"Neither will I."

"Portugal?" Mathieu mimicked in a high, disdainful voice. "That small country? I can't believe it! Why, practically nobody outside of Europe even knows where it is!"

Marie-Thérèse giggled, fighting the nausea the action brought. "Mom was excited because she has friends there, but Josette won't even be serving in their mission."

"I hope serving is what she'll be doing. Not sitting around complaining."

"She wasn't excited to learn the language, that's all," she said in her sister's defense. "You know how she struggled with English. And it took her totally by surprise. Hardly anyone I know here has been called out of France."

"I knew two guys who went to England, and one to Germany."

"Well, there has to be a reason for it. I wonder what?"

"Maybe so she would be humbled," he suggested. "There's nothing like being plopped in a foreign country all by yourself without knowing much of the language. That took me down a peg or two, I tell you. I mean when I first went to BYU."

"That could be part of it." Marie-Thérèse was the first to admit that Josette had always been a little arrogant. Maybe this mission would be more for her own good than for anyone else's.

With that, Mathieu left to heat up the dinner in the microwave that Marie-Thérèse's mother had given her last Christmas; it was quickly becoming her best friend.

A crinkling sound reminded her that she had been reading Josette's latest letter before Mathieu came in. She lifted her back and fished it out from where it had fallen. When the queasiness had passed, she began to read.

* * * * *

She was transferred to Campo Grande after three long months in her first area. The president had pulled out the two elders in the area and sent Josette and another sister in their place. Finally, she was the senior companion and would direct the work! Maybe now she would discover why she had been sent to this small country.

Her new companion was a native greenie, Sister Carvalho, who had wiry black hair and a pale complexion. She was generally cheerful and willingly gave her best effort.

"But I'm so tired!" Sister Carvalho complained at the end of their first week, collapsing on her bed. "If I walk another step, I'll die!"

"At least you don't have to worry about the language," Josette said sympathetically.

"You don't seem to have a problem."

Josette laughed. "I think I got some help from—how do the Americans say it?—the man upstairs. I was horrible when I first got here."

"I don't believe it." Sister Carvalho began to scratch her arm.

"It's true. I used to lie in bed at night and wish to be transferred to France. But I got used to it. There wasn't much choice."

Her companion moaned. "Dang these fleas, they never leave me alone!"

"That's another thing you won't have to worry about. On P-Day, we'll scrub this whole place down and get rid of them once and for all."

"But how'd they get here? This is a clean place."

Josette looked around. This tiny apartment was vastly different from the one in her first area. It had only one bedroom and was immaculately clean. The widow member who rented it to them had gone to live with her grown daughter, but came a few times each week to clean and to get their laundry, which they paid her to wash.

"The missionaries here before us must have been working in the shacks," Josette said.

Sister Carvalho stopped scratching at the tone of Josette's voice. "Is there something wrong with that?"

"No, not really. I've met some really wonderful people there." She hesitated. "They have a tendency to accept the gospel, but they don't stay active."

Sister Carvalho pushed herself up on her elbow. "That's not what we need here, is it?"

Josette shook her head. "Someday, I hope the members in your country can reach out better to the poor." The truth was that many people had to work hard to eke out an existence; they had little to share. Those who did were often overburdened because of their generosity.

"Don't worry," Josette said, removing her shoes. "We won't tract in those areas. We have plenty of contacts in this city. And members, too. Let's use them. The fleas will be gone soon."

Campo Grande, for the most part, was similar to the large cities near Paris. Half of the area consisted of older buildings, but on the far north side, expensive new apartment buildings stretched far into sky. On each floor there were eight large apartments. For part of every morning, they knocked doors at these new buildings. First they had to convince someone to let them in the outside door, as the new doors were never left open or broken. Then they would ride the elevator up to the top and start knocking until they reached the bottom. Occasionally people let them in, but most refused to have anything to do with them or their message.

"Is tracting always so fun?" asked Sister Carvalho after three weeks in the area with no success. There was no missing the sarcasm in her voice.

Josette laughed. "It's all in the attitude. You get used to being rejected." But it was getting to her as well. In three weeks they'd had no baptisms—something that had rarely happened to her before. She knew that soon the president would want to know which commandment they were breaking.

Having baptisms each week was common in Portugal, especially among the sister missionaries. If the missionaries worked hard, were obedient to the mission rules, and prayed, baptisms would literally follow their path. It was the one thing Marc envied about her call to serve in Portugal. Thoughts of her brother brought a wave of homesickness, a feeling she usually managed to keep at bay. He had come home from his mission in late April, and was probably immersed in his studies by now. André was eighteen and serving his mandatory time in the French army. Before she returned, he would be on his own mission. Marie-Thérèse would also have her baby before Josette left Portugal. Life at home, it seemed, had continued on without her. *At least I'll be home next year for Louis-Géralde's sixth birthday,* she thought.

On the way home for lunch, they sang hymns to cheer themselves. "It's beautiful here," her companion said.

Josette lifted her face to the warm sun. It would be a normal August day—hot and sweaty—but for now there was a fresh breeze in the air. On the other side of the street lay a large strip of undeveloped land where trees, bushes, and grasses made up a small forest. She felt her feet nearly skip on the new cement sidewalk, so like those in America instead of the more common cobblestone. "It is," she said softly. "Thanks for reminding me." Sometimes she became so involved in finding people to baptize that she didn't take time to notice the world around her. "Your country has some great beauty. And the people are nice."

She remembered how only yesterday they had asked directions, and a man had insisted on personally showing them where the address was. He refused to give them his own address, but Josette was sure he would have given her his shirt, shoes, or even money had she asked for it.

They passed a large area where wooden shacks crowded in upon each other, most with peeling paint—if they had any at all. Toward the edge of the settlement, a woman in a long black skirt collected water in a basin at the communal water spigot. Aside from an occasional weed, there was no grass or greenery anywhere in the little settlement—only dusty earth.

The wind died and the sun beat down on them relentlessly. Before long, the heat would make walking outside almost unbearable. "Let's walk through the woods," Josette said impulsively. "It should be shady there. We can get the bus for home."

Crossing the street, they walked into the woods. Josette felt her face relax as the shade chased away the heat. Green spread out in every direction before them. Birds called, and unseen things moved in the brush. Her companion plucked a stem of long grass from the ground and chewed on its sweetness.

All at once, Josette's smile left faster than it had come. To their left, deeper in the woods, she could see another settlement of shacks, much smaller and poorer than the others. They were made of cast-off wood of varying lengths; a few had rough shelters big enough to protect the blanket mounds they called beds. Josette counted at least three hovels that were simply two pieces of wood propped together in a short A-frame. A couple of children played in front of one of these, and Josette's heart went out to them. But what could she do? She had nothing to give.

In silence, the sisters made their way to the bus stop at the edge of the forest. Not for the first time, Josette felt inadequate to carry the burden placed upon her as a missionary. *I want to do my best,* she prayed. *I just need help and direction.*

They had to wait for a few minutes at the bus stop. A man dressed in a dark suit and carrying a black briefcase waited at the first of the short line. Already sweat beaded on his forehead. At least he wore no tie—odd to Josette, who was used to seeing the elders and other men at church.

Two women carrying empty wicker shopping baskets talked animatedly some space behind the man. One wore a black dress, signalling mourning; the other's dress was a simple plaid, and she had a matching scarf tied around her hair.

Josette and Sister Carvalho came up behind the women. They looked at each other, knowing they should use this time to make contacts. After all the rejections of the morning, their confidence level wasn't very high.

Josette sighed and waited for an opportunity to approach the women without interrupting their conversation. It wouldn't be too hard; already the women were eyeing their black name tags. But when Josette moved toward them, the women promptly turned their backs and began talking again rapidly.

More people came up behind the sister missionaries—two more women, both short, stout, and poorly dressed. They had four children with them, including a babe in arms. Curious brown eyes gawked at the missionaries from the depths of dirty faces.

"What's them tags for?" asked a young boy, obviously the oldest of the children. Josette judged his age to be older than Louis-Géralde, probably eight or nine. His hair was dull with dirt, but he wasn't overly thin. At least he was getting sufficient food.

"We're missionaries," Josette explained. "We go around teaching people about our church. And who are you?"

"I'm Valter," he said. "This is my brother, Jorge, and my mom and my aunt. That's my aunt's baby. And the one behind her is my cousin, Zezinha."

"Nice to meet you," Josette said.

"What's your name?" Valter's mom asked. She had her hair pulled back in a ponytail at the nape of her neck, making her face seem even rounder than it was. She ducked her head and giggled like a young girl, a shy smile on her face. Josette shifted her feet uneasily. Was this woman as young as she sounded or as old as she looked? Had her life been so hard?

"I'm Sister Perrault, and this is my companion Sister Carvalho." When she saw their blank stares, Josette added, "Sister is a title we use while on our missions."

"You say you teach people," Valter said. "Why don't you teach us?"

"Sure," Josette said. "If that's okay with your mom."

The woman nodded agreeably. "We live in the shacks on the other side of the forest. In number ten. It's not hard to find."

Josette's suspicions had been correct. These people came from one of the very places she had tried to avoid. She bit her lip and glanced at her companion, who was crouched in the hard-packed dirt, talking animatedly to the little girl with the tangled brown hair. She sighed inwardly and wrote down the name Valter's mother gave her: Elsa Sousa. "And what's your name?" she asked the woman with the baby.

"I'm Claudia Monteiro," said the woman. She transferred her baby daughter to the other hip.

"And your address?"

"Number fourteen. But I don't want you to come there. My husband don't like it. I'd have to ask him first, I mean."

"My sister can come to my place and hear you," Elsa said. "I'll send one of the kids to go get her when you come."

"How about tomorrow at two?"

Elsa's face crinkled in a warm smile, as though Josette were her new best friend. "We'll be waitin'. Thank you so much. We'll love hearin' you."

Josette and her companion boarded the orange and white bus that pulled up at the stop, showing their monthly passes to the driver. Elsa and Claudia and their children piled on after, handing the driver their tickets. They sat near the end of the bus, waving periodically at the missionaries. In a world where children grow up using the public transports, these youngsters were openly excited at the bus ride. Josette knew that this must be a special treat for them.

The next day, her heart felt heavy as they made their way through the cool forest and across the road to the shacks. With her greenie's spirit, Sister Carvalho was excited to teach the family, but Josette fought to keep her aversion hidden. They quickly found number ten, where Valter and Jorge ushered them inside a fenced open area that was littered with straw. Along one edge stood a row of rabbit cages. The smell was unlike anything Josette had ever experienced, and she had to force herself not to pinch her nose.

The blanket covering the doorway moved, and Elsa emerged with a big grin. Behind her a girl of four or five peered out curiously. She was much thinner than Valter. "Go, quick, and get your aunt," Elsa said to Valter. He disappeared at a run.

"How many children do you have?" Sister Carvalho asked.

"Three," Elsa said. "And Claudia has two. She's older than me but I started havin' babies first."

Valter came back, breathing heavily. "She'll be here in a minute. She says to wait."

"Is there anything we can sit on?" Josette asked. Evidently, they were to give their discussion here in this odorous play yard. She was only too happy to oblige, having glimpsed the dark interior of the shack.

Elsa and Valter found old wooden crates that, once propped up on end, made usable seats. The children settled around them on the dirt and straw, giggling in anticipation.

Claudia finally arrived with her two daughters, who settled themselves with the other three. The women folded their arms and waited.

"Do any of you know how to pray?" Josette asked. The children shook their heads.

Something bit Josette's shin, and she leaned over to see a tiny black flea jump from her leg. *So much for getting rid of the fleas,* she thought.

She explained the steps of prayer, using examples of things they might say, and Valter readily volunteered to try it out. Usually Josette or her companion would offer the opening prayer to show them how, but they would never turn down a willing volunteer.

Valter squeezed his eyes shut, his arms folded snug against his body and his round cheeks sticking out like apples. Everyone bowed their head except for the baby, who watched with wide eyes.

"Heavenly Father," Valter began. "Thanks for sendin' these sisters to teach us stuff. Bless us to understand. In the name of Jesus, amen."

Josette opened her mouth to begin, but she hesitated, staring down into the dirty but eager faces of the children. She glanced at the hovering mothers and saw that they appeared equally enthusiastic. At once, the smell of the yard, the stark conditions, the fleas—all meant nothing. These simple people and their faith were enough to invoke the Spirit's presence.

I've been so wrong, she thought. *They need to learn the gospel now.*

The truth had been staring her in the face all along. These humble people had come up to her and had asked to be taught, unlike those of better means who continually turned the missionaries aside. Elsa, Claudia, and their children had a great love inside them that hadn't been dulled by material possessions. Josette knew that Jesus would not have neglected them because they were poor. She couldn't change their circumstances, but she could give them the greatest gift she had: the true gospel. Even if she only soothed their suffering for a short time by helping them understand the Lord's love, it was worth every flea bite and other discomfort she would have to endure. These families were why she had been sent to Portugal.

But would they be baptized only to become inactive?

Josette didn't know, and it wasn't hers to judge. She would teach them with the Spirit and help them gain a testimony; the rest would be up to them and the Lord.

Please watch over them, she prayed.

The baby stood up by the crate, balancing precariously on her unsteady feet. Josette lifted her onto her lap. The other children crowded closer, as if sensing her acceptance.

Josette opened her mouth and began teaching them about Jesus. She had never felt the Spirit so strongly.

CHAPTER TWENTY-ONE

The months had gone by quickly for Marie-Thérèse—except for the last one. She and Mathieu had celebrated their first wedding anniversary four weeks ago and since then, depression had been her constant companion. Had any woman on the entire planet ever been as fat and uncomfortable as she was? She no longer recognized her own ankles—when she managed to catch a glimpse of them at all. And every time she stood, Mathieu had to help her from her chair.

She fingered the letter that Mathieu had brought up from the locked mailbox in the lobby. It was from Josette.

> It's raining here, even as I write. Sometimes the whole sky just opens up and dump its contents onto the ground. The roads become shallow rivers. I've never seen such a thing—or maybe I've never walked around in the streets long enough to notice. I guess that's what comes of having led such a sheltered life.
>
> Here in Campo Grande, I've been teaching several poor families. All of the woman and children have accepted the gospel as though they've been waiting for it all their lives. I feel grateful to be a part of sharing it with them.
>
> Often when we teach, all the neighborhood children living in the shacks will come to hear our stories of Jesus. They are all so incredibly precious, but two have particularly caught my attention. They are a brother and sister, Sara and Miguel. They live in a poor hovel with a miser-

able-looking lady. I don't know if she's any relation to them or not, but they call her by her first name. I know she drinks, and at first I thought she hated the children, but lately I've seen a different side of her. I think she loves Miguel and Sara, but the alcohol prevents her from taking proper care of them. What problems drove her to start drinking? I can only guess.

Sara is the most beautiful, trusting child I have ever seen. She has dark hair streaked with thin bands of a lighter color—all natural, of course—and her huge brown eyes have flecks of gold in them. She sings the hymns perfectly after hearing them only once. I wouldn't believe it if I hadn't seen it myself. Her brother, Miguel, is equally amazing. He's tough-looking and insolent at times, but he is very careful of his little sister and treats her with a tenderness he doesn't show toward anyone else. His eyes burn with intelligence, and I think it so sad no one has taught him to read (though he won't admit he can't to anyone but me). I worry that he and Sara are not getting enough good food, and I always try to bring a little something for them. Besides telling him about Jesus, I've made it a point to teach Miguel about nutrition. Can you believe me teaching someone what to eat? He soaks up my words, and his occasional questions show that he understands exactly what I'm saying. I wish everyone could understand equally well. He's too young for baptism, even if the old lady would allow it. Lately, she has threatened to not let them even listen to our stories at all.

My heart aches for Miguel and Sara, and I wish I could take them home. But I have to remember my purpose here and trust that the Lord will take care of them. As he is aware of the tiny sparrow, so is he aware of these precious children's needs . . .

Marie-Thérèse stopped reading, her eyes overflowing with tears. Josette's letters no longer showed her distaste for working with the poor, or mentioned anything negative at all about the rigors of missionary work, though Marie-Thérèse could sense that it wasn't easy for her, either physically or emotionally. A serenity came through in her communication now—and a searing joy.

It isn't fair! The thought came before she could stop it. *It should be me out there tracting and meeting those people whose lives are so empty without the Lord! It should be me holding their children on my lap and teaching them the gospel! It should be me washing the poor children's heads in the communal water spigot before taking them to church! It should be me filling out those baptismal forms and posing for the baptismal pictures! I would have worked hard. I wouldn't have minded.*

Mathieu came in from the kitchen where he had taken their dinner dishes, the daily newspaper under his arm. "What's wrong?" he said when he saw her face.

Marie-Thérèse wiped impatiently at a stray tear. "I'm just pregnant, that's all."

He sat beside her and pulled her close. She closed her eyes and sighed.

Trade Mathieu for a mission? The idea was ludicrous. She loved him even more than she had loved him when they married. Losing him would have been the biggest mistake of her life.

Yet . . . would he have waited for her? Could she have had both?

Maybe. The thought bothered her. While her love and appreciation for Mathieu had increased over the last year, the urgency of their love had faded. Before their marriage, waiting to be sealed had been such a torturous thing that she could hardly bear to be separated from him at all. Now their months together had dimmed that intensity. In the face of an eternity as man and wife, eighteen months didn't seem like a long time to wait. Maybe she should have gone on a mission after all.

The baby inside her kicked. "I felt that," Mathieu said. He poked her belly where the kick had come from, and the baby kicked again.

Despite herself, Marie-Thérèse laughed.

Mathieu grinned, his eyes meeting hers. "It's going to be all right," he said.

He was probably right. If only she could rid herself of the what-might-have-beens. Josette was doing well on her mission, converting enough for both of them.

She silently prayed for acceptance and understanding.

"I thought we might buy a second car," Mathieu said without warning. "For you."

"I don't want a car," she said. "This isn't Provo, and we're not Americans. I don't like to drive in this city. It's too busy, the traffic's too fast. Besides, I can use the metro if I need to go somewhere while you're at work."

"But it wouldn't be fun hauling the baby."

"I won't mind. It'd make me feel better to know we're less in debt."

Mathieu looked wounded. "I make a good living," he said. "And it's only a matter of time before I'm promoted."

"Then can't we wait until that happens?" Marie-Thérèse said. "I'm still worried about all that baby furniture you charged. The baby could have slept with us for a time. Or my mom still has Louis-Géralde's old crib."

A sheepish look appeared on Mathieu's face. "I just got carried away," he admitted. "It was cute, and the clerk was very persuasive."

Marie-Thérèse sighed. "She probably got a big commission."

"I want everything to be perfect for this baby," Mathieu said, stroking her arm.

"I know you mean well." She still felt irritated—at everything—but a sudden sharp pain attacked her midriff with amazing intensity, pushing away all the unhappy thoughts. It was similar to the false contractions she had been having for weeks, but this time it hurt so much that she could hardly breathe.

"Marie-Thérèse!" Mathieu's voice showed his concern.

"I . . . think . . the baby . . . is coming," she said between gasps.

Mathieu had a silly smile on his face. "Oh!" he exclaimed.

The drive to the hospital was difficult because of late-night traffic. When they arrived, Ariana and Jean-Marc were already there waiting.

"I can't believe we're going to be grandparents!" Jean-Marc said.

Marie-Thérèse felt happy tears on her cheeks. "My baby is finally going to be here!" Her feelings vacillated between apprehension and inexpressible joy.

The labor was short but intense, and Marie-Thérèse cried out with the pain. There was no time for the drugs to take their full effect, and she was forced to bear the brunt of the labor. She almost wished she were dead. But when they laid the tiny, red, wrinkled bundle in her arms, it was abruptly worth every agonizing second.

"Hello there," she cooed at her daughter. The baby opened her dark eyes, and Marie-Thérèse saw her answer in them. A mission was important, but it could never equal the great significance of being a mother. God had entrusted her with this baby and knew that she was prepared to take on the responsibility—unlike Josette who needed to grow spiritually and put her priorities straight.

The baby yawned, but she didn't close her wise eyes. What an incredible miracle!

This child's whole future is in my care. Gratitude to her Father in Heaven flooded all her senses. *I accept my calling,* she said in a heart-felt prayer. The Lord had made known once and for all his feelings in this matter. Marie-Thérèse wouldn't look back again.

"So what are we going to name her?" Mathieu asked. "We don't have any girl names picked out. You were so sure she was going to be a boy."

"Well, it was because of something Pauline said before she died. She said that my little boy would be all right. So I just assumed the baby would be a boy." She grinned up at him. "I guess we should have found out before when they did the ultrasound, but wasn't it better as a surprise?"

Mathieu put his cheek next to hers. "I don't care what sex the baby is, just so she's healthy and you're safe. I love you so much." Marie-Thérèse saw the sheen of tears in his eyes and it touched her deeply.

"I love you too," she said.

"Are you happy?" Knowing him so well, Marie-Thérèse understood what he asked. He had obviously felt her deep regrets at not serving a mission, and it plagued him. She knew he had tried his best in the last year to make her happy, but she had been so caught up in focusing on the opportunities she had lost that she had over-looked one of the greatest blessings of all: her eternal companion. What a waste!

"There's no place I'd rather be than here with you," she said seriously. "No place."

The expression on Mathieu's face was worth more than anything he could have said. His eyes slid down to the baby. "Shall we name her after your mother and your sister, Pauline?"

Marie-Thérèse thought for a long time. "I love them," she said, "but I think it's time for something else. I want our baby to start a new legacy—something removed from AIDS and the death."

Mathieu's expression showed he understood. "How about Juliette?" he said, his eyes dancing.

Marie-Thérèse groaned. "That's even worse. No, I want something less tragic. Something like . . . I've got it! Larissa. I read it once in a book when I was at BYU. I looked it up. It means 'cheerful one'."

"I like that."

Larissa's eyes drooped, as if to signal the discussion closed.

Marie-Thérèse cuddled her baby, and Mathieu put his arm around her. She knew she was right where she belonged.

* * * * *

The next day, Mathieu came to take her home from the hospital. He carried a large basket filled with a variety of different potted plants. Wound among the green and variegated leaves was a thick gold necklace. Marie-Thérèse stared at it for a full minute without speaking, her exclamation over the plants dying on her lips.

"Don't you like it?" Mathieu asked. "It matches the herringbone bracelet I gave you for your birthday when we were in Provo. Every time I see you wear it, I remember about buying it for you. I had a buddy get it at the same store in Provo and send it to me."

"We can't afford this," she said with a tight feeling in her chest. It seemed that each week they sank further into the bog of debt.

"But you should have something to celebrate our baby's birth. It is one of the great days of our lives. Now put it on, love. I want to take a picture. Here, let me help you."

Marie-Thérèse's heart sank further, but in the face of Mathieu's joy she couldn't refuse. What wife would complain because her husband bought her a gift at the birth of their baby? Was she making a big deal out of nothing? Or did Mathieu actually have a problem with spending too much?

She longed to tell her husband exactly how she felt, but she knew from experience that this particular complaint would fall on deaf ears.

CHAPTER TWENTY-TWO

Zack had finished giving the couple's son a blessing when the recognition came. He snapped his fingers. "I know who you are!"

Jacques de Cotte looked at him blankly. "We've never met," he said. He glanced at his wife, Charlotte, who shook her head, sending her shoulder-length blonde hair swinging. She tucked the quilt around her sleeping child, checking his fever again.

Zack lowered his voice. "I had a companion, Marc Perrault. He told me your name and that the last he heard you lived in this area. He said he has a piece of you."

Jacques and Charlotte exchanged glances as large smiles spread across their faces. Charlotte motioned them outside the room.

"Yeah, he has a piece of me, all right," Jacques said once they were back in the sitting room. "My kidney. Would you elders like to see the scar?" He started to untuck his shirt.

"No thanks, Brother de Cotte," Zack said hastily, answering for both himself and his new American companion, who had only been in the country for a week. "I've see Marc's."

"Oh." Jacques seemed disappointed. He sat on the couch, waving them to be seated opposite him on the loveseat. "He's a good boy, Marc. I'm glad he was able to go on a mission."

"He was a great missionary," Zack said.

"Like his father." There was a curious note in Jacques' voice, and though Zack couldn't be sure, he thought it sounded like respect. "His mother was also a good missionary."

He glanced at Charlotte, who squeezed his hand. There was no doubting the love they shared, but Zack felt it hadn't come easily.

"How is the Perrault family?" Charlotte asked. "I meant to keep in touch, but with a three-year-old and another on the way . . ." She patted her gently swelling stomach.

Zack felt his smile leave. "Marc's younger sister died."

Jacques' dark-blond head jerked toward him. "Pauline."

"I saw Marc a few times at zone conferences," Zack continued. "He took it well. I don't know what I would do if my little sister died."

"They had time to prepare," Jacques said. "That helps." He had a faraway expression, but Charlotte cuddled closer to him on the couch and the look disappeared.

A tiny whine came from the hall, forcing Charlotte to her feet. "I'm going to check the baby again."

Zack cleared his throat. "Marie-Thérèse got married and had a baby girl, or so my sister tells me." He shifted his weight to the edge of the loveseat. Since they had another appointment soon, they needed to be leaving. This was their first visit at the de Cottes', and though Zack was grateful it had coincided with their little boy's need for a blessing, there hadn't been time to discuss the possibility of teaching their nonmember friends. He had heard that Brother de Cotte was the president of a large carpet company; he should be a great source of responsible investigators. Since the Leandro family's baptisms, only Madame Legrand and her daughters had joined the Church, and Zack was searching for a better way to find new people to teach.

"She got married. To a member, I'll bet."

"I think so. Marc doesn't write much, but I remember my sister saying the man was a friend of the family who Marie-Thérèse met again at BYU. They got married last year or something."

"And Josette?" asked Jacques. "She was always the beautiful one. And such fire! Just like her mother."

Zack recalled that this man had been Marc's mother's first husband, and despite the love he had for his current wife, he obviously still had tender feelings toward Ariana.

"She is beautiful," Zack said.

Jacques looked at him sharply. "You've got it bad," he said. "Beware; loving her won't come easily, but it will be worth it."

"I haven't even met her!" All thoughts of leaving the de Cottes' fled from Zack's mind. "And besides, I'm a missionary. I don't have time for those thoughts." The truth was that he had only one month left before he returned to the real world. Sadness filled most of his mind when he thought about leaving France and the people who had become so much a part of his soul, but he couldn't deny that another part felt quite differently. That renegade part anticipated the moment he would meet Marc's sister. As much as he loved his old companion, he admitted—if only to himself—that the girl in the picture was the real reason he was going to visit Marc before returning to America. He had to know why he felt so powerfully drawn to her, why he dreamed of her, felt warnings for her.

This last thought reminded him of the attack on Josette and the anger and frustration he had felt at not being there. Jacques laughed at his expression. "One look is all it takes," he said. "From across a crowded room or at a picture, it's all the same."

Zack jumped to his feet. "We'd better be going. We have another appointment."

"But you haven't told us why you wanted to meet with us." Charlotte moved into sight from the dark hallway.

"They want us to give references," Jacques said with a grin. "Isn't that right?"

"You got it," Zack said.

"Come back on Monday night then. We'll have a special family night and invite our neighbors."

"But go gently on them," Charlotte said.

Now it was Zack's turn to grin. "Don't worry, we're trying to save them, not scare them to death."

Jacques chuckled, and Charlotte joined him hesitantly.

Zack whistled as they emerged on the street below the de Cottes' apartment. They would be slightly late for the next appointment, but it had been worth a first contact. The night was going better than expected.

He reached into his shirt pocket to check the address of where they were headed, but instead his hand closed over a snapshot of Brionney. Laughing at her side was Josette. She sat on a couch with her knees pulled up to her chest. The long, straight locks fanned out around her shoulders and knees like a shiny dark coat. Her brown eyes seemed to speak directly to him.

What would he say to her at the instant they met? He hadn't decided—perhaps he wouldn't until that crucial moment. But whatever, he would be true to the feelings in his heart. He could only hope that her real self matched the woman he dreamed she was—not shallow, heartless, and vain, but spiritual, caring, and intelligent.

With effort, Zack put these thoughts aside and locked them in the most tender part of his mind. *I am yours, Lord,* he prayed silently. *Please, lead us to those who are ready. For this month, at least, my whole heart is dedicated to this mission.*

And then . . . his heart said, but his mind was too bent on the work at hand to answer.

* * * * *

The words of the letter in Marc's hand blurred before his eyes. Had a whole year passed since he had finished his mission? Where had the time gone? Josette would be home in another three and a half months, and Marie-Thérèse and Mathieu already had a six-week-old daughter. And now Elder Fields was finishing his mission and coming to Paris for a visit before leaving France.

Marc had written Zack once after Pauline had died and at Christmas last year, but he had been too involved in his engineering studies to write much. He managed to write to Josette each week, remembering how much he had craved hearing from her on his own mission. To his surprise, she answered him. Most of the letters had been lighthearted and typical of his sister, but during the last six months there had been a change. Josette seemed to be more thoughtful about things, and she hadn't complained for at least the last four letters. It was odd, but not unwelcome.

He checked the dates in Zack's letter and went to find his mother, who was reading a novel in the television room. "We're going to have company, if that's all right," he said, showing her the letter.

Ariana looked pleased. "Of course it's all right. I've been looking forward to meeting the Fields after all they did for the girls while they were in Provo. Is it just them and your companion?"

"They don't mention anyone else, so I guess that's all."

"Well, we've enough room, with the girls gone."

"What's up?" André's feet clomped in the boots they had given him during his army service.

"One of my old companions is coming to visit," Marc said as his brother sat beside their mother on the couch, placing an arm lovingly around her shoulder.

"Yes, war stories!" André exclaimed. Next month he would leave on his own mission, and he loved any opportunity to hear about mission experiences.

"He can stay with me in my room," Marc said, "now that André and I don't share anymore."

"And his parents can sleep in Josette's room," Ariana said. "I hope they don't mind single beds."

"They won't care."

"We'll have a big dinner to welcome them," Ariana continued. "Do you think we should invite Emeri and his parents?"

Marc laughed. "Good idea. Let's have a big party."

Their father came in the room with Louis-Géralde hopping at his side. "Look what we got, look what we got!" he sang. In his arms he carried a small package from Josette. "Can I have the stamps, Mom?"

Ariana smiled. "Of course. I'm sure she picked them out just for your collection."

"The package is addressed to André," Marc said, peering closer.

Louis-Géralde handed André the box. "Be careful of the stamps."

André ripped off the brown paper and opened the box. Nestled inside were a set of scriptures with bite marks and a note that read: "These have already kept two Perrault missionaries safe. Since I'm nearly finished, I thought it was your turn to have them."

"Cool," André said.

Marc laughed. "That's Josette for you. Always trying to take care of us." But it had been the younger Josette who had been thoughtful—before she had become so self-centered. Had she actually changed for the better? A mission would do it, if anything could. More than anything, Marc wanted her to be happy.

* * * * *

The next week, Marc opened the door to Elder Fields and his family. "Look at you!" Zack said, giving his old companion a bear hug. "You've lost weight."

"A bit," Marc admitted. "My mom doesn't feed me as well as the members did on my mission."

"Force-feed you, you mean. Boy, it's good to see you."

The Perrault family, including Marie-Thérèse and Mathieu, gathered around for introductions. "And these are our friends, the Faurés," Marc said, motioning to an older couple and a thin, intense-looking young man.

"Nice to meet you all." Zack presented his parents and translated for them. He lost interest when he learned that Marie-Thérèse could also translate, and left her to help his parents.

He walked over to Marc. "Where's your other sister?"

"Josette?" Marc asked in surprise. "I thought you knew. She's on a mission. She's in Portugal, if you can believe it."

The light went out of those blue, blue eyes. Zack swallowed hard. "You didn't mention that in either of your letters."

"I didn't think it would make a difference," Marc said, but he knew he had purposely avoided mention of Josette. Protecting his twin came naturally to him, but was there a need to protect her at all? Perhaps he was wrong about her and Zack. "Besides," he added lamely, "didn't your sister tell you? I know she writes to Josette."

Zack frowned, then licked his lips as if tasting something sour. "She didn't say." He paused for a moment, his gaze resting on a large family picture in the hall. It was an old one, taken before Marc's mission when Pauline was still alive; Marc supposed his mother would always keep it there.

"I guess it wasn't meant to be." Zack made a rolling movement with his shoulders that approximated a shrug. "It's just that I don't understand why I felt—" The words broke off. "So are you going to show me the Eiffel Tower, or am I going to have to find my own way there?"

Marc clapped his friend on the back. "We'll probably have to eat first—you know how mothers are. But don't worry, I have a whole list of places to take you and your parents. Be prepared to see the Paris you've always imagined and more!"

* * * * *

"I can't believe you didn't tell me that Marc's sister was serving a mission!" Zack said to Brionney. Outside the car, the landscape along I-15 streamed by. In the front seat, their parents talked quietly.

"What! You're back in Utah less than fifteen minutes, and that's all you have to say to me?" Her eyes twinkled.

He put his arm around her. "I'm glad to see you, Bri, I really am. You're so grown-up, though."

"I'll be a senior in the fall."

"You think I don't know that? Man, you make me feel old."

"So why did you want to know about Josette?"

Zack shrugged, feeling suddenly very idiotic. "I don't know. I just think it's odd that you didn't tell me. Or Marc. He sure doesn't like the idea of . . ." Brionney stared eagerly at him, but Zack didn't feel like finishing the statement.

"Josette didn't want me to tell you," she said.

He felt as though she had punched him in the stomach. "Why?" he managed.

"Oh, don't take it personally. She didn't want anyone to know. I think she was a little embarrassed to be going at all."

Zack didn't understand why, but the way his sister said the words made it obvious that he should understand. He opted not to say anything and reveal his ignorance. If he listened closely, he might figure it out without embarrassing himself further.

"She's pretty sour on guys," Brionney continued blithely. "Ever since the attack. It's a sad thing, too. Guys were always lining up at the door to take her out." The words had a touch of envy mixed with admiration.

This new idea of Josette's being afraid of caring for a man made Zack abruptly hopeful. He could show her how a real man acted and how a woman should be treated. But when? They were separated by an immense ocean, and she didn't even know he cared. Would it even matter if she knew? Could Marc be right when he said Zack wasn't good enough for her?

"In fact, the only guy she writes me about at all is someone named Emeri. He's a friend of the family, and he and Josette are close. They write all the time."

"I met him," Zack said shortly. In his opinion, Emeri was a great young man and it was plausible for Josette to be interested in him. Now that Zack thought about it, Emeri did have an air of tragedy about him, despite the happy smile and apparent good health he had showed in their brief meeting. Maybe he had that certain something that attracted beautiful women. Zack gave a long sigh.

"What's wrong?" Brionney asked him. Something about the way she said it made Zack stare. *Oh, she was speaking in French!*

"It's nothing," he replied in the same language. He and Brionney had always been close, but his irrational feelings about a girl he had never met were too private to share with anyone.

There was instant hurt in Brionney's eyes, and Zack felt bad. He searched for some way to change the subject. "Your necklace," he said, noticing for the first time. "Where's your half of the charm?" Loosening his tie, he brought out the jagged half of the heart he had kept tucked inside his shirt.

Brionney flushed. "Oh, that. Well, you see, it's like this. Josette and I got to be good friends, and she gave me a pin. It's really beautiful. It's gold and has sparkly diamond dust all over it. She was wearing it during the attack, and she just couldn't bear to see it anymore. She was going to throw it away, but I liked it so she made me keep it. And then I wanted her to have something to remember me by, and all I had was that charm. I meant to go and buy another set before you got back, but I didn't have the money. You're not mad, are you? I just wanted two of the people I love most to have something from me."

Zack tucked the necklace back inside his shirt. "I'm not mad," he said. "You were very unselfish to give it to her." In fact, the idea of Josette having the other half appealed to his romantic side.

"I thought you'd say that. Besides, it's not like you'll be using it anymore, now that we're back together. I mean, most men in the Church don't seem to wear necklaces—not that I've noticed, anyway."

Zack understood what she meant. When she had first given him the necklace, he had been embarrassed to wear it at all. He had given in only when he had seen how much it had meant to Brionney. His views had changed considerably since seeing a different part of the world. For a man to wear a necklace in France was more common than not, even among the Church members he had met. He wasn't embarrassed anymore; in fact, quite the opposite. And now that he'd learned who had the other half, he wouldn't give his up for the world. As long as he wore the necklace, he had some link to Josette.

"Why don't you write to her?" Brionney said, breaking into his concentration. "I mean, if you want to." She smiled at him to show she was teasing, but Zack didn't take the bait.

"That," he said, "is exactly what I'm going to do."

CHAPTER TWENTY-THREE

During the last two months of her mission, Josette served in Benefica, where the city was divided between the sisters and the elders. The sisters' half of the city was mostly solid buildings with few open areas except for the large city zoo. There were no makeshift shacks or poor cement houses that Josette ever encountered. Despite the tender experiences she had shared with the poor in other areas, she felt grateful she would not have to confront the emotions that churned inside her when she thought about how little she could do to better their physical circumstances. At first, she had trouble sleeping at night in the new area, spending many hours worrying about the fragile, impoverished converts she had left in her previous area. Finally, she begged the Lord to take care of them and relinquished them to his care.

Unlike most of her other areas, their district didn't hold street meetings; and though the ward in the area was exceptionally supportive, most of the members lived in the elders' side of the city. This meant Josette and her companion spent nearly all their time tracting. Josette no longer felt even a twinge of fear when she knocked on strangers' doors. When they were lucky enough to get someone to open up, she always found a way to keep them talking to her, and rarely was anyone rude.

"You make me laugh," said Sister Nabb, her new American companion. "Three months in the mission field, and I never knew knocking doors could be so fun."

Josette laughed, flattered, but her body sagged in weariness. She felt as though she could go to bed and sleep for days without awakening. "It's time we headed home," she said. Once again they rented a room from a family, but this was the first time she had lived with non-members. Josette wanted to pave the way to teaching them someday, though they showed no interest . . . yet.

"They're very good people," Sister Nabb said, as if reading her mind. The Tiza family were devout Catholics and the mother, Graziela, spent a portion of each day doing some kind of charity work. After three weeks in the area, Josette had grown quite attached to them.

When they arrived home, the whole family awaited them: Senhor and Senhora Tiza, their teenage daughter Tininha, and Roc, the large red Labrador whom the family treated like another member.

"Oh, Sister Perrault," Senhora Tiza said the minute they walked in the door. "Mail came for you; the elders dropped it by."

"Great. Where is it?" When the elders had mentioned they were going into the mission office for supplies, she had asked them to check for any forwarded mail. She had begun receiving mail from her family again, but since her parents and Marc wrote her faithfully every week, she knew a few of the letters sent to the previous address were still missing.

Thin Graziela wrung her long hands with a nervous laugh. "There were six letters," she said. "I put them on the table, and when I came back Roc had them. He chewed half of them, and one is missing completely." She grimaced. "I'm really sorry."

No one said anything for a long second, and then Sister Nabb doubled up with laughter. "The dog ate the letter! If that isn't a first!" She laughed so hard that tears came to her eyes. Josette saw the absurdity and joined in. Soon her laughter threatened to make her faint from lack of air.

"In school," Sister Nabb said, gasping for breath, "I always tried to get my teacher to believe my dog ate my homework, but she'd never believe me. 'Dogs don't eat paper!' she'd say. Well, I guess good old Roc proved her wrong!"

The Tiza family laughed with them. "I'm really sorry," Graziela repeated when she finally could speak.

Josette wiped her eyes and took the letters. "That's all right," she said. Five letters in one day was still a good thing.

The two mauled letters were from Marc, and by piecing the shreds together she could read them. He mentioned Zachary Fields' visit, and for a moment Josette wished she had been there to meet him. But would he have been interested in her? And if he had been, would his interest stem from her beauty or who she was inside? Better not to know.

Two of the other letters were from her parents, and there was also a thick one from Brionney. So who had written the sixth—and by now partially digested—letter? Perhaps Marie-Thérèse had written to recount her daughter's latest abilities or her husband's virtues. Josette sighed. As envious as she was, she would have enjoyed hearing the details. Or maybe André was writing to tell her about his own mission.

Shrugging, Josette opened Brionney's letter.

Dear Josette,

I hope this letter gets to you, what with your being transferred and all. I can't believe you're almost done with your mission. Are you sure you won't come back to BYU? I miss you like crazy. Maybe I'll come to France to visit you, if I can get my parents to pay for it. I was going to go when Mom and Dad went to pick up Zack, but I really couldn't miss two weeks of school since we were nearing finals. My good grades are about all the enjoyment I have in life. Anyway, you wouldn't have been there, so what was the point? Maybe I'll come after you get back. Then it'll be just you and me roaming the streets of romantic Paris!

Zack is different since he came home. He still teases me, but he's more spiritual—or something. I don't know. I'm glad he's back. We do stuff all the time now. I tease him that he'll never find a wife this way, but he just laughs.

That reminds me. Boy, was Zack ever irritated that I didn't tell him about you being on a mission. He didn't yell or anything, but I could tell. He wouldn't say why. I bet he has a crush on you (like practically every other guy in the world). I told him he didn't stand a chance since you didn't like men anymore. And besides, with all those romantic French hunks, you don't need a boring American. Ha! Ha! He didn't like that. But don't worry, he has a date this weekend with a girl in one of his summer classes at the Y. I'll try and get him safely married so you can come and visit me with no worries of being hounded.

Josette stopped reading, and thumbed through the photographs Brionney had sent. There were many of her and Zack, but looking at them made Josette strangely depressed. She threw them into a deep corner of her suitcase and didn't look at them again.

All at once, she wished she could talk with Pauline. She needed one of her special hugs now. That night she prayed harder than she had ever prayed. The veil seemed very thin, and Josette felt comforted.

"You know, it's funny how things work out," Josette said to Sister Nabb. "When Grady attacked me, I thought my world had ended. And then they told me about my sister, and I wanted to die, but when I saw her and hugged her, and she seemed so peaceful, it was okay. Then there was Emeri; I had to help him join the Church for Pauline, and that led me here. It's strange to say, but if the bad things hadn't happened, I wouldn't be here, and I couldn't have helped any of the people I've met."

With regard to her missionary service, Josette's joy knew no bounds. She looked backward on her life and mission and saw a chain of connected events, some horrible, some pleasant, but each making up a vital part in the intricate tapestry of her life.

She cried when it was time for her to leave Portugal. How could she ever have thought she would serve her time and never look back? In her heart, she felt a mixture of satisfaction at a job well done and sadness at leaving it behind. The country would be a part of her forever.

Before the plane landed in France, she forced herself to wipe the tears from her face and look forward. Aside from the joy of being reunited with her family, her future didn't seem very exciting. What could equal working single-mindedly for the Lord and feeling his Spirit so strongly each day? It would be a hard act to follow.

* * * * *

The entire Perrault clan waited for Josette at the airport in Paris. Marie-Thérèse carried the newest addition, five-month-old Larissa, in her arms. At her side was Mathieu. He looked much the same, but the attraction Josette had felt for him was completely gone. Had she ever really loved him? Compared to the feelings she had for those she had baptized in Portugal, those once devastating feelings meant absolutely nothing.

"Your daughter is beautiful," Josette said as she hugged Marie-Thérèse. "Look at those cheeks! Hello, little one, I'm your Aunt Josette." The title sounded odd to her, but no one else seemed to notice. The baby reached out and grabbed a lock of Josette's hair that had grown back almost as long as it had been before her mission. She had been meaning to get it cut, but had never found the opportunity.

"It's so good to see you," Marie-Thérèse said as she untangled her daughter's hand.

Josette laughed. She didn't know until seeing her family how much she had missed them, especially Marie-Thérèse and Marc.

"Hey, Josette, what about me?"

Josette faced the voice she recognized, but was startled at the change in Emeri. He was much thinner than he was when she had left on her mission, and he wore a hat to hide the loss of hair. She knew that meant his cancer had returned. Why hadn't he mentioned it in his letters? She held out her arms to hug him. "Oh, Emeri! It's so good to see you. I've sure appreciated your letters."

"I'm an elder now," he said. "Just last week. And I've been doing some splits with the missionaries. It's fun!"

Josette laughed. "I'll bet you're a great missionary. Look how fast you converted your parents."

"It wasn't me," Emeri said humbly. "It was the Spirit. You know that."

"Yeah, I guess I do."

Marc put an arm around her. "Come on, Jose. You look like you could use a soft bed."

"A bed? I could sleep for a week!"

And she nearly did. But at the end of that week, she got out of bed and went to her mother. "Did you take care of it?" she asked.

"Yes. But are you sure about this, honey?" There was concern in Ariana's eyes, and more than a little reluctance.

"I've got another three weeks before I need to leave," Josette replied. "And it's not like it's forever. I may not even finish my schooling at BYU." She hesitated. "But I have to go there for at least a semester. It's like I said in my letter; I just feel I have to face it. You know, what happened with Grady and all." There was more to it that she didn't expect her mother to understand. How could she, when Josette didn't understand it completely herself? She only knew it had something to do with proving to herself that her life was actually as changed as she felt it was. At BYU she could face her demons, both real and imagined.

Ariana dug something out of the cedar chest at the base of her bed. "Here are your school papers and the address of the apartment we rented for you."

"You didn't tell Brionney's family, did you?" Josette hadn't told anyone except her family about the decision to return to BYU. After she resolved whatever it was that pulled her to Provo, then she would call Brionney and surprise her.

"No, the missionary who baptized me helped," Ariana said. "He still works at the university."

"Good." Josette smoothed the gentle creases in her mother's cheeks. "Oh, Mom, don't worry. I'm following the Spirit."

Ariana hugged her. "I guess you've learned to do that well enough in these past eighteen months. I'm so proud of you. Do you know that?"

Josette's heart filled with exhilaration. It meant everything to have her mother say those words, especially because she knew they hadn't always been true. She wished she didn't have to leave again at all.

* * * * *

Three weeks later at the airport in Paris, Josette said good-bye to Marc and Emeri. "You've got to give up this man-hating thing," Emeri told her. "Just because one guy turns out to be a creep doesn't mean that all guys are. Take me, for instance. Underneath my creepy exterior was this incredibly sweet guy."

Josette laughed. "Right, Emeri. But alas, you're taken. Pauline would kill me if I made any moves on you."

Emeri's return laughter ended in a bout of coughing. Josette peered at him worriedly. "Maybe I shouldn't go," she said.

He held up his hands. "Oh, no. Don't stay to fuss over me. I've got my parents for that. That's all I need—another weepy woman." His kissed her good-bye. "Now, behave yourself. Marc, I'll be waiting in the car."

Marc walked with Josette to the gate entrance, where he hugged her and kissed both cheeks. "I wish I could go with you," he said. "I don't like the thought of you going by yourself."

Josette laughed. "You just don't want me to go at all. But don't worry, I'll be all right. And I'll be back soon, I promise." She touched his face briefly. "I'll always come back to you, brother. You're my other half."

"Just so you remember who's the younger half," Marc said. "The older sibling always has to look out for the younger."

"I'll be back to do my duty," Josette said with a grin. "But why five and a half minutes makes a difference, I'll never understand. Now can I go already? The plane's about to leave."

"Just one thing," Marc said. He hesitated, as if making an important decision. "I'd like you to look up Zack for me, if you will. Tell him I sent you. He'll understand."

"I'm through with men. I told you that."

"Zack's not a man. I mean . . . well, he's my friend. Come on, you'll be seeing his sister anyway."

Josette didn't have time to argue. "Okay," she said. Blowing him a kiss, she turned and made her way to the plane.

CHAPTER TWENTY-FOUR

The mid-September morning carried a brisk breeze, unexpected after the heat of summer. Zack's T-shirt let in the cold, but he knew that later in the morning the sun would burn away the clouds and heat the world again. He opened the car door and let Brionney inside.

"How's Suzy?" Brionney asked as he settled in the driver's seat and started the engine.

Zack shrugged. "I haven't called her."

"But I thought you liked her." She checked her makeup in the passenger-side mirror.

"We were just friends," he said. "I think she's going out with a football player now."

"So, fight for her."

"Have you seen those BYU football players lately?" he asked, faking amazement. "Boy, one would think you don't want a brother at all."

Brionney laughed. "You're nuts. And if you don't start dating those girls who are always calling the house, you're going to end up an old bachelor."

He knew he should make a better effort to find a spouse, but his heart simply wasn't in it. There was only one girl he wanted to date. *Why didn't she answer my letter?* he thought. Aloud he said, "I've only been off my mission for four and a half months. It's not like I'm old yet; give me some time."

"No way. I'm your sister. I'm supposed to bug you." She waved as she got out of the car at Provo High School. "Thanks for the ride."

Zack put the car into gear and drove to BYU.

Josette had never answered his letter, and he was embarrassed to have sent it at all. What had he been thinking?—writing to a girl he had never met. He couldn't really blame her for not answering, could he? And what was it he had written? He had tried to come across suave and debonair, but maybe he had been maudlin and gauche. One thing for certain: he had bled all over the page, laying bare his heart and soul. What had she thought when she read it? He would give anything to know.

Since he had received no response, he had put aside all ideas of returning to France to meet her. He still thought about her in his spare time, and she even appeared in his dreams. Not that he had much free time to dream. He worked full time now at his father's real estate office, and also had three college classes. Maybe next semester he would cut down and go out on more dates.

Soft drops of rain left splotches on the cement, and Zack took a moment in the parked car to breathe in the smell. From his child-hood, he had loved the pungent aroma of rain on the pavement. Tucking his head down against the pelting drops, he hurried toward his first class. The rain came faster now, and he wished he had thought to bring a jacket.

He looked up as a girl sprinted toward him on the wide cement pathway, her dark head bent against the rain. Before he could dodge, she barrelled into him, sending the backpack on her shoulder tumbling to the ground. She scrambled after it in a mess of incredibly long, damp hair, and Zack went down with her, trying to help.

"I'm sorry," she muttered in accented English. Her voice was low and attractive. A gold necklace around her graceful neck glinted dully in the dim light. "I didn't see you."

"That's all right. The rain—" His words broke off as they arose together and he saw her clearly for the first time. He felt his pulse race, and for a moment he couldn't make his mouth work. She stared back at him, her dark eyes wide and full of emotion.

Students streamed past them, but it was as if they were in a world alone. For so long Zack had been waiting for this moment, so long that he had almost let go of the hope or the desire that it might ever happen. And now here she was, the woman he had grown to love on his mission and who had haunted his dreams ever since. Between them flowed a recognition that went far beyond a few pictures and shared friends. Zack imagined he knew her, clear to the deepest part of her soul, and he felt she knew him as well. There was only one thing left to say.

"Vous voulez me marier?"—Will you marry me?

"Oui," she answered.

Zack leaned down and kissed her. Nothing had ever tasted so sweet.

* * * * *

The first thing Josette noticed when the man drew back and she finally managed to open her eyes was the black mole on the lower part of his left check. The extraordinary blue eyes, the white-blond hair, the handsome angular face, were as she remembered from pictures, but that little mole was something new.

She marveled at the emotion she felt. How could she love a man at first sight? That was ridiculous, wasn't it? But she felt as though she had known him somewhere before.

Elder Fields—no, Zack, she had to remind herself—bent to kiss her again. He was taller than she imagined he would be, but with a little bending and stretching, they fit together perfectly.

The cold breeze, the falling rain, the jostling students, nothing penetrated their world. Then, as if even the heavens were seared by the passion in their hearts, the rain stopped and the clouds parted.

Zack chuckled. "Amen," he said, looking up into the warm face of the sun.

Josette smiled, and Zack did too. He watched her with an odd expression on his face, one Josette had never seen before—except perhaps on her father's face when he stared at her mother.

"What are you thinking?" he asked in French.

"I'm wondering if you can see how fast my heart is beating." Even as she said it, she recognized that once she would never have confessed such a thing.

He gave another warm chuckle. "Like a freight train going down a hill without brakes? Oh, I know the feeling."

Josette laughed, experiencing an astonishing joy, rivalled only by the times when those she loved had accepted the gospel. This feeling was a hundred times stronger.

The path was clearing of students, and Josette knew she'd be late for her first class. She pictured what she might say to the teacher. "Excuse me for being late, but a man I've never met before just asked me to marry him."

And she had said yes!

Oh, dear.

Josette stared at the ground.

Zack bent down, twisting his head around to see her face. "I'm holding you to it," he said softly. "Don't worry, I'll prove myself to you."

He kissed her again, but it was too quick for real enjoyment. "You're going to be late to class, aren't you? Me too. We'll have to talk later."

"But . . ."

He withdrew a necklace from his shirt. "See," he said, pointing to the half-charm on her chain as if that explained everything. Then he left, whistling cheerfully.

Josette felt relieved to be alone to sort out her feelings. Love? Was this love? It all seemed like a dream, and by the end of her first class, she had almost convinced herself that she had imagined the whole incident.

That afternoon when she arrived at the apartment, Zack was already in her front room with a bouquet of flowers. Her roommates giggled and made themselves scarce.

"How did you find me?" she asked with sudden shyness.

He handed her the flowers. "I have my ways."

"Yeah, right. I bet you called campus information."

"Maybe."

"How did you know I don't like roses?" The bouquet he had brought her had just about every flower she was familiar with except roses. Roses. The flower most men had brought her.

"You are too beautiful for only one type of flower," he said, standing. "Now, I've got to go back to work for a while, but what I came for was to ask if you'll come to dinner tonight . . . at my house."

"I haven't even told Brionney yet that I'm here."

"She'll understand, especially when we tell them we're getting married."

Josette held her breath. She really hadn't been dreaming earlier! "But . . ."

"Yes?" He stared at her, as if daring her to go back on her word. What could she say, that he was crazy? That they were both crazy?

"You're not really going to tell your parents."

"Why not? Maybe we should call your parents, too. And your brother. I'd like to hear his reaction when you tell him."

"He told me to look you up," Josette said, remembering. "He said you'd understand. Do you?"

Zack laughed until his face turned red. "Old Marc's finally come to his senses, that's all. I don't know how or why, but I'm grateful. It'll make things easier."

Josette didn't know what to say.

"That's funny," Zack said. "I'd never figured you for the speechless type, especially after knowing Marc. Man, that guy never shut up. But that's okay. I guess there'll be time to get to know each other before the wedding. Which temple do you prefer?" He glanced at his watch. "Oh, dang! I've got an appointment to show someone a house. I'll be back at six-thirty." He leaned forward and planted a soft kiss on her cheek, then ran out the door. Josette heard his voice float back to her as he plunged down the stairs, "And leave Saturday open, so we can go look for a ring."

Josette sat down on the couch and stared at the flowers. "Oh, boy," she murmured.

After a while, she picked up the phone and dialed home. She waited the few seconds for the call to go through and start ringing. To her relief, Marc picked up at the other end. "Hi, Jose," he said brightly. "Had enough? Are you coming home?"

"Zack asked me to marry him," she said.

"Did he? You've only been there, what, two weeks? Don't you think that's a little soon?"

Two long and lonely weeks, Josette corrected silently. Weeks that she had been walking around feeling empty, wondering if coming back had been a good idea at all.

"I only met him today."

"You *what?*" her brother sputtered.

"We just met, and he asked me."

"Well, I guess he's been waiting a long time. But . . . is he rushing you?" Marc sounded angry.

"I said yes."

"Oh. Well, then congratulations . . . I think."

Josette said nothing.

"He's a good guy, Jose. I couldn't recommend better. He's one of the most spiritual guys I know."

"Then why didn't you try to set us up?"

"I just didn't think you'd be good together, that's all."

Josette was close enough to her twin to know when he lied. "You didn't think I was good enough for him, did you?" she asked slowly.

Marc's reply came even slower. "I just didn't want him to hurt you; please believe me. And for what it's worth, I think you and he will make a great couple. But don't let him rush you into anything. You're entitled to your own revelation."

"I know that."

"You could always tell him to get lost, or I will for you, if you want."

It was an option Josette couldn't consider. To go back to what her life was before? To deny what the Spirit had told her? "I love him," she said simply, and knew it was true. Joy filled her heart, but fear was there as well. What had she gotten herself into this time?

"Isn't that funny?" Marc said. "Sometimes true love can be just under your nose, and you don't see it."

"Zack wasn't under my nose, thanks to you."

"Well, you know what I mean."

They talked for a long time before hanging up. Marc agreed to keep her news a secret until she felt more comfortable with it.

As promised, Zack picked her up later that evening and took her to his parents' house. Terrell and Irene were just as Josette remembered them. Brionney was still short and plump, but had grown out of some of her awkwardness. Josette knew she would soon be eighteen.

"I can't believe you didn't tell me you were coming!" Brionney said, flinging herself into Josette's arms. "When Zack called and said he'd found you and was bringing you home, I couldn't believe it. Why didn't you tell me?"

"I wanted to surprise you . . . after I got settled. And I've been trying to find a job."

"A job! You're kidding. Well, no matter. I bet Zack and Dad can use you at the agency, can't you?" Brionney looked at them expectantly.

"That's a good idea," Zack said. "It'll all be in the family, anyway."

Everyone fell silent. "What?" Brionney finally asked.

Josette stared at the ground, wishing Zack wouldn't say anything more, but also praying that he would.

"We're getting married," Zack said. "That's why I wanted Josette to come to dinner tonight. We wanted to make the announcement."

There's no going back now, Josette thought, panicking. *Is that why he's rushing to tell them?*

"Oh, now I know why you haven't contacted me," Brionney said with a smirk. "You've been too busy going out with Zack. You must have gotten his letter." She glanced at her brother. "Oh, I know you sent one, but when Josette didn't say anything, I didn't want to pry."

"What letter?" asked Josette, looking at Zack. "I never got a letter. Did you write one?"

Zack grinned. "You didn't get it? Oh, that explains everything!"

"It was about the time you were transferred to your last area," Brionney added.

"That is strange," Josette said. "There was only one time that . . . . Oh, the dog ate it!"

"Now that's a new excuse," Zack drawled. He put his arm around her shoulders.

"But it's true." Josette tried to explain, but her heart had begun that curious, rapid beating, and the English words fled from her brain. She held her hand to her heart.

"Is something wrong?" Zack asked.

She gave a short laugh. "No, it's just the freight train again," she said in French. He pulled her closer and planted a kiss on her temple.

During the whole announcement and discussion, Irene and Terrell Fields had said nothing, and Josette hadn't dared meet their eyes. What would they say if they knew that today was the first time she and Zack had ever met?

Irene touched her shoulder. "Welcome to the family."

Behind her, Terrell smiled. "We'd just about given up hope on old Zack," he said. "But now we know he was holding out for the best-looking girl in France."

Josette felt an emotion in her breast that she couldn't name. This wonderful family accepted her! Zack loved her! A good and worthy man, not someone just out for a good time.

"Come on into the house for dinner," Irene said.

Zack let his arm fall from Josette's shoulders and gripped her hand instead. On the other side, Brionney hooked her arm through Josette's. "Tell me, if it wasn't for the letter, then how did you meet, Zack?"

"In our dreams," he said. Josette didn't know him well enough to tell if he was joking.

Brionney snorted. "Well, that's okay, don't tell me. I don't need to know. But thank heavens you chose each other. I didn't like the idea of my brother marrying just anyone. And I guess that's why I never bought another heart charm," she said with a satisfied smile. "I knew you belonged together."

Zack laughed. "Okay, sis, I guess I'll let you off the hook."

"So when is this wedding anyway?" Brionney asked.

"Next week," Zack said.

Josette glanced at him quickly and saw a twinkle in his eyes. "Are you crazy?" she asked in French, not caring that Brionney would understand.

"I'm kidding." He squeezed her hand. "We'll take it slowly—for now."

CHAPTER TWENTY-FIVE

Zack felt that everything went perfectly during the dinner. From the way his parents acted, they liked Josette. Of course Brionney was crazy about her, and his three married sisters would also love her when they met her at the customary family dinner, held twice monthly. How could they not? She was so beautiful.

Only one thing about the evening disturbed Zack. Josette wasn't as outspoken as he had imagined she would be after hearing about her from Marc. Was this the same girl at all? Or was something wrong?

Each time anyone mentioned their coming wedding, she paled and fell silent. *Maybe she's overwhelmed,* he thought to himself. *Heck, I'm overwhelmed.*

To him, it didn't matter if she said nothing. They were together, and that was what counted. Still, he wondered if her aloofness meant that she was unsure about them. He would have to work harder at showing her how right they were for each other.

That night he kissed her chastely, fighting the urges inside him. "You are so beautiful," he whispered. "I love you."

A hesitant smile played on her lips, but she didn't meet his eyes. "I had a nice time, Zack. Thank you."

He hugged her then, and it was all he could do to let her go. "See you tomorrow night," he said.

"Tomorrow?"

"Do you already have plans?" How dumb of him to assume that a girl as desirable as Josette wouldn't have plans on a Friday night.

"I'm free," she said. "What are we going to do?"

"Dress casual. Jeans or something. I'll surprise you. Okay?"

To his delight, she gave a low laugh. "Okay, Zack." He loved the way she said his name.

* * * * *

The next evening Zack was at her door at six-thirty. He had wracked his brains for something original—something that would not only relax them both, but make her happy.

"Hi," she said when she opened the door. She wore jeans that were exactly the right fit for her slender curves, and a simple white cotton blouse with tiny buttons down the front. Her long hair swung down her back in a thick braid, showing the fine planes of her face. Her eyes traveled to the two pair of roller blades he held in his hands. She laughed, and her whole face seemed to shine with pleasure.

"Here. These are my old ones from junior high. I would have borrowed Brionney's, but she's got such tiny feet. I mean, I thought these would be more comfortable."

"That's the first time anyone's ever said I have big feet," she said.

"That's not what I meant—" Then he saw she was teasing. His plan to relax her was working already!

"Marc and I always used to go blading," she said as she laced the roller blades.

"I know. He told me. That's practically all he ever talked about. You and those roller blades."

She stopped. "He didn't tell me much about you. Of course, in the last three and a half years, we haven't been together much."

"You miss him."

Her eyes became luminous. "I do. I mean, we've always been so close. Have you ever felt like a part of you was missing?"

He had to clear his throat before he could say, "Yes. I felt exactly that way until I met you."

Her hand reached out to his, and she didn't have to say anything because Zack knew she understood.

"Where are we going?"

"You'll see," he said. "But bring a sweater. It might get cold before we get back." He wore his own denim jacket.

At first he led the way down the sidewalk, but Josette soon skated ahead, her red sweater tied around her waist. "Race you," she called.

She was better than he was, and he had to use all his strength to catch up. "It's all those stairs on my mission," she said with a laugh. She glanced at a group of passersby who watched them with indulgent smiles. "I've never felt so conspicuous," she said.

They slowed and skated hand-in-hand. At each street corner, Zack indicated which way to turn. Soon their destination was in sight.

"The temple," she said.

He took her to the grassy hill on the east side of the temple. They sat for a long moment without speaking.

"I'd like to get married in this temple," he said, trying to sound matter-of-fact.

"I don't even know what you're majoring in," she said. As usual, she spoke French with him, and Zack loved the sound. He could listen to her all day.

"Business management," he said. "But I'm already working full time as a real estate agent with my dad. And you?" For all of the times Marc had talked about his twin, he had never said what she was studying.

"Interior design. I know, it sounds kind of stupid. Unimportant. I mean, what eternal significance will that have on anyone's eternity? I've been thinking about changing, but I enjoy it. I just don't know what else I should do."

"I think it's perfect," Zack said. "Picture this. Besides selling houses, I'd like to invest in a few old ones and restore them. You know, fix what's wrong and decorate. You could help me. We'd make a great team."

Her smile came again. "That sounds fun. It really does." She leaned over to hug him, but pulled back after a brief embrace.

"What is it?" he asked.

"I just don't know how to act. It's been a long time since I dated. I . . ." A sudden frown covered her face.

"Don't do that," he said. "You're so beautiful when you smile." The truth was, she was beautiful no matter what she did. But he wanted more than anything to see her happy.

She looked away, and Zack wondered what he'd said wrong. Instinct warned him not to push.

They talked for a long time and were surprised when the outside lights of the temple began to show in the twilight. He took her hand, and it felt soft and warm.

"Tomorrow," he said, "we have to find a ring."

* * * * *

Josette must have tried on a million rings before both agreed they had found the perfect one. During the search, they giggled like small children and held hands every chance they had. When one of the sales clerks tried to convince them to settle for a ring they weren't sure about, Josette firmly refused. Zack was glad to see that no one could push her around. Maybe it eased his conscience.

He felt his luck too good to hold when the third store they visited had the ring for them. To his surprise, Josette wasn't interested in a big diamond, and he even had to convince her to get one that was a little larger. "Wouldn't you like it?" he asked.

"Oh, yes," she replied hesitantly. "But I don't want to be too showy." Then she added in an undertone, "I can't believe I just said that."

He threw back his head and laughed. "Well, I don't want to be called a cheapskate. I have four sisters, you know, who'll never let me forget it. Besides, what would your parents say?"

"They wouldn't care. At least my mom wouldn't. She doesn't go in much for jewelry. Besides her wedding ring, the only jewelry she wears is a rose pin my dad gave her."

"Even so . . ." Zack looked at the sales clerk. "Put in this larger stone," he said, pointing out the size.

"That's a good choice," the clerk said. "We can have it ready for you by next week."

After grabbing a warm pretzel to munch on, they took a drive in the mountains, and Josette made him stop the car so she could gather a bouquet of colored leaves. Without warning, she tossed them onto his head and ran up the trail. He caught up to her and dumped a handful over her. The stems and pieces stuck in her braid.

"Oh yeah?" She put her foot behind him and pushed him to the ground, piling more leaves on top of him. Zack fought back, and both of them began giggling uncontrollably.

"Enough!" Josette cried after a while.

Exhausted, they fell back onto the leaves, still laughing. Josette tried to brush the leaves out of her hair.

"You'll have to take out the elastic." Sitting up, Zack pulled out the elastic and began to undo the braid. "Besides, I love your hair loose. Like that day in the rain." Had it only been two days ago? It seemed like he had known her forever.

"You should always wear your hair like this," he added, his fingers combing through the long strands. "Did I tell you you're beautiful?"

Her smile faded. "Yes."

He released her hair, and the ends fell to mix in with the leaves on the ground. "Why do you look away when I say it? Don't you believe me?"

For a moment, he thought she would answer; instead she laughed. Not a real laugh, but forced. "Of course I believe you."

"Is there anything you want to tell me?" he asked, feeling there was something more.

"No, silly." She picked up the ends of her hair and swatted him playfully.

He hugged her then, and everything returned to normal, but the incident worried Zack. He hoped that in time she would learn to trust him.

* * * * *

Business was slow as Josette waited for Zack to come back to the office with the couple he had taken to show a house. Josette had finished her work at the reception desk, but she wanted to see Zack before she went home. They would probably end up doing something together as they had every night for the last two weeks.

The new engagement ring on her finger still felt awkward. It was beautiful and she was glad Zack had insisted on a larger stone, though she had been reluctant to admit it was what she had always wanted. Did a large diamond really matter in the eternal scheme of things? No, she had to admit. She had learned only too well that jewelry was no substitute for the real love she felt for Zack.

Her cheeks burned at the thought. Love. This was love. Could it be too good to be true?

Her head ached from the weight of her single braid. Zack liked her hair free, and it certainly felt better that way. During school and work hours, she kept it pulled back, but now . . . She undid the elastic and shook out the braid. Already, her scalp felt relief from the pressure.

She gave a short laugh and refocused on the stationery before her. Last week she had received a letter from Emeri, urging her to return to France and the people who loved her. He and his parents had recently attended the temple, where they had been sealed as a family. Josette wished she could have been with him, but she knew that her place right now was with Zack. The urge to come to BYU had been too strong for her to deny. She wanted to tell Emeri about Zack, knowing he would be happy for her.

Josette's attention was pulled away from Emeri when Zack came into the office with a young couple. He gave a thumbs-up signal behind their backs. That meant they liked the house he had shown them and would make an offer. Now he would have to fill out the earnest agreement and present it to the owners. For him that meant working late, but the commission would be worth it. Maybe she would tag along. It would be better than facing her apartment alone.

She scribbled a few more words to Emeri, then gave it up. *I'll just call him tomorrow,* she thought.

Josette felt as though the past sixteen days with Zack had been better than any dream she had come up with in her childhood. Why did she feel as though she had never been out with a boy before? Or ever kissed a boy? Until Zack.

She still felt she wasn't good enough for Zack, but the feeling that their relationship was moving too fast had subsided to a faint memory. At the moment, to be with Zack was her one great desire. She didn't want to think about life without him.

Only one thing made her nervous. What if he woke up one day and didn't love her? What if he grew tired of her beautiful face? She knew that beauty alone could never hold a man.

Zack came out of his office with the couple. "I'll let you know as soon as I have their answer," he said to them. "If it's yes, or just a little different, I'll swing by your house and get it taken care of tonight."

"We'll be waiting." The man shook Zack's hand, and the wife gave a happy nod.

When they were gone, Zack flipped the "closed" sign on the glass door and sauntered over to her desk. He pulled her out of the chair and into his arms. "I missed you," he said, burying his face in her hair.

She clung to him. "I missed you, too."

"So will you come with me?"

"Of course." She bent down to scoop up her book bag.

"I like your hair like that."

His words made her flush. "I know."

They drove to the house the couple wanted to buy. It was the largest house Josette had ever seen. "But why does that couple need something so big?" she asked.

"They have six children."

"They didn't look that old."

Zack laughed. "The children are still small, and besides, they had to use fertility drugs. They got triplets the last time."

The owners of the mansion accepted the offer, and Zack whistled as he drove the car to another section of town. Josette assumed they were going to tell the couple and their six children that the mansion was theirs, but Zack stopped at another house instead. Dark windows signalled its vacancy. "I want to show you something," he said with a mysterious smile.

He led her up the cement walk to the house, where he pulled out a key and opened the front door. "It's a repo," he said. "The people couldn't pay the bank, so the bank repossessed. It needs a little work, but for the price, it's an excellent deal. Look at this wood floor and the tile in the kitchen. That's expensive stuff, and it won't have to be redone."

"I like that bay window," Josette said. "And this entryway. It's small, but I like the idea of not having to walk into the front room when you want to go to the kitchen."

"It reminds me of France," Zack said.

Josette wondered why he had brought her here. Was this a new house he had been commissioned to sell? No, it was a repo. Just exactly why were they here?

Zack took her into the empty front room. "This rug needs replacement," he said, poking the large area rug with his shoe, "but underneath the wood is better than in the entryway. "Do you like it?"

"Yes, but—"

He looked at her earnestly. "It can be ours, if you want. We'll need a place, and this is too good to pass up. Even if we decide we don't want it later on, we could sell. What do you say?"

Contrasting emotions bubbled up inside Josette. One part of her wanted to sing out with happiness and run wildly through the house, making plans for renovation. To think—a whole house for only the two of them! With plenty of yard to plant things. To a woman who had been raised in a city apartment, the large plot of earth was the greatest pull. Her children could play on swings in the backyard. She could plant a garden, though she didn't know where to begin, and they could . . .

The other emotions were just as strong. Buying this house meant that they would be making their home permanently here in America. It was the one subject they had not discussed. How could she give up her native land and everything she held dear?

Images of her family flashed before her. Several stood out in her mind, but strangely she remembered most the look on Emeri's face when he finally understood how much his parents loved him. How much time did he have left on earth? The separation from her family during her mission and for school had been different because it was only temporary, but this was for life. How could she live without her family, especially her other half? *Oh, Marc!*

But there was also no life for her without Zack. While she had insecurities regarding their relationship, the circumstances leading to their meeting left no doubt in her heart that he was her soul mate. As heartbreaking as it would be for her to give up her family, for him she would do it.

"You look so sad," Zack said, touching her cheek tentatively. "Don't you want to marry me?"

"Oh, yes, I do." Josette pushed her homesickness out of her mind, letting her love for Zack fill the emptiness. "I love you, and I love this house."

He picked her up and whirled her around. "Then hurry outside," he said. "We've got to do this right."

Puzzled, Josette followed him to the front step.

"We'll build a porch here," he said. Before she could reply, he scooped her up and carried her over the threshold. "It's an American tradition," he told her. "The groom always has to carry his bride into the house."

"Why?" She nearly choked on her laughter.

"I don't know, they just do it."

She struggled in his arms. "Well, we're not married yet. Put me down!"

"Hey, I'm practicing. I want to get it right that day. You don't want me to accidentally drop you or something, do you?" Zack set her down, his eyes dancing.

They examined the rest of the house, planning what they would do. "This is so fun!" she said.

"I know. But we can't live here until we're married. Maybe we ought to set the date." His words were gentle but probing.

"I haven't told my parents," she protested. Why was she stalling? She knew she loved Zack. The problem was the look in his eyes when he told her how beautiful she was. But that didn't mean–

"Well, now's a great time to tell them. We can call them from your apartment." Zack looked satisfied, and Josette didn't have the heart to object.

"Okay," she said.

Zack whooped and nearly knocked her over with his exuberant hug. "Let's go finish this business with that mansion, and then we'll call."

Less than thirty minutes later, they arrived at Josette's apartment. "You know, I did tell Marc that first day we met."

"Then maybe your parents already know."

"Marc would never give away my secret."

"Maybe he's hoping you'll change your mind." Zack's voice sounded serious.

She punched his arm. "Let me handle Marc."

After dialing the number, she listened to the beeps on the phone that signalled the different paths making up the overseas connection. Finally, it began to ring. Her mother picked up the phone.

"Hi, Mom," she said a bit breathlessly. "It's me, Josette."

"Oh, honey, I'm so glad you called. Something's happened." From her tone, Josette knew it wasn't good news.

* * * * *

Zack saw Josette's face drain of color beneath the remnants of her summer tan. She made a desperate noise in her throat. "No," she moaned. She was quiet while her mother continued to speak. Zack could hear the soft, melodic voice coming from the phone, but Josette didn't appear to be paying attention. The receiver slipped from her ear, and only Zack's quick catch stopped it from hitting the linoleum floor.

Josette walked out of the kitchen, moving like someone in a trance. Zack put the phone to his ear. "Hello?" he said in French.

"Who's this?"

"Zack Fields."

"Oh, yes, I remember you. Marc's old companion. Is Josette all right?"

"I think so. I'll take care of her."

"I appreciate it. She and Emeri were close. She didn't expect him to die before she came home. None of us did, really. He had actually started to improve, but . . ."

Zack stopped hearing the words. Emeri was dead! No wonder Josette was so upset. He remembered Brionney saying how much Emeri meant to her. He had even felt jealous of him before meeting her, and still suspected that Emeri was the reason for her reluctance to set a wedding date. Hadn't he seen a letter addressed to him on her desk earlier? What had she been writing?

"When did it happen?" he asked.

"Just this morning. He died peacefully in his sleep. He'd been in a little bit of pain since he and his parents returned from the Switzerland temple a few weeks ago and he'd had to take medication."

"How is his family taking it?"

"Remarkably well. Emeri helped prepare them, and we are all here to give them support and help. I think they'll be all right. They are wonderful people and have great faith. They actually have plans to adopt a young orphan boy who also has AIDS."

Zack felt amazed at their willingness to mourn another son. "I'll talk to Josette and we'll call you back," he said.

"I'm so glad she's with your family. Maybe your mother can—"

"We're not with my family. We're at her apartment."

There was a long pause and then, "Tell me." The comment showed Ariana's perceptiveness. It wasn't easy to reach across the thousands of miles separating them, but she did it easily.

"I love her," he said. "And I'm going to marry her."

He expected to hear outrage at the uncompromising way he had made the statement, but Ariana laughed. "I'm glad you're there, then. Have her call us later."

Zack hung up and went to find Josette. She was in her room, lying stomach-down on the bed with her hands pulled under her chest and face turned to the wall, covered by the disarray of her dark hair.

He had never been in her room before. Besides the single bed there was a small desk and chair, a dresser, and a closet. Clothes were piled on the chair, giving him the impression that Josette wasn't quite as organized as he liked to be. He didn't care. On her dresser was a picture of her family, a jewelry box, a small stack of opened letters, and a bottle of perfume knocked on its side.

"Josette." He sat on the bed. When she made no move to turn to him, he reached out and uncovered her face. His hand came away wet from her tears. Frowning, he let the hand fall to caress her back. "I'm so sorry," he murmured.

She turned toward him, curling her body around his, and he saw that in her hands she clutched a brass-framed photograph of two laughing young men, one of whom was Marc. Was the other this Emeri? Zack had only met him once briefly when he had visited Josette's family after his mission, and he couldn't remember his face.

"I was writing him a letter," Josette said. "I've meant to do it for weeks now, but I just kept putting it off. He's written me three times already in the month I've been here. I only sent him a postcard."

"You couldn't have known."

"Why now?" She started to sob. Zack gathered her in his arms, feeling close to tears himself. He rubbed her back awkwardly as she clung to him. When the tears subsided, she pulled back slightly. "Thanks for being here."

"Where else would I be? I love you. We're supposed to be here for each other."

Her face crumpled, and tears once more slid down her face. Strands of hair caught in the salty water and stuck to her left cheek.

"You loved him," Zack said. "Is he why you didn't want to set the date?"

She shook her head. "Oh, no. Emeri is Pauline's."

"Then shouldn't you be just a little happy for them?" he asked. "They're together now."

Josette blinked twice. "You're right," she said. "And I know that—with my mind. But my heart just feels like I'm losing so much."

"What do you mean?" he asked. "You've got me."

She watched him for a full minute before replying. "And that's enough. I'm so lucky to have you."

"No," he said, brushing the hair from her cheek. "I'm the lucky one. You're so beautiful."

She looked away as she always did when he said this, and Zack felt disappointed at her reaction.

"Don't say that," she said.

"What?" He couldn't keep the annoyance from his voice completely. "Why shouldn't I call you beautiful? You are."

"What if I'm not always beautiful?" she asked, not looking at him. "What if I got in an accident or something? Or when I get old and wrinkled?"

"I'll still love you."

"Not if that is what makes you love me. Oh, Zack, I know you mean well, but I'm tired of men telling me how beautiful I am. I want you to love me for *me.*" She tapped her chest. "For what I am inside."

Now Zack understood. He moved his head into her line of sight. "What if I looked any different? Would that change how you feel for me?" She shook her head reluctantly. "Well, neither would it for me. When I say you're beautiful, I don't mean just physically. I mean what I see inside. I love you because when I'm with you I'm happy, because when you look at me I know I can do anything." He took her hands in his. "Josette, I fell in love with you before we met, but it wasn't just because of your picture. It was because of what I learned about you from Marc and Brionney, and from the Spirit. I know we're meant to be—twin flames on a single candle. I just want to be with you. No matter what, you'll always have all of my heart."

She hugged him then, fiercely. "For that I'll marry you tomorrow, Zack Fields."

He laughed. "I don't know if I can get the house that soon."

She kissed him, and he tasted the salt from her drying tears.

"Well, get started then."

"Uh, we have to call your mom back first. She's worried about you. Besides, I told her I was going to marry you. I think she wants an explanation."

Josette's mouth opened in astonishment. "You told her?"

He grinned. "Sometimes if you want something done, you've got to do it yourself." He paused, fingering the folds of the blanket. "Actually," he said, hating the catch in his voice, "your mother sounded worried. I wanted her to know that someone who loves you is here to help."

"That just moved the wedding up again," Josette said. "How does tonight sound?"

He hugged her. "Just about right."

They called France and had a long conversation with the Perrault family. Everyone, including Marc, acted pleased with the wedding plans.

"Boy, you never give up, do you?" Marc teased Zack when it was his turn to talk.

"The best is worth fighting for," Zack said. "But between you and me, I don't think she remembers I'm a year younger than you guys. Don't remind her, okay?"

When he said good-bye, he found Josette in her room again, reading a letter. He sat next to her on the bed. "It's the last one Emeri wrote," she said. "Listen. 'I can't imagine where I would be if I hadn't met Pauline and learned about the gospel. I was lost and she found me. It was nothing short of a miracle. There are no words to thank you for helping me recognize the truth. God loves me! There is a plan! I'm no longer afraid.'"

"He sounds like a great guy," Zack said. "I wish I could have met him."

Josette leaned against him. "One day you will."

CHAPTER TWENTY-SIX

Marie-Thérèse finished the last of Madame Cerro's ironing as she heard Larissa calling from her room. She put the iron to cool on the counter, making sure the cord was out of reach of curious hands.

Larissa waited in her crib with arms outstretched, looking like a chubby angel in her fluffy pajamas. "Good afternoon, baby. Did you sleep well?" Larissa grinned and babbled something Marie-Thérèse didn't understand. She picked the baby up and kissed her.

"Dolly blahda fahma," Larissa said, pointing to a doll on her shelf next to the window.

Marie-Thérèse walked to the shelf and picked up the rag doll that had belonged to Pauline. She hadn't let the nine-month-old Larissa hold Dolly more than a few times because she wanted to keep it nice for her when she was older and could understand how special it was.

Larissa hugged the doll and kissed it before trying to peel off the embroidered eyes. "They don't come off, Larissa," Marie-Thérèse said. "But her clothes do. Want to see?"

The door buzzer interrupted their play. Marie-Thérèse left Larissa with Dolly and went to the door.

"Oh, hello, Madame Cerro. I'm finished with your ironing." Marie-Thérèse stepped back to let the bulky woman through the door. "Larissa just woke up from her nap, and I was going to bring it over."

"Goodness, it's cold in here," the woman observed. "Don't you have the heat on?"

Marie-Thérèse didn't want to admit that she kept it down on purpose to avoid the high bills. Every franc she could save was one more she wouldn't owe later. She was accustomed to the cold now, and she dressed Larissa warmly so the baby wouldn't suffer. Besides, Marie-Thérèse kept busy, and it wasn't often she had time to think about it. "I like it this way," she said. "When I do the ironing, I get hot."

"Well, I suppose," Madame Cerro said doubtfully.

Marie-Thérèse led the way to the kitchen, where she had installed a bar to hold the rows of shirts and dresses she ironed. When Ariana had announced Josette's impending marriage in America, Marie-Thérèse had been determined to attend the wedding. But because of Mathieu's impulsive spending habits, she was already having trouble making his wage stretch to cover their bills. The only alternative was to earn the money herself by doing something at home. Taking in ironing seemed the perfect solution. Their landlady, Madame Cerro, who lived in the same building, had been one of the first to take her up on the offer.

Madame Cerro bent her graying head and examined the clothes. "You do a good job," she said grudgingly.

"I really try," Marie-Thérèse said. She refrained from mentioning that Madame Cerro's dresses contained twice the material of most women, and the fabric was one of the most difficult to pleat.

The older lady gathered her clothes, careful to hold them by the hangers. "Well, thank you. And I'll bring you more when I have some." She turned to leave.

"Uh, Madame Cerro. What about . . . I mean, the payment." Marie-Thérèse was embarrassed to remind her, and wouldn't have if she hadn't been counting on the money to help pay her way to America.

Madame Cerro was shorter than she was, but the woman did an excellent job of looking down her long nose at Marie-Thérèse. "Well," she said. "I thought you knew. Yesterday when your husband came by with the rent—two weeks late, I might add—I simply didn't charge him the late fee because I knew you were doing the ironing." She looked down at her burden. "This makes us about even, don't you think?"

Marie-Thérèse tried not to grimace. "But you said you understood. It was the first time we were late."

"I do understand. That's why I allowed you to do ironing. I know things are tight when you are first getting started. Regardless, a contract is a contract." She gave Marie-Thérèse a patronizing smile.

"But don't worry, dear. I'm sure I'll be bringing a lot more ironing. And don't bother about seeing me out. I know the way."

Marie-Thérèse sat down on a kitchen chair. It was part of a nice set Mathieu had bought her for her birthday last week. She had wanted to continue to use their hand-me-down table, but his boyish enthusiasm had made her relent. Now the purchase meant one more monthly payment.

Marie-Thérèse opened a drawer, took out an envelope, and counted the money she had saved. It wasn't enough to get one person to Utah, much less a couple and a baby.

Frustration welled up inside Marie-Thérèse. *Things have to change.* She had thought it before, but hadn't the will to carry through. *Tonight I'll talk with Mathieu. We can work it out.* Mathieu earned good money, and she knew if they could live frugally for a few years, they could get out of debt—perhaps even buy a house like Zack and Josette were doing in Provo.

Larissa crawled into the room, her large eyes bright and happy. In one chubby fist she gripped Dolly's hair, dragging her rag body across the tiled floor. She pulled herself to her feet next to the chair and laid her head on Marie-Thérèse's knee. After studying her mother quietly, she offered the doll and a coaxing grin.

Marie-Thérèse smiled. "Thank you, Larissa."

The baby wandered away on hands and knees while Marie-Thérèse stared at the doll. Without warning, emotions boiled up inside her and she burst into tears. *Pauline! I miss you!* A pounding wave of longing crashed into her being, reaching deep into a part of her that she hadn't felt for a long time. *My sister is gone!* her heart cried. Tears coursed unbidden down her cheeks.

Oh, why did it hurt so much? Why now? In three weeks it would be two years since Pauline's death. Two long years since she had seen that sunny smile.

Frantically, Marie-Thérèse seized Dolly to her chest as she remembered how Emeri had held Pauline that last day, and closed her eyes against the affront of her emotions. What was Pauline doing now? Did she ever think of Marie-Thérèse? Was she happy?

Of course, Marie-Thérèse thought. *She's with Emeri and our parents . . . and with Jesus.* This time the assurance didn't ease the hurt. She remembered how Pauline had made her smile, her positive attitude in the face of suffering and trials, and her trusting, all-encompassing love. Marie-Thérèse missed her dreadfully.

Gradually her tears seeped away, and when Larissa came to sit in her lap, love for her daughter eased the terrible grief. Marie-Thérèse took several deep breaths. "I must remember the greatest lesson Pauline taught," she told Larissa. "Endurance."

Larissa giggled, and Marie-Thérèse managed a soggy smile.

When she had calmed down, Marie-Thérèse went to see her parents. The walk in the brisk air and the brief ride on the metro helped clear her head.

Ariana opened the door with a smile. "I was just going to call you," she said, holding out her arms for Larissa. "Well, hello there, beautiful. Give Ga-ma a kiss." Obediently Larissa gave one of her famous open-mouthed kisses.

"Come in and sit down a while," Ariana invited.

"I still don't have the money for the tickets," Marie-Thérèse blurted as she followed her mother to the sitting room. "Maybe you should just buy yours without us. I don't want you to miss finding a place on one of the planes."

Ariana waved the words away and sat down on the couch. "That's all right, don't worry about it. Your father had to pay for the tickets yesterday, so it's all taken care of. That's why I was going to call you. We want you to accept them as our gift."

"I can't do that, Mom. You've done too much for us already. Mathieu and I will pay you back." Marie-Thérèse wished she had the courage to tell her mother about their financial situation, but she felt doing so would somehow betray Mathieu.

Ariana looked at her with concern. "What's wrong, Marie-Thérèse? There's something you're not telling me."

"I'm fine, really, Mom. I just . . ." Marie-Thérèse stared after Larissa, who had decided to investigate behind the couch.

"It's Pauline, isn't it?" Ariana said softly.

Marie-Thérèse nodded and bit her lip. "It's like I only now felt her gone," she said. Her voice wavered, and the tears she had thought were all cried out threatened to return tenfold.

Ariana slid closer and put her arms around Marie-Thérèse.

"Sometimes that happens to me, too," she said. "And it's pretty over-whelming. But it will get better. I've been worried that it might affect you like this. I was grateful at the time that you had your new rela-tionship with Mathieu to help you cope. But it's rather hard to mourn properly when you're so much in love."

"I never really mourned her." Marie-Thérèse felt a keen sense of guilt at the words. She remembered feeling numb when Pauline had died, which she knew was often the first step in grieving, but Mathieu had been so comforting. Her sorrow had been consumed in the joy of their love.

"You've had so much going on in the past years—a husband, a pregnancy, a new baby," her mother continued. "You've had a lot to keep you busy. It's no wonder it has only hit you now. It does that sometimes with me, and I went through the whole grieving process."

Grief. Now Marie-Thérèse recognized her emotions for what they were. She knew the feelings well. For several years after her parents' deaths she had seen a counselor to help her understand that her varied feelings were not only valid, but common to those who had lost a close loved one. After Pauline's more recent passing, Marie-Thérèse had congratulated herself several times on how well she had dealt with losing her beloved sister and only blood sibling. But at this moment of glaring revelation, she felt as though she might never be all right again.

Why now? Marie-Thérèse searched herself for the answer, exam-ining her feelings as though they came from someone else. Once she had been protected by the walls of newfound love, but her anger at Madame Cerro for her uncaring attitude and at Mathieu for his spending habits had left her with no safe barrier. That must be why she was able to feel the freshness of Pauline's death as she hadn't years ago. *My dear little sister, how I wish I could hold you!* A part of Marie-Thérèse relished the pain. It was almost better than thinking of facing Mathieu.

Why can't he live within his means? Marie-Thérèse knew he had had a humble upbringing by his widowed mother. So where had he learned to spend without apparent restraint?

Ariana held her and rubbed her back, and despite Marie-Thérèse's unwillingness to release the hurt, she felt comforted. For that moment, Pauline wasn't far away. And now that she knew why she was feeling the way she did, perhaps she could better deal with the emotions.

Later, when she and Larissa were making their way home, Marie-Thérèse felt much better. "I love your daddy," she told Larissa. "I just have to make him see. I only wish he wouldn't get so defensive every time I bring it up. Maybe I'll wait until after Christmas." Larissa nodded her head as though she understood.

Marie-Thérèse kissed her daughter's dark hair, feeling love for her blot out every other emotion. "And I'll earn our way to Josette's wedding—even if I have to iron every shirt in the entire neighborhood!"

CHAPTER TWENTY-SEVEN

Brilliant white blanketed the earth. It was two weeks before Christmas, and colder than Josette ever remembered any day being—in Utah or France. But Zack's smile as he picked her up at her apartment warmed her. In seven days they would be married in the Provo Temple. Her family would arrive today from France to join in the last-minute preparations. After Christmas another celebration would be held in France, where they planned to spend their honeymoon.

"I hope their plane isn't delayed because of the snow," she said as they plodded through the mound of white on their way to the van Zack had borrowed from one of his married sisters.

"It's stopped now. There's not a cloud in the sky. Look at all that blue."

Josette slipped her gloved hand in his and scanned the sky. Sure enough, it was clear, and the biting cold indicated that new snow wouldn't be falling any time soon.

"We'll have plenty of time to do some Christmas shopping and check out the lights at Temple Square before we go to the airport," Zack continued. "The roads ought to be fairly clear."

Catching a glimpse of a snow-laden tree near the walk, Josette purposely steered him under it and tugged on the branch. A flurry of dry, powdery snow rained on Zack, carrying with it a few crustier pieces that hadn't come with the snowfall the night before.

"Why, you . . ." Zack lunged toward her. Josette gave a short cry of alarm before they both fell into the snow. He scooped up a handful and hurled it toward her. Most of the powder fell short, but enough hit Josette in the face to make her eyes sting. She pushed more snow back at Zack.

"This stuff's no good for snowballs," Zack said. But he picked up a huge armful and dropped it on top of her.

The snow fight went on until they were both too cold to move. Zack tried to kiss her, but Josette shook her head. "Are you kidding? Our lips will freeze together."

"Let's run to the van. We can dry out on the way to Salt Lake." Zack brushed the snow from her hair and coat as he talked.

Josette darted away, but she was no match for Zack's long legs. He had the van door open for her by the time she reached it. She was glad to slip into the warmer interior.

They fell into an easy silence. Josette watched Zack out of the corner of her eye. In seven days they would be married! She could hardly believe it was true.

Despite her brave words to Zack, they hadn't gotten married the day she found out about Emeri. Because of school and her parents' schedules, they agreed to wait until the Christmas break. The two months had seemed much longer at the outset, but now it seemed the time had gone by quickly.

She was anxious to see her family again. Everyone was coming except André, who was still on his mission, and Grandma Louise, who wasn't able to make the long trip. At least she would be able to see Grandma Louise when she and Zack arrived in Paris. Josette could thank her parents for that; if they hadn't offered the plane tickets as part of their wedding gift, she and Zack would have spent their honeymoon in their own home.

Everything wasn't as perfect as Josette would like to pretend. Marc wasn't too happy about her staying in Utah, and neither was her mother. Josette had never mentioned the objections to Zack and felt relief when her family had finally become resigned to her decision. As had she. She tried not to worry about the future.

At the airport, Josette hugged and kissed her family. Everyone looked the same except Marie-Thérèse's daughter, who was nearly walking. Marie-Thérèse herself looked rather thinner than normal, but she assured Josette that she was fine.

"Snow! I want to play in the snow!" Louis-Géralde said, dancing from one foot to the other.

Josette laughed and ruffled his hair. "Tomorrow morning will be soon enough for you. I even bought you some snow boots."

"Where are we going to sleep?"

"At the new house Zack and I bought. It's not big, but it's got a huge yard. And tomorrow you can come to my apartment and help me move in the rest of my things."

"Will you be able to build a snowman with me?" he asked.

"Well, the snow we have right now isn't much for packing, but it'll probably snow again before you leave."

Louis-Géralde's face grew solemn in thought. "I didn't know there was different kinds of snow!"

"Well, there are. Besides, I still have classes tomorrow. But I promise I'll spend the rest of the day with you. I took the time off work just to be with all of you."

Marc put his arm around her. "So this is America." He grinned pointedly at Zack. "I hope you have some sights to see. I don't want to spend the whole week I'm here watching you two make eyes at each other!"

"You think we don't have anything to compare with the Eiffel Tower?" asked Zack. "Well, you've got another think coming. I'm going to show you the building that houses the prophet of God! That's certainly something you don't have!"

"I'm hungry," Louis-Géralde put in. "You have a McDonald's, don't you? Or haven't you got them yet?"

"Of course we have," Zack said. "We're the ones who started the restaurant chain."

The boy blinked at him. "Oh? I thought your dad sold houses."

Zack faced the laughter with a good-natured grin, giving up the explanation altogether. With one arm encircling her twin and the other her fiancé, Josette was happy.

* * * * *

A week later, Josette married Zack for time and all eternity in the Provo Temple. During the ceremony, as they knelt across from each other at the altar, the elderly gentleman officiating fell into an abrupt silence. The room was utterly quiet as he stared into the distance without completing the words of the ceremony, his head bobbing slightly as if he couldn't keep it still. Josette wondered if he was too old to remember the words. Or was he falling asleep? Her worry must have shown in her face because Zack's fingers tightened on hers, giving much-needed reassurance.

With a sharp movement, the sealer moved his eyes back to Josette and Zack. His mouth opened, but he didn't pick up where he had left off. "It has just been given to me to know," he said, "that you two made a promise in the premortal world to find and marry each other." He paused and stared, his gaze moving back and forth between them. "It is very rare for individuals to have made such promises; and of the ones who do, most do not find each other but end up marrying someone else. I thought you would like to know."

Twins flames on a single candle! thought Josette. Zack had been right all along. She met his eyes and saw eternity in their blue depths.

Josette knew everything in her life had prepared her for this moment. She and Zack had found each other despite the distance between them and their different circumstances. How grateful she was for parents who had raised her in the Church! How grateful for gospel principles that had kept her feet from treading too far from the straight and narrow way! No longer did she worry about Zack falling out of love with her, or about her own unworthiness. The past was gone, the future yet unwritten.

Only one thing marred the day: the look on Marc's face when she and Zack left the reception held at the church house. "I'm going to miss you," he said in her ear. "It's not the same at home without you."

"I know," she whispered back, feeling her own heart torn in two, "but you'll find someone yourself one day, and then it'll be okay."

* * * * *

Zack couldn't believe that two months had gone by since their wedding. Both he and Josette worked and attended school, and they didn't have a lot of free time. Zack knew Josette missed her home and her country, but she seemed content enough with his family as a substitute. He was glad Josette had no friends besides Brionney to interfere with their marriage. As it was, Zack often had to hint for his sister to leave so that he could be alone with his wife.

Josette hadn't been to work for two days. "I think I'm coming down with something," she had said yesterday morning. "I keep falling asleep in class. And I feel kind of sad. I don't know why. It doesn't make sense."

"Are you sure it's not because you miss your brother?" he asked. A week earlier she had celebrated her twenty-third birthday, and Zack knew that except for their missionary service, it had been the only time in their lives that the twins hadn't been together on that day.

"No. It's not that," she insisted.

Maybe she's working too hard, Zack thought. Josette studied almost constantly, and the office had never functioned so smoothly. Even his father had noticed the change and had mentioned the additional business she had brought to the firm. Today he had talked about hiring an assistant for her, and Zack planned to tell her about it tonight.

Darkness still came early in February, and Zack found himself longing for summer. He would take Josette camping and show her all his favorite spots–just the two of them, with no interruptions. Life was so good.

The smell of cooking meat came to him before he opened the door to their home. Good, that meant Josette was feeling better.

She didn't wait for him to even close the door, but raced toward him and hugged him. Her exuberance, her love of life, was one of the things he adored most about her, but today there was an added excitement.

"I see you're feeling better," he said.

"Of course, it's night," she said.

"What does that mean? Do you need to sleep?"

She grinned at his confusion. "No, but tomorrow morning, I'm going to feel bad again."

Zack felt his eyes open wide. His heart pounded as his mouth moved without speaking.

"We're having a baby!" Josette said. "I should have thought of it before, but today I went and got one of those tests. Come on, I'll show you." She led the way to the bathroom, where the proof was sitting on the counter top.

Zack felt like dancing and shouting the news to the world. He was going to be a father! "Who have you told?" he asked.

"Why just you, silly. Isn't the father supposed to know before everyone else?"

Zack waltzed her around the room. "I'm so happy," he said. Then he stopped dancing. "But are you? I mean, I know we agreed to let the Lord decide whether or not we were ready to have children, but you hoped to finish school first . . ."

"I'm glad," she said. "I think a baby will make this place more like home."

Her solemn words reiterated the loneliness he knew she felt. Home to her was still France, not America or even this house they had worked on so hard together. But a baby could help with that, couldn't it?

Before he could say anything, she drew away from him with a groan. "Oh no, the meat." She rushed to the stove and threw it open. Her tiny nose wrinkled at the smell. "It's a little overcooked," she said with a self-derogatory laugh. "I guess I got carried away dreaming."

Zack grinned. Neither he nor Josette had much luck at cooking, although they were better than in the beginning. "I like my meat well done," he said.

"Nobody likes it *this* well done. No humans, anyway. We might want to think about getting a dog." She flipped off the stove. "I guess it's cold cereal for us. Or maybe pizza—I'm hungry enough to even endure that. Hey, maybe your mother has extras. We could go by just to tell them the news, and . . . ," she let the sentence dangle, already heading for the hall closet and her coat. Zack felt so full of happiness he wondered if his heart would burst.

I'm going to make you as happy as you have made me, he vowed silently. *Just you wait and see.*

* * * * *

It was Saturday, and finals were over at last. Josette was looking forward to a long vacation from school. She knew she should take at least a few summer classes, but she couldn't bring herself to do it. More than anything, she wanted to rest.

She wandered into one of the two spare bedrooms. She had set this up as an office, with Zack's desk, her father's old laptop, and two large easy chairs bought second-hand from an ad in the *Daily Herald*. They had spent many late-night hours here studying since their marriage, but it was also where Josette came to write letters and to dream. The room was on the east side of the house, and the morning sun made it cozy.

"Honey, I'm going out to till the garden." Zack was dressed in his oldest jeans and a faded flannel shirt. "It's a beautiful day outside." He leaned over and put his mouth next to her stomach. "In a few months, we'll go camping," he said to the baby. "I know you won't be able to see the mountains from in there, but I'll tell you all about them!" He straightened and grinned at her, bringing a laugh to her throat. If possible, Zack was more excited about this baby than she was.

"Are you going to come out?" he asked.

"In a while. I want to write a letter before the mailman comes."

"If you're not out by the time I finish tilling those rows, I'll come back in to get you. I need your opinion on what we should plant."

He blew her a kiss as he left, and Josette grabbed it in mid-air and slapped it to her cheek as her father had always done with her blown kisses as a little girl. Homesickness came in a drowning wave, and for a moment she shut her eyes and let it wash over her.

When she opened them, she could see Zack out the window, breaking the earth with his parents' tiller. The two rows of peas they had planted last month had already sent sturdy tendrils from the earth. She knew she should go out and help, but bending over made her worry about hurting the baby, even for all of Irene's assurances.

During the past three months, her body had changed with the pregnancy. Her emotions had changed too, and that left her sometimes feeling desperate. Like now.

She left the window and sat at the desk, pulling her feet under her. Still on the desk was the letter she had begun to Marc the night before. She hadn't written him since they talked on the phone on their birthday in February. Somehow the letter didn't fill the void, nor did anything she tried. What was wrong with her? She had the most wonderful husband in the world and was expecting a baby—all her childhood dreams were at last in place. Then why wouldn't the sadness leave? She couldn't remember feeling so unhappy since Pauline's death.

Had it been almost two and a half years since she had said good-bye to her sister? Memories came filtering through the months that separated her from the actual occurrences, like sunlight through a shuttered window. Josette threw open those shutters and let the memories envelop her: the family pulling together, their mourning tempered by the assurance of eternal life; Marc's loving arms around her and his ready smile; André's steadiness; Marie-Thérèse and her unwavering love; Louis-Géralde with his innocence; her parents' warm laughter. Oh, how she missed them!

Homesickness worse than she had ever felt assaulted her. More than anything, she wished she could have a few hours alone with her mother. She longed to discuss the baby, her marriage, and life as she never had before. Why hadn't she appreciated Ariana before? *I wish I could tell her.*

And Marc. Josette felt her heart would break. She longed to go blading with her brother, to walk along the Seine, to see the familiar skyline of Paris, to eat warm chestnuts from the vendor's cart at Christmastime. All that was now lost to her. Tears fell from her eyes before she could stop them. She laid her head on the desk and sobbed quietly, smearing the words she had written on the page.

"What's wrong?" Zack's voice came from the doorway, followed almost immediately by his warm hands on her shoulders, kneading, caressing. As always when they were alone, he spoke French, which was considerably better than her English. The concern in his voice brought a sense of guilt.

"Nothing." She sobbed harder. "I'm just emotional, that's all. The pregnancy—"

"I know you well enough to know it's not the pregnancy," he said, pulling her up from the chair and into his arms.

As their bodies touched, Josette was conscious of the growing life in her stomach, though she couldn't yet feel its movements. Again the thought came: she had Zack and her baby. Why couldn't she be happy?

"Tell me," Zack said.

"I was writing a letter to my brother, that's all."

"Josette, tell me."

She wiped at her face with her hands. If she could just stop the tears, her contentment with Zack would make everything all right.

"You miss him."

Josette sniffed.

"Tell me," he urged again.

Her resolve broke. "I feel like part of me is gone. I'm so lonely— even when I'm working or whatever." There was pain in Zack's eyes, and Josette faltered. "I just wish I could see my family more, that's all," she finished lamely, feeling selfish and mean. Why couldn't she stop herself from hurting Zack?

"Do you want to go home?" he asked, holding her back to see her better. "Do they mean that much?"

"Not more than you. I love you more than anything."

"But that doesn't stop you from missing them."

Josette replied softly, "No."

There was a silence between them, but their love flowed through their joined hands.

"I've been thinking about us moving there," Zack said finally.

"But your future is here!" Even so, his words brought a leap of hope to her heart.

He met her gaze. "My future," he said slowly, "isn't in a country, but with you. Wherever you are, I want to be there. And if you're not happy here, then why can't I go to where you will be happy?"

"But what would you do there?"

"That's one thing about real estate. Everybody's got to have it, even in France."

Josette looked out the window, feeling the warm sun on her face. Was this too good to be true? "But what about your family?" she asked. "If we move to France, won't it be hard for you?" She held her breath, waiting for the answer.

"I don't know," he said. "But I have to try."

"Do you really mean it?"

He hugged her tighter and laughed. "Yes, I do."

"When—when will we go?" It was all she could do not to run into their bedroom and start throwing things into her battered suitcase.

"Well, my passport is still valid, so there's no problem there. But there's the house . . ." He released her hands.

"Where are you going?"

"To my parents', and then to place a newspaper ad on the house," he said. "No use in finishing the garden, since we won't be here to take care of it. It's better that we start making plans to move. I'll need to give Dad notice at work. There are a few accounts I'll have to finish up."

"Can you wait until I grab a snack? I'm feeling a little nauseous."

He pushed one of the easy chairs into the sunlight. "Why don't you sit right here and eat? I'll tell my parents and come right back."

Josette sighed with relief. Still, she knew that Irene and Terrell would be as happy about their son moving to France as her parents had been with the idea of her staying in America.

As Zack left the house, Josette cuddled into the easy chair with a hunk of french bread from Storehouse Market heated up in the microwave. The crust was chewy and a poor substitute for the real thing, but it didn't matter now. Soon she would have all the real french bread she could ever want.

I won't finish the letter to Marc at all, she decided. *I'll surprise him. Imagine his face when I arrive home!*

The heavy shroud of despair vanished, leaving her heart as light and warm as the sun streaming through the window. She tried not to think about what Zack was giving up for her. He would be happy in France. He would!

* * * * *

Zack should have known that loving an exceptional girl like Josette would exact a large sacrifice, in this case his country and his family.

"It's no more than she was willing to give for me," he said aloud. In truth, Josette's sacrifice was greater because unlike her, he not only had an excellent command of French, but also a deeply ingrained missionary's love for the country and her people.

He knew his parents wouldn't be happy about his decision. His three married sisters had stayed close, and everyone had assumed that he and Brionney would do the same. But this was the only choice he could make for his wife. He smiled wryly. Love certainly shook things up.

He hoped his parents would understand. Didn't the scriptures say that when a man married he should leave his parents and cleave unto his wife? That was what he planned to do.

Even if it meant in another country.

His parents were in the kitchen, eating a late breakfast. Brionney was nowhere to be seen. Zack took the proffered chair. "I have to talk with you," he said. His mother paused at the dish cupboard. She held very still, as if knowing her life was about to change.

"Josette's not happy here," he said.

Irene set the dish in her hand carefully on the counter top. "I've seen it in her eyes. But we've tried to make her feel welcome. We love her like we do you and the girls."

"It's not your love that's the problem." Zack said. "I think you've made her as happy as possible, but she misses her family, especially Marc. Even though she's tried to hide it from me, I can tell. I thought the baby might change things, but it's not getting better. I've been praying about what to do, and I've felt we should move to France and try it there for a while."

Resignation filled Irene's eyes. "I guess I always knew it would come to this."

Terrell placed his fork, prongs down, on his half-eaten pancake. "I think we all knew it would be hard on you and Josette. Not so much because of the merging of cultures as because of the distance separating the two countries. It's nice to be on your own, but that's a little too far."

"Especially without enough money to visit," Zack said. He was surprised that his parents were taking this so well.

"Your mother and I have talked about this already," Terrell said. "Leaving your country is not the same for a man as it is for a woman. Especially if she stays home with her children. Even in France, you'll have your job and business associates, but once she finishes school, Josette will have none of that. It can get lonely with the language barrier."

"That's what I think," Zack said. "There, she'll have her mother and Marc and Marie-Thérèse."

"Especially at this time," Irene added. "Having your first baby is wonderful, but it can also be very scary." Her words sounded calm, but she looked as if she was fighting tears.

Zack's own eyes felt moist. "I'm not saying it's forever, Mom. It's just for now. Who knows? Maybe after we have a few children and Marc's married, things will change. I mean, you live far away from your parents."

"We still see them every few months," Irene said. "Montana's not that far away. At least not compared to France."

Terrell slapped Zack lightly on the shoulder. "For what it's worth, I think you're doing the right thing, son. But it's going to take us some getting used to."

"Well, we still have to sell the house. We'll make a good enough profit, with the restoration we've done. Enough to have a little investment to start out with in France." Zack grinned at his mother. "You always said I had it in me to make a million. I guess now we'll have an added incentive—so we can visit more."

Irene gave him a watery smile. "Just promise me one thing. Teach your kids English, too. I'm too old to learn French."

Zack left them, feeling more determined than happy. What if this change didn't work? He heaved a long sigh. The Spirit had confirmed beyond any doubt that Josette and he were meant to be together. He just hadn't understood how difficult making that happiness would be.

* * * * *

"But now *I'm* losing *my* brother!" Brionney wailed as she saw the plane tickets.

Josette hugged her, understanding exactly how the younger girl felt. "I know, and I'm sorry. But there is good news." She fanned out the tickets. "Remember how you said you were going to visit me in France? Well, you are. Look! There are three of them! You're going to stay with us for the whole summer! We leave the last week of May. You need to make sure your tests are all over by then."

Brionney grabbed the tickets. "Yay!" she shouted, jumping to her feet. "Now you're talking!"

"And maybe you'll meet one of those handsome French guys you're always dreaming about."

"Yes," Brionney said dreamily. "And he'll be a multi-millionaire, so we can have two houses—one here and one there."

"I guess that lets my brother out," Josette said. "He hasn't made a million yet."

"He's cute. But I don't know if he likes plump girls, much less ones who are nearly five years younger than him."

"How do you know? When he was here for the wedding, you didn't even see him long enough to say two words to him."

"My French is so bad. I didn't want to be embarrassed."

Poor Brionney! Josette felt embarrassed by her English, but it had never stopped her from meeting men. She could relate to the fat thing, though. In the past weeks while searching for a buyer for their house, her stomach had grown tremendously. She had taken to watching pregnant women, and wondered how long it would be before she began to waddle.

She heard the car outside. "Zack's home."

"Did you make dinner?"

"No, I just got here myself. I think we'll have to get pizza. You know, I think I'm actually going to miss that junk."

Brionney smiled wickedly. "If it'll make you feel better, I'll go out and see if I can find any snails in the bushes."

"Would you?"

Both burst into laughter as Zack came through the door. "Did I do something funny?" he asked.

"I was just telling Brionney how I was going to take you both out for escargot when we get to Paris."

Zack's face twisted in a slight grimace. "You and Brionney can go," he said. "I think I'll be too busy."

"Coward!" Brionney punched his shoulder.

"Hey, I've tried those slimy little gray things before, and I still have nightmares of being trapped in a room full of them." He put an arm around Josette. "I vowed to love you for eternity, but I don't remember any mention of having to eat snails."

"I guess you're off the hook, then."

"That's a relief." Zack's voice took on a note of suppressed excitement. "But guess what? I found a buyer for the house. It's a good offer, too. Nothing will stop us now."

.

CHAPTER TWENTY-EIGHT

Josette's father picked them up at the airport in Paris on Friday shortly before noon. Only he and Ariana knew they were coming, but they had gathered the family at the apartment under the pretense of a special announcement.

"Rumor has it that I'm receiving a new church calling," Jean-Marc joked. "It's kind of funny, really. You see, the stake president is going to be released, and now they're looking for a replacement. People think our bishop will be the new stake president, and the children tease that I'll take the bishop's place. Imagine that! Me as a bishop. I don't think so. Serving as a counselor is as close to that as I ever want to get. So the kids think we've called them in for an announcement. They have no idea that you are coming."

Josette and Zack laughed with him, but Brionney stared blankly. Josette repeated the conversation slowly so she could understand. They had agreed to speak only French so that Brionney could gain more fluency.

"Marie-Thérèse wasn't there when I left," Jean-Marc added. "I hope she and Mathieu get there on time. Their car's in the shop and they'll probably use the metro to get to the house."

Brionney said little during the drive, her face showing the wonder of being in the famous City of Love. Josette also fell silent, her heart singing with joy at being back in her beloved France. She clung to Zack's hand while he and her father discussed the steps Zack would have to complete before being allowed to sell real estate in the country. Since her father was so widely known and respected, he would be a great help in making the transition.

When they arrived at the apartment, Ariana let them in. "Everyone's in the living room," she said after hugging Josette.

The room burst into a cacophony of questions as they entered. Before anyone else could move toward her, Marc jumped up from the couch and enveloped her in a bear hug. "You didn't write," he said. "I was just about ready to go to America and kidnap you!" He pumped Zack's hand before pulling him into another bear hug. "How long are you staying?"

"We're moving here," Josette said, releasing him to greet her grandparents, Aunt Lu-Lu, and the two young cousins. *Where is Marie-Thérèse?* she thought.

Marc's jaw dropped, and his eyes went to Zack's for confirmation. "I knew how much you missed me," Zack quipped. "And I thought with you and André going into engineering, we could work together. You build 'em and I'll sell 'em."

"Well, I don't know anyone who'll buy a bridge or a road," Marc said. "Except a city. But maybe I can work in an apartment complex or two."

"That's a guy," Zack said.

There was a silence, and then Marc added in a choked voice, "Thanks for bringing my sister back."

"Well, I won't be going blading anytime soon," Josette said, touching her belly.

"I haven't been since you left anyway," Marc said.

"Look who else is here." Josette propelled Brionney forward. The girl immediately turned a bright shade of red.

"Hello," she said timidly.

Marc grinned at her and then at Zack. "Your sister is very pretty," he said.

"I remember saying something similar about yours."

"Exactly." Marc moved closer to Brionney. "Consider me your official tour guide while you're here," he said. "That is, when I'm not in school. I'm going to be a civil engineer, you know."

Brionney stared at him blankly.

"You're speaking too fast," Josette said. "She speaks and understands well, but is not quite fluent yet."

Marc shot a teasing glance at Zack. "That's okay. There's one language that doesn't need translating—the language of love."

Brionney did get that, but instead of turning a darker shade of red, she giggled. "You are exactly like Zack," she said. "I know how to take care of you." She punched him in the shoulder hard enough to make Marc rub it with his hand.

Josette extracted herself and went to talk with her grandparents. Her mother's parents, Géralde and Josephine, were as she remembered, but Louise, her father's mother, seemed older. It struck her that had she stayed in America, she might never have seen Louise again.

Josette excused herself a short time later to go lie down in her old room where she and Zack would be staying until they found an apartment of their own. On her way, she had to pass through the kitchen, where she lingered for a moment with her mother.

Ariana was on the phone, but she hung up when she saw Josette. "I was calling Marie-Thérèse's, but she's not there. She must have already left. It's not like her to be so late."

"When she gets here, tell her I'm in my room. I need to lie down for a while. To rest."

"Are you feeling all right?" Ariana asked.

"Yes, I'm just tired from the trip. And the time difference. For us it's the middle of the night, not early morning. But I'm so glad to be home."

Ariana inclined her head, a warm smile on her lips. "I'm happy you're here, too. I've missed you."

Josette hesitated. "I wanted to tell you that it may not be forever."

"We'll take each day as it comes."

There was a heavy silence. Josette wished her mother could see into her heart instead of her having to piece the words together. How could simple words convey her depth of feeling? "Mother, I've wanted to tell you how much I love you," she said hurriedly. "Appreciate you, I mean. I don't think I've ever told you before."

Her mother seemed to understand what she was saying, though the words were dreadfully inadequate. "I know. I remember feeling the same way about my mother after I had you and Marc." She smoothed Josette's hair. "Thanks for telling me."

Happiness filled Josette's heart as she made her way to her room. Already her father had put their suitcases near the bed. Nearly everything they owned was in those four suitcases and two flight bags, but Josette felt rich. She was back where she belonged!

* * * * *

The lights in the underground train had been off for ten minutes, and there was still no word from the engineer. Baby Larissa had tried constantly to escape her mother's arms, and Marie-Thérèse had finally let the fifteen-month-old down to toddle near the seats. The other passengers smiled and waved at the baby as she approached.

"Don't let her go too far," she warned Mathieu. He grabbed the baby as she passed him and pulled out a pen to entice her to stay on his lap. Larissa pushed it away and struggled to get down again.

"We wouldn't be here if we had a second car," he said.

Marie-Thérèse sighed. He was right, but that didn't mean they should buy one. How could they possibly afford one more bill?

"We have to live within our means," she replied. No matter how nicely or thoroughly she explained it, he didn't seem to have a grasp on their circumstances. The money he earned simply wasn't stretching to cover the never-ending pile of bills. Sometimes she thought if she had to iron one more shirt from someone else's wardrobe, she would go crazy.

The overhead lights flickered and a weak cheer went up from the crowd. The train lurched a few times before beginning its smooth humming. Larissa stopped struggling and stared out the window, laughing at the occasional light in the dark tunnel.

"We're going to be late," Marie-Thérèse said.

Mathieu shrugged. "They'll understand. It couldn't be helped."

Marie-Thérèse felt his words as an accusation, but this time she would not relent. As much as she loved Mathieu, things had to change. With his impulsive spending, she couldn't plan for anything in the future. Nothing was assured. She might have tried to save for a new set of dishes or cutlery, but any extra money was immediately gone for bills or for whatever Mathieu thought appealing. Both she and Mathieu recognized there was something wrong between them, but neither could agree on what it was or how to fix it.

Mathieu leaned close to her and put his arm over the top of her shoulder. His physical gesture told her that he wasn't upset, but Marie-Thérèse couldn't relax. She could only identify the emotion in her heart as a looming fear. What would come next?

She didn't have long to wait. At the base of the stairs leading out of the metro, an old woman dressed in black sat on a dingy gray blanket with a chipped coffee mug in her frail, thick-veined hands. She was only one of the hundreds Marie-Thérèse had encountered in the subway over the last few years.

The old lady pushed her mug toward them in silent pleading. Marie-Thérèse fished in her pocket for some change, but Mathieu reached into his wallet and pulled out several bills. "Here, old woman," he said kindly.

Marie-Thérèse couldn't believe her eyes. One part of her commended the unselfish gesture he had made, but with that money she could have made a payment on one of their credit cards or bought food for three days. How could he give away so much money when she couldn't sleep at night for worry? The possibility that the old woman might use the gift for drink, or to give to a family member to buy alcohol, made Marie-Thérèse even more upset.

She clutched Larissa to her chest and bounded up the metro stairs ahead of Mathieu. He caught up to her, talking blithely about the possible reasons her father had asked them to the house. "Maybe he got a new calling," he guessed. "Or maybe he's planning a surprise party for someone."

Marie-Thérèse walked stiffly, her teeth clenched in hostile silence. It took a long while before Mathieu perceived her anger. "What's wrong?" he asked.

She turned on him, letting her anger take control. "The bills aren't paid, I need grocery money, but you're more concerned about a beggar than your own wife and daughter!" Even as she said the words, she felt stingy. For all she knew, that old woman did need the money more than she did.

Mathieu stopped. "We're supposed to help people," he said defensively.

"We're supposed to get out of debt so that we can be in a position to help people," she retorted. "We're not supposed to live beyond our means."

"We're not. I make enough to pay the bills."

"To pay the interest on the bills, you mean."

"But I'll be getting a raise soon—"

"And you'll get a new bill to use the money."

"Marie-Thérèse, that's not fair."

"Isn't it? You know how we need to pay off the bills, but what did you do when you got that bonus? You bought that crocheted bedspread from Sister Gill. Never mind that I know perfectly well how to crochet and would like to have money to buy the thread to do one myself."

"But now you won't have to do it."

"I *want* to do it. I like crocheting, and I want to have something to pass on to Larissa. She's not going to give a hill of beans for a stupid bedspread that someone else made. It's not going to be a family heirloom."

Mathieu's eyebrows drew together and he stared hard at her. "You know Sister Gill needed the money to support her son on his mission."

This was the point in their argument where she would normally break down and admit that he was being the better Christian, but not today. Something in what he said didn't agree with what was in her heart. Either her feelings were wrong, or he was. There was no compromise. "She doesn't need it any more than we do," she insisted. "And if she can't pay, the ward will help. What do you think we donate money to the missionary fund each month for?"

In her arms Larissa whimpered, and Marie-Thérèse knew her daughter was reacting to their argument. Mathieu glanced at her and the tenseness in his voice relaxed. "I just don't know what to do," he said. "I don't see the problem."

Marie-Thérèse grimaced. "And that's the biggest part of the *problem,*" she said scathingly. "If you could admit you have trouble managing money, we could talk about it and work something out. But you just don't see anything."

The fact that he didn't lash out at the ugly tone of her voice showed what kind of a man he was, but Marie-Thérèse didn't want to count his good qualities. The money situation threatened to drive her to a nervous breakdown, and it all but consumed her.

She started walking again, rapidly, with Larissa still whimpering in her arms. "Shh. There, there. I'm sorry, honey. It's over now." Marie-Thérèse knew it was a lie, but saying it made them both feel better.

When they arrived at her parents' apartment, Louis-Géralde let them in. "Finally," he said. "We've been waiting for you." He smiled, bursting with a secret. "Josette's here, and she came to live with us. She's staying forever! Well, in France anyway."

Marie-Thérèse's mood lightened. Josette back in France! This was just what she needed. "Where is she?"

"She's in her room. I think she's tired. She's got a baby inside her, you know."

Larissa kicked to get down and Marie-Thérèse let her toddle off with Louis-Géralde, knowing he would watch her closely. Without a word to Mathieu, or even glancing in his direction, Marie-Thérèse went into the kitchen and down the hall. She felt relieved that she wouldn't have to face all of the relatives while she was still so angry. By the time she returned, maybe she would be able to put the fight behind her.

Until the next time.

Marie-Thérèse sighed heavily. Then she forced her mouth into the semblance of a smile and rapped on the door to the bedroom she and Josette had shared while growing up.

"Come in," said a tired voice.

Marie-Thérèse pushed open the door. "Are you sleeping? I can come back later."

"Oh, no. I'm so glad to see you!" Josette eased off one of the beds and hugged Marie-Thérèse.

"You look great. I mean, you barely look pregnant. How far along are you—four months?"

"Yes, but I feel like I weigh a ton already."

Marie-Thérèse wrinkled her brow sympathetically. "I remember that." They sat together on the bed. "So what made you decide to come home?" Marie-Thérèse asked.

Josette's face softened and her eyes began to water. "It was Zack's idea. He thought I would be happier here. I've been so lonely, especially without you and Marc. And with the baby coming and all, I . . . ."

Marie-Thérèse squeezed her sister's arm. "You don't have to explain. I understand. Everything's suddenly different when a baby comes."

"That's it exactly. I thought that if anyone was independent, it was me, but I've been fooling myself. I need my family."

"What about Zack? Do you think he'll be happy here?"

Josette's lips turned slightly downward, not quite a frown, but almost. "We'll just have to wait and see. I couldn't bear for him not to be happy."

Marie-Thérèse thought Josette's words showed how much she had changed over the past few years. She was no longer the self-centered, greedy playgirl of the past.

Josette's fingernails slid over Marie-Thérèse's arm. "Why are you so sad?" she asked.

Sudden tears came, and Marie-Thérèse blinked rapidly to keep them from falling. Lately it seemed she was always crying. "Since when did you get to be so perceptive?"

Josette's smile flashed and was gone. "I think it was the mission. You have to listen to what people aren't saying. Tell me."

Marie-Thérèse opened her mouth to say it was nothing, but to her surprise the problem flooded out before she could stop it. Instead of laughing it off or making a negative comment about Mathieu, Josette listened without interruption.

"Have you told anyone about this?" she asked when Marie-Thérèse finished.

"No, I've been too embarrassed. I mean, everybody loves Mathieu so much, and I don't want them to think badly of him. Besides, it kind of makes me sound selfish, doesn't it?"

"Not to me. It sounds like you want some security."

"That's it exactly! I don't want presents, a second car, or even furniture, I just want security. And freedom, I think. I want to be free to do a few things without worrying about owing on them for the rest of our lives."

"I think you should counsel with the bishop," Josette said. "I'll bet he'd have some suggestions or know someone who does."

"I'd be embarrassed to tell anyone."

"You told me."

Marie-Thérèse had to admit she felt better with someone knowing how she felt. "But we're getting a new bishop."

"Oh, that's right. Well, that's as good a time as any, isn't it? I'm sure it'll be someone experienced. But what about Mathieu? Would he go?"

"I think he will, if only for the bishop to straighten me out. He doesn't see that we have a problem. He thinks it's something else entirely, but he doesn't know what. My uptightness, probably."

They fell into silence, but Marie-Thérèse's heart was lighter now. Then Josette giggled.

"What's so funny?"

Josette made a face. "Oh, I'm sorry, Marie-Thérèse. I was just thinking what would have happened if it had been me who had married Mathieu before my mission. Can you imagine it? We would have been so far in debt, they'd have to dig us out with one of those huge machines. You know, one with those big claws on the end. They'd keep digging and find me at the bottom with a stack of worn-out credit cards!"

Marie-Thérèse couldn't help joining in her sister's laughter. "That's for sure," she said.

"Zack tears up any cards we get."

"That's good." Marie-Thérèse sighed before adding thoughtfully, "I wish I had known about Mathieu's problems with money before we married."

"Why? Wouldn't you have married him?"

"Of course I would have. But maybe we could have talked about it beforehand. I mean, now that I look back, there were signs, but I didn't really notice them. Remember how he always took us out and paid for it with his credit card?"

"Yeah, I remember."

"Well, we're still paying for those meals." She sighed. "I just think it would have been fairer to get the whole scoop before marriage, so I could be prepared. I don't like surprises."

"Those are the kind everyone could do without. My poor Zack . . . I think he got one of those with me. He has to do a lot of the cleaning."

"I'll bet. I've lived with you, remember?"

"So what are you going to do with Mathieu?"

Marie-Thérèse grabbed her sister's hands. "Please don't think I don't love Mathieu. I do, I really do. If not for this, I think we'd be perfect for each other."

"Twin flames on a single candle," Josette murmured.

"What?"

Josette seemed very far away. "Something Zack said once. It's nothing."

"For some reason it made me think of Pauline and Emeri," said Marie-Thérèse.

Josette smiled. "Oh, yes! I like that."

"I think they would, too."

* * * * *

"But Josette just got here and we're going to eat. You can't leave now!" Louis-Géralde said to his parents.

Ariana kissed his proffered cheeks, thinking how much he looked like his father. "Don't worry, we won't be gone long."

"Where are you going?" Marc asked. "I'm starving."

Ariana adjusted the strap on her purse. "We've been called down to the church for an interview with the stake president. We'll be back in a while. Grandma Josephine will put the finishing touches on the food, and we'll eat when we get home."

Zack grinned. "Uh-oh. I sense a new calling. Funny how you brought the family together on the pretense of receiving a calling, and then you are summoned to the church. Hmm, what a coincidence."

"Yeah, someone up in heaven has a sense of humor," Marc added.

"I'm sure he just wants to talk about some of the leaders in the ward," Jean-Marc said. "Since I was a counselor in the bishopric until a few months back, they'll want to know about the capabilities of our members. I remember they did that when the last stake president was called."

"Sure, Dad," Marc said. "Dream on."

"Dream on," Louis-Géralde echoed in his high child's voice. Jean-Marc grabbed him and tickled his stomach.

"We'll be right back," Ariana said. "Tell the girls if they come out of the bedroom."

"They may never come out," Mathieu said. "Marie-Thérèse is mad at me." He picked up his daughter who pulled at his leg, asking for a drink of water.

Zack chuckled. "So you're in the doghouse, as we say in America. What happened?"

"Oh, it's nothing," Mathieu said, shrugging. "It'll pass." He took Larissa into the kitchen for a drink.

Ariana frowned at his retreating figure. She had felt for some time that Mathieu and Marie-Thérèse were having problems—ever since last December, when Marie-Thérèse had belatedly mourned Pauline's death. Before that they had always seemed so perfect together, but now Ariana felt a distinct tension between them. She knew from past experience the torment of being in a bad marriage, and she couldn't help being worried. Even strong love couldn't hold a relationship together when other key elements were missing. She wished Marie-Thérèse would confide in her, but until she did, Ariana could only wait and give her love. The gentle probing wasn't working, but maybe prayer would.

At least Josette seemed happy. Now if only Marc could find someone special. Ariana's eyes went to the sitting room where she could see Zack's sister on the sofa, trying out her French on Grandpa Géralde. Brionney was very pretty with those beautiful blue eyes, and she seemed nice, which was more important. *Who knows? Maybe she's the one for Marc. We'll wait and see, I guess.*

* * * * *

Ariana came out of the stake president's office, smiling at the dazed look on Jean-Marc's face. "I can't believe it," he said. "Me as the new bishop. I was pretty sure our bishop might be called as the new stake president—everybody thought that. But me, a bishop? That's something I never expected. What about you?"

"Well, I've known you had the potential," Ariana said.

"But are you willing to sacrifice the time it'll take?" he asked, taking her hand in his. "I mean, we've been talking about going on that extended trip this summer and spending more time together. Now the trip will have to wait, and . . ." He shrugged. "It's a big responsibility."

"Yes, it is," Ariana said, hugging him. "But you can do it, and I'll support you. We'll be fine. I think we've learned how to keep our family together by now, don't you? This'll be one more adventure."

Jean-Marc gave a short laugh. "Some adventure. But if you're willing to do it, then I guess so am I." His arms tightened around her. "I love you, you know. Just when I think I couldn't love you any more, the feeling increases."

"I love you too," Ariana said, kissing him. "So are you going to say yes?"

"Now, now," Jean-Marc chided jokingly. "He told us to go home and pray about it."

"But we already know, don't we?" Ariana said.

"Yes, we do. What we have to do is pray for me to be equal to the task." He grinned, and his green-brown eyes sparkled. "And just when I was getting comfortable!"

Ariana laughed and hooked her arms through his. "Be careful of complacency—it'll get you every time. Come on, let's go tell the children."

When they arrived at the house, the family gathered and Jean-Marc made the announcement. There were slaps of congratulations and good-natured teasing.

"Next time, you'll listen to me," Zack said.

"Does this mean I have to call you Bishop?" Louis-Géralde asked.

Jean-Marc rumpled his hair. "No, son. It most certainly does not." The boy appeared relieved.

"Well, I think it's about time we had our meal," Ariana said. "I don't know about you guys, but I'm pretty hungry."

"I could eat a horse," Zack said.

Louis-Géralde laughed and followed the others into the kitchen, saying, "I bet I could eat an elephant. No, a whale. Maybe even a tyrannosaurus rex!"

Ariana noticed Marc and Brionney trailing the rest. "I guess it's up to me to show you Paris this weekend," Marc said to her, "since I'm the only one not married and boring. How about it? We could start after we eat. The night is still young."

Brionney's grin matched his. "Sure," she said. "But I want to see the Eiffel Tower."

Marc laughed. "That is *so* American. You know, the only times I've even gone there have been with Americans."

"Get used to it," Brionney said. "I'm going to be here all summer."

"I guess I can make the sacrifice." Marc didn't act like it would be too painful.

Ariana was glad to see him so content. He had been too quiet since Josette had left for America. Maybe now that she was back, he could find his own happiness.

CHAPTER TWENTY-NINE

Zack walked in the door before five o'clock after a busy and satisfying day. He couldn't wait to share the details with Josette. "Honey?" he called. "Are you home?"

There was no answer, and he experienced the same letdown as he had on the other days she had not been there. He set down his briefcase and read the note she had left on the counter.

Gone with Marc, be back soon. I'll bring some dinner.
Love, Josette.

He poured himself a glass of juice from the refrigerator and sat down to wait. After almost two months in France, he felt he had made good progress. He had been given a work visa and started a new job at a promising real estate firm owned by a business associate of Jean-Marc's. Zack was having great success. The Parisiennes loved his American accent and were intrigued with his height and blond hair. Many happy customers sent friends and family his way.

Eventually, Zack planned to open his own agency, but only after he learned the business and received the appropriate licenses. One of the first things he had done after securing a job was to find a small apartment. It had only one bedroom, a bathroom, a kitchen, and a tiny living room where Brionney stayed when she wasn't out with Marc or Marie-Thérèse. It was inexpensive and an excellent investment.

At first Josette hadn't seemed to mind the small size of the apartment, but lately he wondered. Often she went out with Marc or her friends when he wasn't home. Zack found himself remembering with longing the closeness they had shared in their house in Provo, when she had been all his.

He frowned. Where was she, and why was she taking so long? Well, no sense wasting time; he opened his briefcase and pulled out some papers that needed his attention. Concentration didn't come easily.

It was another hour before he heard Josette's laughter at the door. He arose quickly and ran to the hall to meet her. "Where have you been?" he asked gruffly.

Josette kissed him before replying. Zack could smell her familiar perfume. She was six months along with their baby, and he thought her more radiant than ever. Her hair lay loose around her shoulders, long and thick. "Oh, Zack, we went to the cutest little place! It was an entire old-fashioned village in miniature. They had windmills where they actually ground real flour, a cobbler shop, a bakery, a pub. And so much more. There were even short castle walls surrounding the whole place. It was so cute. Wasn't it, Marc?"

Marc leaned against the door. "It really was interesting how they set it all up. We'll have to take you there. It's free to the public."

"I was worried about you," Zack said.

Josette looked puzzled. "Why? I wrote you a note so you knew I was with Marc. And we had so much fun! It was better than sitting around here, wondering how many more days until I can't see my feet. Marc knew that, and since he had some time off from school, he came and took me away."

"I helped her wash the dishes first," Marc said with a grin.

"And we brought dinner." Josette shoved a white paper bag at Zack. "It's from the bakery at the miniature village—not from the miniature bakery, of course. From the real one they have there to sell to visitors. They have a pottery shop, too, with all sorts of stuff. That's how they make money to take care of the village. But go ahead, look in the bag. It's bread with meat inside. I tasted it already, and it's good. So let's eat!"

Zack didn't reply, and Josette made her lips pout. "Come on Zack, don't be upset. You know I'll always be careful, especially since I'm carrying our baby."

She turned a cute pink, and Zack's irritation vanished. He began unrolling the top of the paper bag. "Okay, then, let's see what you have here. You call this a meal?"

"Try it."

Zack did. "Mmm, it is good."

"Well, I'll leave you to your gourmet feast." Marc moved toward the door.

"You won't stay?" Josette asked.

"No, I'm going to pick up Brionney at Marie-Thérèse's. I can't hang out with you old married folks all the time." He kissed Josette's cheek, gave Zack a salute, and went out the door.

"Poor Marie-Thérèse," Josette said. She walked down the short hall, past the bathroom to their tiny front room. "All that ironing she's taking in because Mathieu can't control himself. I don't know how much longer I can stop myself from interfering."

"It's Marie-Thérèse's call," Zack said, sitting next to her on the couch. "You know as well as I do that Marie-Thérèse is enabling him to act that way."

"Enabling," Josette said with a sigh. "Such an ugly-sounding word. But I guess you're right."

"As long as she keeps making excuses for him and keeps scrambling to make enough money on her own so she doesn't have to depend on his earnings—"

"She's started to clean apartments now, too. She usually can take Larissa with her, but sometimes she leaves her with Mom." Josette looked up at the ceiling as if remembering. "Marie-Thérèse always did the same thing with me when we lived together. Enabling, I mean. When I didn't want to clean something, she'd do it. Or when I wanted something, she'd find an excuse to let me have it. In fact, the only time she ever stood in my way when I thought I wanted something was when she and I were both sort of dating Mathieu. Then she fought for him."

"He was important enough," Zack said. "And I think as soon as she feels their problem is important enough, she'll put a stop to it. But make no mistake; it's Mathieu's fault. I've tried talking to him, but it's like talking to stone. He just doesn't see what I'm getting at. I'm embarrassed that a priesthood holder can be so oblivious to the Lord's counsel to stay out of debt."

Josette slipped off her shoes and tucked them under her, cuddling up to Zack. He put his arm around her shoulders. "I'm glad we don't have problems like that," she said.

Zack thought of his earlier aggravation at finding Josette once more gone with Marc. "Why do you like being with Marc so much?" he asked casually.

Josette looked surprised. "Oh, I don't know. We've always been together, I suppose. He makes me laugh when I get uptight. You know how he is, always joking around."

"Yeah. He's a great guy."

"He's promised to take me on a boat ride soon. But I'm a little nervous with the baby and all." She touched her stomach. "What do you think?"

"Give me a few days' notice, and I'll go with you," Zack said.

"Oh, Zack, that would be wonderful! You're such a great husband." She turned around in his arms and began kissing his face an inch at a time. "I love you, did you know?"

Zack felt fire in his reaction to her touch. He kissed her back. "Yes," he said, "but I don't mind hearing it again."

"I love you, I love you, I love you." She kissed him each time she said the words.

Zack laughed, feeling content. Josette was happy as she had never been in America, and he loved seeing her this way. Whatever challenges he would face in sharing her with family and friends, the move had been the right thing to do.

* * * * *

Marie-Thérèse felt weary. Her arms ached from the extra ironing, and her heart felt compressed and heavy like a ball of steel in her chest. But then Brionney had shown up unexpectedly in the afternoon and helped iron a tall mountain of clothing. The tight grip on her heart began to loosen.

When Brionney skipped off somewhere with Marc, Marie-Thérèse went down two flights to apartment 2-A and spent an hour cleaning for the widowed dentist who lived there. Larissa doubled the amount of time it normally took by getting into everything. Marie-Thérèse felt happy the dentist was still at work and wouldn't fire her.

When she went back upstairs to make dinner for Mathieu, who

usually arrived home at seven-thirty, she found two strangers waiting outside her apartment. "Madame Portier?"

Marie-Thérèse adjusted Larissa's weight to her other hip before answering. "Yes?"

One man whipped out a paper and handed it to her. "We're from Retrieval Incorporated, and we've been assigned to collect a bill for your new bedroom set. We've talked several times on the phone with you, and still you have made no headway on your loan as promised. I'm afraid we'll have to repossess the items in question. Of course, we'll keep what you've already paid for the usage fee. Now, if you'll be so kind as to show us the furniture?"

A sense of panic grew inside Marie-Thérèse as she cleaned out the drawers to the dresser under the men's impassive stares. Her face felt hot and embarrassed, and it was all she could do to hold back the tears as she watched the men haul out her bed. Where were the old mattresses her mother had given them? Gone to charity with all the other perfectly useful items Mathieu had replaced.

Marie-Thérèse sat down in the living room to fan herself. The heat was terrible, but she didn't dare turn on the air-conditioning because of the added electric charges. She was glad Larissa had missed her nap earlier and now lay sleeping on the couch opposite her.

Marie-Thérèse's body rested, but her brain flew at top speed. She wouldn't miss the bedroom set—she hadn't wanted it in the first place. But would the repossession make Mathieu take notice of what he was doing?

She doubted it. The increasingly frequent phone calls from bill collectors hadn't seemed to do a thing. The calls bothered her greatly, and her embarrassment grew each time she had to promise another person she would try to pay. It was impossible.

When the doorbell rang, she was almost glad for the distraction. "Hello, Madame Cerro," she said. "Oh, your clothes are all ready."

"Good, because I have to wear that purple dress tonight."

Even the thought of Madame Cerro looking like a purple grape didn't make Marie-Thérèse smile. "Well, it's done. Here." She handed the clothes to the older woman. "And I guess just take it off the rent."

"Uh, you are already five weeks late. For the second time," Madame Cerro said. She looked uncomfortable, but her expression was rigid. "I feel I've given you ample notice, and I really just can't delay any longer. You know I have bills to pay, too."

Marie-Thérèse felt light-headed. "What are you saying?"

"I'm saying that you and your husband have two weeks to find a new place to live. I've found someone else for this apartment—someone more reliable. I'll of course keep your deposit money to cover my expenses."

"But I could ask my parents," Marie-Thérèse said. "They could help." She had known they were overdue on the rent, but since it was the one thing Mathieu had been paying, she hadn't realized just how late they were.

Madame Cerro drew herself up to her full height. "Well, I would think you would have already asked them by now, before those men came to get your furniture." Marie-Thérèse colored, but Madame Cerro plunged on. "But it's too late now. I've already promised the apartment. I trust there will be no problem getting out?"

"No," Marie-Thérèse said faintly.

She walked numbly through the house, searching for something she couldn't identify. The room she shared with Mathieu was now empty of everything but a pile of clothes and sheets on the floor against one of the walls. If the bed had been there, she might have thrown herself on it and cried out the anger and frustration. But instead, she simply stood in the doorway and looked at the jumble of her life, epitomized by the unorganized heap.

Oh, dear Lord, she prayed. *What now? I don't know how much more I can bear.*

When Mathieu came home a short time later, she was sitting at the kitchen table with a large pile of bills. "Hi," he said, giving her his winning grin. "What's for dinner?"

"I don't know yet," she said. "I've been busy."

"What's up? You look depressed." He kneaded her shoulder with a strong hand. "I must have sensed you'd be depressed, because look what I picked up for you at lunchtime." He took a little box and set it on the table, pushing it over to her with a flourish.

Marie-Thérèse thought she was going to be sick. Unwillingly, she opened the box. A pair of smooth gold earings glinted up at her, as wide as her little finger.

"They'll match the necklace and bracelet set I've given you better than anything else I've seen," Mathieu said. "And I wasn't even looking for it. I was at the store to check out those candle holders we talked about, and when I passed the case, I saw them."

"You talked about them," Marie-Thérèse said.

"What?"

"*You* talked about the candle holders. And I don't want them."

"Okay, we won't buy them."

"No, I don't want the earrings." She snapped the lid shut and tossed them back to him. Rage filled her, a desperate out-of-control feeling that she couldn't control. "I don't want you to buy me anything!" she shouted. "Nothing! I want you to pay the bills you have. I don't want to iron anymore, or clean other people's dirt! I'm sick of it, do you hear? I'm not doing it anymore. You can do it yourself—at least for two more weeks until you're kicked out of this apartment!"

Mathieu stared at her, amazed. "Marie-Thérèse, we've had this discussion before. You don't have to iron."

Marie-Thérèse had to stop herself from slapping him. "I want to eat," she hissed. "I want to feed my daughter. And I want to hold up my head with pride."

Tears finally found their way to the surface, but Marie-Thérèse stalked out of the kitchen and down the hall to the living room. She picked up her purse and the sleeping Larissa and headed for the door.

"Marie-Thérèse, what are you doing?"

She stopped for a moment and faced him calmly. "I don't like sleeping on the floor."

"What?"

"Go see." She pointed in the direction of their room.

"Wait right here," he pleaded. "Let me go look."

Mathieu took her silence as agreement. Marie-Thérèse waited until he was out of sight, then opened the door. Without another look, she turned her back and left the apartment.

* * * * *

When Marie-Thérèse arrived at Josette's apartment, she was happy to discover her sister there alone. Larissa, who had awakened during the trip and was cranky and cross, brightened when she saw her Aunt Josette.

"Oh, good, I'm glad you came to visit!" Josette said, tickling the baby. "One of Zack's home teaching families called for a blessing. Zack wanted me to go along, but since I'm pregnant, I didn't want to risk getting sick."

"Well, that's understandable."

"I thought so, but Zack is kind of different here," Josette said. "Possessive. It's like he wants to know what I'm doing all the time. It's kind of cute, but sometimes it can be annoying."

"There are a lot of changes when a baby comes," Marie-Thérèse said mechanically. "A lot of men feel left out. There's so much they don't understand about us."

"Well I don't think Zack's problem has anything to do with the baby, but . . ." Josette's voice trailed off. "You've been crying. What happened?" She put her arms around Marie-Thérèse, whose tears once more came to the surface. "Oh look at me babbling on when you're so upset. I'm sorry! Come and sit down here on the couch and tell me what's wrong."

Marie-Thérèse let Josette lead her to the couch, where she let Larissa down to play. "I've left Mathieu," she said through her sobs.

"You what?"

"I left him." Marie-Thérèse cried harder. "Men came to repossess our bedroom furniture. I had to clean out the dressers with those men watching. It was so awful. All our underclothes and personal items heaped in a pile. They didn't say anything, just stared at me." She put her cold hands against her hot cheeks, trying to calm down. "And then Madame Cerro came to pick up her ironing and told me she's kicking us out of the apartment. She's tired of waiting to be paid."

"Oh, I'm so sorry!" Marie-Thérèse felt her sister's arms tighten. She cried until her anger and frustration was spent. Josette went to the bathroom and returned with a wad of tissue. "Here. Are you feeling better now?"

"A little," Marie-Thérèse admitted. "But I need someplace to stay. I'm not going back there."

"Well, we should go get your clothes."

"I do have ironing I need to deliver to people, but I can't face

Mathieu again. It tears my heart out to see him. I love him so much, but I can't live like this any longer."

"You could stay at Mom's," Josette said. "They have plenty of room."

"Can't I stay here?"

"Of course you can stay here. I was only thinking you'd be more comfortable there. Mom would love having Larissa around."

"But I can't face her either! Not knowing how badly I've failed."

Josette's eyes flashed angrily. "How you've failed? You? You mean how Mathieu has failed. The only thing you've done wrong is letting it go so far!"

Marie-Thérèse blinked in surprise. "Really? Do you really think that, or are you just trying to make me feel better?"

"Oh, Marie-Thérèse." Josette hugged her tightly. "For an intelligent woman, you can be awfully blind."

"But why does Mathieu act this way?"

"I've thought about this a lot," Josette said. "Maybe Mathieu's making up for all that poverty he dealt with as a child. I think deep down, he just wants to take care of you. To give you all the things his mother didn't have because his father died and couldn't help out."

"I've thought that, too. I've even tried to tell him that, but he just tells me what a great job he has and how he'll pay for it. He keeps promising me that we'll buy an apartment soon, but I think the credit companies are finally learning something."

"Maybe they won't give him any more money. That'll actually be good."

"I wonder where he'll go," Marie-Thérèse said. Mathieu's mother lived too far away for him to stay with her and commute to work.

"Probably after you."

"I don't want to see him." Marie-Thérèse grabbed her sister's hand. "Promise me you won't let him see me."

"I promise. But at least let me call Mom."

"She won't understand."

"Yes she will. Come on; use that brain of yours. Mom's been through a lot, and she'll understand. And I'll bet she knows more about what's going on than you think."

"You didn't say anything!"

"No. But it's easy to see that you're not happy."

Marie-Thérèse looked sadly at her hands twisting in her lap. "I thought love was enough, you know? Romance, love, being together. But there are other things, aren't there?"

"Well, I think whatever is wrong between you and Mathieu can be fixed with love. I mean, if he didn't love you and want to please you, then he wouldn't care. But he does."

"He listens, but he doesn't hear what I'm saying. And now we don't even have an apartment to sleep in."

"That old witch Cerro could have at least told you before you ironed her tent dresses," Josette said. "Talk about rude!"

Against her will, Marie-Thérèse smiled. "I don't want to iron anything ever again!"

"So don't. Wrinkled is in, haven't you heard?"

Marie-Thérèse laughed. "I love you, Josette. Thanks for being here."

"Heaven knows you've pulled me out of enough trouble. Maybe I can finally help you." She rose to her feet.

"Where are you going?"

"To call Mom. She should be here."

Marie-Thérèse didn't object. Maybe talking to Ariana was a good idea.

Before Josette could lift the receiver, the phone rang. Marie-Thérèse bounded the few steps to the small kitchen and stopped Josette from answering. "Let the answering machine pick it up," she said. "It might be him."

They waited until the message came. "Uh, Josette, it's Mathieu. I'm looking for Marie-Thérèse. I'm trying to find her, and I'm a little worried. She's not at your parents' apartment either. If you see her, ask her to call home. Thanks."

* * * * *

When Ariana arrived less than half an hour later, Marie-Thérèse was already beginning to feel crowded in Josette's tiny apartment. Zack had returned, and he and Josette were discussing a boat ride they were planning with Marc and Brionney. Marie-Thérèse saw now that there was no way she could stay with them in this small space. There simply wasn't room.

Ariana must have sensed her feelings. "Why don't we take a walk together?" she suggested after greeting everyone. It's dark, but the streets here are safe."

"Would you watch Larissa?" Marie-Thérèse asked Josette.

"Sure. It'll be good practice, won't it Zack?" She patted her swollen stomach with a complacent smile.

"Take your time," Zack said. "As long as you need."

Marie-Thérèse felt a rush of gratitude. "Thanks."

As she went out the door, Josette squeezed her arm. "You'll get through this, you'll see." Trite as the words sounded, they made Marie-Thérèse feel better.

Marie-Thérèse and Ariana walked slowly along the cobblestone sidewalks. A few cafes along the street lit up the darkness with light and noise. "You and Larissa are welcome to stay with us," Ariana said quietly.

"How much did Josette tell you?"

"She said you and Mathieu were having problems and that you needed a place to stay tonight. That's all. She said you'd fill in the rest."

Marie-Thérèse stopped abruptly. "I left him, Mom. And I'm not going back. Not unless he changes."

Ariana put a hand against Marie-Thérèse's back and propelled her gently forward. "Let's keep walking," she said. "Tell me about it."

Marie-Thérèse found herself explaining the details of Mathieu's spending habits and her constant struggle to make ends meet. Ariana nodded sympathetically. "Why didn't you tell me before?" she asked. "I could see you were unhappy, but every time I tried to ask, you would change the conversation."

"I was just so embarrassed, Mom. This was never supposed to happen to me, a finance major."

"Well, an education in finance doesn't guarantee freedom from money problems."

"But it could. I mean, Mathieu makes good money. And if we were careful, in a few years we could have all of those nice things."

"Mathieu has to want to change," Ariana said.

"You're thinking I shouldn't have left him, aren't you?"

"Me? Heavens no! Maybe this is the wake-up call Mathieu needs."

"I thought you wouldn't be proud of me anymore."

Ariana gave a low laugh. "Marie-Thérèse, I've always been proud of you. And I know you tried everything before you left Mathieu. Now the next step is up to him."

They walked on in silence for a few minutes, then Ariana said, "Jean-Marc left me once. Or rather, I kicked him out of the house."

Marie-Thérèse gasped in disbelief. "You what?"

"It was before you came to live with us, when your parents were alive. Jean-Marc was spending too much time working, and I felt I was raising the children alone. I only had the twins and André then, but it was overwhelming. Jean-Marc was off starting a new branch for my father's banking firm, and I would sit home praying he'd come home early enough to tuck his children into bed. For their part they didn't really know him, or care when he cancelled promised trips. Well, one time he had promised them a ride on the Canal Saint-Martin, and he cancelled on them for the third time. I'd finally had enough. When he came home that night we argued, and I repeated all the arguments I'd given him for months about spending time with his family. When he wouldn't listen, I gave him his suitcase. He was so angry that he packed and left."

"I can't see him doing that," Marie-Thérèse said. "He's so calm and understanding."

"Well, he has come a long way. We both have. But at that time he had a tendency to run away from conflict; so when I confronted him, he ran."

"What did you do?"

"I cried, I ranted to myself, and I took the children on the canal ride without Jean-Marc. You and your mother came with us."

Marie-Thérèse thought for a moment. "I think I remember. Wasn't that about when my mom started to get sick?"

"Well, she'd been sick for a number of years, but it was right after the canal ride that we found out about the AIDS."

"So how did you and Dad get back together? Did he come back?"

"Yes, he did. He only stayed away a couple of nights—I can't even remember exactly how many. But I do remember feeling so ashamed when my father pointed out to me that Jean-Marc hadn't left, but that I had kicked him out." Ariana laughed. "It's funny to me now, but at the time, we both really suffered. When he came home and we made up, he almost ran right back to work when I told him we had to be tested for HIV. But in the end, he stayed and we faced it together."

"So kicking him out was the right thing to do?" Marie-Thérèse asked doubtfully.

"Yes. The experience was the beginning of waking Jean-Marc up. Of course, we had a lot of work left before we found a satisfactory compromise. We both had to give. For example, I found that I was so competent with the children that often I didn't let him do anything for them. Consequently he wasn't very close to them, so he buried himself in his work where he could find satisfaction. It was hard for me to relinquish control, but I did. I had to realize that things done halfway by Jean-Marc were better for the kids than me doing them all the way."

"And he got better."

"Oh, yes. With practice, he became a lot better at some things than I was."

"I have no control," Marie-Thérèse said bitterly. "Mathieu does whatever he wants."

Ariana was silent for a minute. "Perhaps you've let him off the hook too long." The words were gentle, but they bit into Marie-Thérèse's soul.

"Josette said the same thing. She's happy I left him." She looked earnestly at her mother. "But without me, I don't know how Mathieu will get by."

"Maybe that's what he has to find out. For now, why don't we go get Larissa and go home? I'll call Mathieu and at least let him know you're all right. He called the house three times before I left, and he sounded very upset. I would have called him once Josette told me where you were, but I thought it might do him a little good to worry for a while."

"I don't want to talk to him—yet."

"You don't have to. I'll do it. Better yet, I'll let your father. That'll give him more practice as a bishop."

Marie-Thérèse smiled gratefully. "Thanks, Mom."

"Just don't give up, honey. Not yet, anyway. Mathieu's a good man. He just has a few problems to work through. You take a rest and when you feel ready, then talk to him."

"Sometimes I'm afraid he'll never change," Marie-Thérèse admitted. "And it hurts so bad that I want to die."

Ariana put an arm around her. "I know that feeling well. But maybe I have an idea to help you. Think of Pauline and Emeri. I have seen no greater example of love helping someone to change. Pauline continued to love Emeri, never giving up, and that gave Emeri a chance to find his Heavenly Father."

Marie-Thérèse didn't reply. She thought of Pauline and her brave refusal to marry the man she loved in order to share eternity with him. If Pauline was so courageous, then maybe Marie-Thérèse could also risk losing Mathieu temporarily, if that meant in the end their marriage could be saved.

CHAPTER THIRTY

Two days after Marie-Thérèse left Mathieu, Marc took Brionney to a stake-wide dance for all members thirteen and older. He hoped he would see Marie-Thérèse and Mathieu together tonight. Maybe they would finally talk things out and life could get back to normal. Marc wished he could beat some sense into Mathieu.

"They're not here, either of them," Brionney said, reading his thoughts as she often did. Her sensitivity was one of the reasons he liked her so much. "I'm going to go look for them."

As she left, Marc noticed that she was no longer the plump girl he had met when she first arrived in France. Their morning roller blading outings, weekend hikes, and constant tourist playing had helped her lose the weight Marc knew she had despised, though with her sky blue eyes and her white-blonde hair, he had always thought her beautiful. Marc didn't know when he had begun to feel attracted to her, but he knew the feeling was strong. Could she be the woman he was supposed to marry? Tonight he vowed to find out.

Yesterday, Josette had reminded him that Brionney would return to America in less than a month to attend school at BYU. "You have to find out how you feel about Brionney," she had urged.

"I like her," he said.

"Well, have you kissed her?"

"Not yet. I didn't want to rush anything."

"Not rush? You've been dating her two months already."

"She's a good friend," Marc said. "I don't want to ruin that."

Josette sighed. "You men are impossible."

"What's Zack doing now?" Marc asked with a teasing grin, glad to change the subject.

All of a sudden, Josette became serious. "You've got to talk to him, Marc. I don't want to hurt his feelings, but he's smothering me. I love him and I love being with him, but sometimes he acts suspicious about what I do in my free time. The other day I went out to lunch with some old school friends—all girls except Fábio, who's married to one of them. I didn't know Zack planned to come home for lunch. Well, he waited for me to make sure I got home all right. He even missed an appointment." Josette took a deep breath and rushed on. "I've been wondering if . . . well, he knows I used to go out a lot. I'm worried that he thinks I'm going to, you know, fall into my old ways."

"That can't be it," Marc said.

"No, I guess not. I'm truly different now, and I love Zack so much. He's a great guy."

"He is," Marc said. "But I'll have a talk with him when I get the chance."

Josette smiled. "Thanks, Marc. I appreciate it."

"What are younger brothers for?"

She laughed and slugged his arm. "For getting me more nieces and nephews. Now remember to talk to Brionney tomorrow."

Marc's thoughts turned back to the dance. He saw Josette out on the floor, dancing with Zack. She made kissing motions toward Marc, and he knew exactly what she was trying to tell him. He looked around for Brionney and found her laughing with a group of young men near the door. He sauntered over and touched her arm possessively. "May I have this dance, Mademoiselle?"

Brionney nodded her assent. "Mais oui." But yes.

Rebekka Massoni flew up to them. "Oh, there you guys are. Finally! Marc, you have to dance with me. You promised!"

Marc smiled and patted the girl's shoulder. "Of course we'll dance. Don't we always?"

Rebekka's laugh tinkled through the cultural hall. She still showed the awkward edges of being thirteen, and though her body was quickly filling out into graceful curves like her mother's, Marc still saw the pesky five-year-old she had once been.

"The two beauties of the ball," he said, putting an arm around them both.

"I concede him first to you, Rebekka," Brionney said with an exaggerated curtsey.

Rebekka nodded regally. "Thank you, Brionney. I accept." They both giggled.

Marc stifled his irritation at being interrupted by Rebekka. Tonight was supposed to bring magic for him and Brionney, but how could it with Rebekka in the way? He ended up dancing three songs with Rebekka. He noticed that Brionney didn't sit on the sidelines but danced with some of the single men.

Marc finally extracted himself from Rebekka. "Come on, let's dance," he said, appearing at Brionney's side. "I got rid of the pest, at least for now."

"Rebekka is not a pest."

"No, but sometimes she can be very annoying." Marc took her hand and led her out to the floor. Other couples crowded after them.

"Tonight is for us," Marc said nervously. It might have been the most romantic thing he had ever said to her. His heart thudded oddly in his chest.

The music changed to a slow song and he took her into his arms, closer than he had ever been to a woman. He guided them to one of the more secluded corners of the room and stopped dancing. His face was very close to hers.

This is it! he thought, stifling the sudden urge to laugh. The crowd of people faded, and they were alone in the room. Marc's lips met hers, tentatively at first, then more demandingly. Brionney responded in kind, and a pleasant feeling spread throughout his body. He waited eagerly for the fireworks and the rush of passion he expected would follow.

Nothing happened. He faltered and drew away.

"I wondered when you'd do that," she said. "I was beginning to think we were only friends."

"I—I—I," Marc stuttered. He wasn't sure how he felt or how to voice anything. Maybe the fireworks show was overrated. He certainly enjoyed kissing Brionney, even though it wasn't what he had expected.

He scratched the raised scars on his arm, old markings from the dialysis treatments he had received before his kidney transplant.

Finally, he found his voice. "I see the relationships my sisters have, and my parents. I want that. I like you, Brionney."

He lapsed into silence and Brionney said, "I like you, too."

"Well, I guess I mean that I more than like you. I mean, I see your potential."

"You mean now that I've lost weight."

He snorted impatiently and took her hand. "It doesn't have anything to do with your weight, but what's in your heart. You're not only beautiful on the outside, but on the inside where it counts. I think you'll make an excellent wife and an even better mother. You have a strong testimony of the gospel. You have everything I've wanted in a wife. I'd like us to get to know each other better."

"I'd like that too, Marc."

Marc gazed into the dark room, pleased with her response, but not knowing what to say next. His eyes fell on Danielle Massoni, Rebekka's mother, who was dancing with her husband. Her auburn hair caught the lights. *She is beautiful as no other woman could ever be,* he thought.

"You're in love with Danielle, aren't you?" Brionney said quietly.

The realization that Brionney easily saw what he had tried so long and hard to hide hit Marc like an iron fist to his stomach. He jerked his head toward her, his mouth open to speak. Then without utterance, he shut it again.

"I guess I am in love with her," he admitted after a long while. "I didn't realize it was that obvious. Not in so many words, anyway. I think I've loved her since I was fifteen."

"You saved her life in the bombing; it's natural you would care for her." Brionney's words were soft but questioning, and Marc had to tell her the truth.

"Oh, Brionney, I wish it were that. How I've prayed for something like that!" He turned his head back in Danielle's direction. "But it's much more. I've never admitted this to another person, but I really love her." He grimaced and gave a self-deprecating laugh. "Boy, do I feel stupid. Here I am trying to start a relationship with you, and I'm telling you that I'm in love with another woman."

"She's very beautiful."

With effort, Marc took his eyes from Danielle. "And very much in love with her husband."

Brionney studied the dancing pair. "I don't see why. He's handsome, but he can't take her to the temple. And he seems a little arrogant to me."

"A little?" Marc said in amazement. "The guy's an idiot." He paused before rushing on. "No, that's not fair. He had a hard life as a child. I think he's come a long way. And he treats Danielle like a queen. He makes her happy. Oh brother, now I'm defending him!"

"Defending him when you wish he'd go away?"

Marc shook his head slowly. "No, she'd never look at me. I'm only a boy to her. I've long ago given up any idea of having a relationship with her. And I do want a relationship, Brionney." He took her hand and continued earnestly. "I think we could try for one. I think with you I could forget Danielle."

Brionney's eyebrows drew together in thought. "We're both looking for someone," she said. "And we don't want to settle for anything that's less than perfect for us. I really like you, Marc. But I've seen how you act around Danielle, although I've tried to tell myself it was nothing." She frowned. "The truth is, I could fall in love with you all too easily. But I'm not ready to settle for loving a man who's in love with someone else. I want someone to love me and only me."

"I want to," Marc said. "I really do."

"I know, but I think you need to resolve how you feel about Danielle before you try another relationship. It's not fair. Not to me or to you. We might both just end up getting hurt."

"So the answer's no."

"That's not what I'm saying. I'm saying let's go back to being friends; and when you're ready, maybe then it'll be time for us. With modern technology, America's not so far away; and we're both young—or at least that's what my parents keep writing me. In the meantime, I don't want to lose you."

"You've told your parents about me?"

She grinned, and the tight clench of Marc's stomach eased. "Of course I have. Since losing my brother and Josette to each other, you're the best friend I have."

"I know what you mean," Marc said. "And I guess I can live with us just being friends—for now. But my family isn't going to be happy about it. They really like you."

"They'll get over it."

"Can I have just one more kiss? It might help me to get over Danielle."

"All right." Her voice held amusement. "But just one more, and then that's it."

He kissed her again, and this time he didn't see Danielle in his mind. Maybe eventually the part of him that loved Brionney could overshadow the part of him that adored Danielle. Then Brionney drew away, her eyes catching the dim light. Were those tears? Was she as sad as he was that things hadn't worked out between them?

"There's just one thing, Brionney," he said sincerely. "Just in case . . . I mean, when you go back to America, don't settle for the first good-looking guy you see. Not unless he's like . . . well, like me. What I'm trying to say is, don't marry a man unless he treats you right and you can be yourself around him. He shouldn't care what you weigh or how much makeup you have on. That stuff doesn't matter—only what's inside. I just want you to be careful." He didn't know how to put it better. Sometimes she was so vulnerable, and he wished he could protect her.

"I will," she promised. "But don't worry so much. I look back now and see how far I've already come. Once I would have jumped at the chance to have any sort of a serious relationship with a man as wonderful as you; but being with you has taught me what I'm worth as a person and as a woman. That's a gift I can never repay." She smiled and added, "But who knows? Maybe I'll just wait for you."

Marc glanced once more toward Danielle, feeling desolate. The ache in his heart was unbearable. Brionney suddenly grabbed his hands. "Come on, the music's changing. Let's go boogey to some American rock!"

"Boogey?" asked Marc. "Is that another of your untranslatable English words?"

"Yeah, come on and I'll explain."

Marc was relieved that the awkward moment between them was over. Now that they weren't in love, things could go back to normal between them. They danced for two more songs before Brionney began to limp. "I think I have a blister," she shouted over the music.

Marc picked her up and carried her to the row of chairs lining the gym. "I really should stick around and marry you," Brionney joked.

"You're a true gentleman, and besides, at least then it would be possible for me to have twins."

He faked a wounded look. "You just want me for my genes," he said. "I hate to break it to you, but the tendency to have fraternal twins passes through the mother's genes, I think."

"Well, then, I guess I'm off the hook. What a relief!"

Marc grinned. "Just for that, I'm leaving you. They've got to have some girls around here that don't have lousy shoes. Besides, I promised Rebekka on the threat of death that I would dance with her again. Or would you rather I stay?"

"No, thanks. I'm going to go see a man about a dog."

"You Americans and your euphemisms. Can't you just say you have to go to the bathroom?" With that parting shot, he disappeared into the crowd.

Marc couldn't find Rebekka anywhere inside the cultural hall. Where could she be? He didn't feel much like dancing, but he had promised to save at least one dance for Rebekka, and he might as well get it over with. In the hall he passed laughing couples and families. When he reached the end, he wandered into the next corridor where the lights were off. The sound of soft sobbing came to his ears. He followed the sound and pinpointed the darkened room where it came from. "Hello?" he said.

The sobbing stopped. "Go away," came a tear-filled voice.

"Rebekka, is that you?"

"No!" The door slammed shut.

Marc turned the knob, pushed the door open a crack, and peered through. On the other side, Rebekka tried to shut it again. "Open up," he said.

"No."

"Rebekka, let's talk about it. Come on."

"I don't want to," the girl wailed. "Now go away and leave me alone!"

"I'm your friend, and I'm not going anywhere. If you don't open the door, I'm going to force it open!"

The pressure on the door gradually released, and Marc swung the door inward. Rebekka sat down on a chair in the middle of the room, her face turned away. "Don't turn on the light," she said. "Someone might come in. I don't want anyone else to see me like this."

Marc crouched in front of her chair. "Okay, what's wrong?"

By the dim light coming from the door, he saw Rebekka clamp her mouth shut, her lips puckering stubbornly.

"If you don't tell me, I'm going to go get your mother."

The threat worked. "I saw you kissing Brionney out there." Rebekka's eyes filled with tears that spilled slowly over and coated her cheeks. "I guess now you'll be getting married. I hope you're happy together, I really do." Her voice rose on the last words, and she began to sob again.

Marc hugged Rebekka and stroked her hair. "You don't sound happy," he said softly. "But you don't have to worry; Brionney and I are just friends." He felt a little guilty as he said it, because he hoped someday he could become more than that to Brionney.

Rebekka's lower lip trembled, and for the first time Marc noticed how much she looked like her mother. "You don't love her? Really?"

"Really. I mean I love her as a friend, but that's all for right now. Just friends. And later this month she's going back to America. She's going to major in French at BYU."

Rebekka smiled through the tears. "Her accent's better than it was when she came," she said generously.

"But if we did want to get married, why would that make you sad?" Marc asked. He had been sure Rebekka had been over her crush on him for at least a year.

Her expression changed to a melancholy one that belied her young age. "You think I'm just a little girl, don't you?"

Marc studied Rebekka. Her wavy auburn hair fell becomingly around an oval face. Her cheeks were streaked with tears and her eyes more red than their usual striking gray, but the potential for beauty was undiminished. "You are a beautiful young woman, Rebekka," he said sincerely. "And I know you're beautiful right here, where it really counts." He thumped his chest. "And some day you are going to find someone who loves you more than life. But don't be in such a great hurry. You've got a lot of time."

He paused, not knowing if he should say more. "And I do know what it's like to love someone who can never return that love."

Rebekka's eyes grew big. "Who?"

"I can't tell you," he said. "But now it's up to me to decide what

I'm going to do with it. I think mostly I have to move on and find a way to be happy without her."

Rebekka touch his cheek, a light touch that was different from anything Marc had ever felt from her. "I'll help you," she said.

He smiled. "Thanks. I appreciate that. And you can do that by dancing with me again. Would you?"

"Sure," she said, coming to her feet.

Marc rose with her. "And I guess I might have to share you with that bunch of boys I saw you with earlier. I'll bet they're still out there searching for the most beautiful thirteen-year-old girl in the ward."

"They always do want to dance with me," Rebekka said with childlike frankness. "But not one of them is like you."

Before Marc could reply, she grabbed his hand and pulled him to the door. When they neared the cultural hall, Rebekka slipped into the rest room. "Wait here," she ordered. "I have to make sure my eyes aren't red."

Marc decided to rest on the couch in the foyer while he waited. Zack was already there, moving his head in time to the music. He made room as Marc approached.

"Hey, what's up?" Marc asked.

"Bathroom stop. Josette spends a lot of time there nowadays. Something about the added pressure on the bladder."

"Good, then she can help Rebekka with her face."

"What's wrong with Rebekka's face?"

"Nothing. I think she still has a crush on me and is feeling a little neglected."

"She'll grow out of it," Zack said sympathetically.

"That's what I keep hoping." Marc sat without speaking for a moment, then recalled Josette's request of the day before. "What's going on with you and my sister?" he said bluntly as only good friends could. "I sense there's some tension going on. Are you upset because she's been hanging out with me?"

Zack stared at him for a moment, as if debating what to say. "Well," he began, "now that you mention it, I guess it does make me a little . . ."

"A little jealous."

"Jealous? No, that's not it. Okay, maybe it is." Zack shook his head. "I don't know what I feel exactly, but I do want to get it over with before it becomes a big problem. I mean, look at Marie-Thérèse and Mathieu. Whew! What a mess!"

"So what do you think is wrong?"

"She's so happy."

Marc blinked. "So what's wrong with that?"

"I don't know."

"Aren't you happy?"

"Yes, when I'm with her."

"Ah-hah! You don't understand how she can be happy when you're not around." Marc knew the feeling well, from his experience with both Danielle and Josette.

Zack shut his eyes. "That sounds so stupid—but it's true." He groaned. "Man, what an idiot I am! She wasn't happy in America, so I decided to move to make her happy. And now that she's with her family and friends, she is happy—and I'm jealous!"

Marc stifled an urge to laugh. "You think that's bad! She's my sister, and I still felt betrayed when she went to America to marry you. And I even like you. But I couldn't believe she could be happy without me. Think about it! We grew up together; we've been every-thing to each other. And then in one day, she's your wife first and my twin sister second. That was a shock."

Zack looked at him warmly. "I see what you mean. So how did you get over it?"

"I found some hobbies, some other friends, and when you came back, I kept going to see her. She's changed, but she's still my sister and I know she loves me. I'd rather be second in her life than lose her completely. Besides, I keep hoping that someday I'll find a woman who will put me first, like Josette does with you."

Zack ran a hand through his blond hair. "She's so beautiful," he said softly. "And I love her so intensely. It's a feeling I never imag-ined I would have about another person. It's an eternal type of thing—it's so huge."

As his friend talked, Marc knew that was what had been missing with Brionney. But that didn't mean it couldn't happen someday.

"Sometimes I can't believe she's chosen me," Zack continued. "I think I'm afraid that one day she'll wake up and find I'm not the man she thought she loved. Look at Marie-Thérèse and Mathieu."

Marc snorted. "Mathieu's being blind," he said. "You don't have that problem. Well, maybe you do. Would it help to know that when you're not with us, Josette always talks about you? It's Zack this and Zack that. She's crazy about you." Marc lowered his voice. "And just because she's beautiful doesn't mean she's going to leave you one day. Take Danielle Massoni, for example. She is beautiful and everyone knows how she adores her husband, even though he's not a member and a jerk most of the time." Marc hoped the longing in his heart didn't reach his voice.

"He treats her well."

"And you treat Josette well."

Zack sighed. "Except I'm rather possessive."

"Yeah, but don't worry about it too much," Marc said. "It's an emotion women are willing to deal with if it doesn't get too serious. They like being adored. Now, if you were in love with another woman . . ."—he made a chopping motion—"they'll cut you off in an instant. But possessiveness is definitely something you can work on." He forced a laugh to express mirth he did not feel. He couldn't let Zack know how much Brionney's refusal to deepen their relationship bothered him, though he understood and agreed with her reasons. "I knew you had a tendency to be single-minded," he added. "In fact, looking back, I can see that's part of what made you such a successful missionary. Once you had a hold on those investigators, you never let them go! But I never thought that stemmed from insecurity."

Zack groaned. "Is it that obvious?"

"Yep, your secret is out." Marc slapped him on the back. "But tell me, how are you feeling about everything else? You've got to be missing your family."

"I do," Zack admitted. "But with Brionney here, it's been all right."

"Does Josette know how you feel?"

Zack shook his head. "No. I promised myself I'd never let my homesickness affect her happiness. Sometimes it's not so much my family I miss, but America or some aspects of my life there. Not that I want to go back now," he added hurriedly. "Not with Josette missing you all so much. She needs her family, especially during this pregnancy."

"You should tell her your feelings so she can be there for you," Marc said. "Like you were for her. You need to trust Josette. I don't think she'll let you down."

"I trust Josette," Zack said.

"Do you? Well, maybe you should show her."

Whatever Zack was going to say next was cut off by the return of the women. Or the woman and the girl, rather. Josette smiled and accepted her husband's proffered hand. "Sorry I took so long."

Marc glanced at Rebekka, but saw no traces of the tears. She smiled at him shyly. He grabbed her hand and started for the cultural hall. "Thanks, Josette," he mouthed over his shoulder. But his sister's attention was focused on her husband. *As it should be,* Marc thought. His step quickened. If he hurried, he might be able to talk to Danielle before the night was over. Maybe even dance with her.

To his delight, Danielle herself met him at the door. "Don't look now," she said, "but my cousin and your sister are both here and about to run into each other."

Rebekka clapped her hands. "Your plan worked, Mom!"

Danielle gave them a radiant smile. "Well, all I did was ask Ariana if Marie-Thérèse was going to be here and then tell Mathieu. I hope that on this neutral ground they can work things out."

Marc hoped so, too.

CHAPTER THIRTY-ONE

Marie-Thérèse went to the dance only because she was sick of being cooped up in her parents' apartment, which despite its comfortable size didn't feel like home anymore. Of course she wouldn't dance with anyone other than her brother or father, and even that didn't seem right without Mathieu there.

She missed him more than she wanted to admit—especially at night, when they had usually curled up together and talked about the future. Even though she had started to consider most of his financial dreams as delusions, it had still been a special time. They would talk about Larissa, and often about the gospel. At times the old sensations of love would fill her heart until they absorbed all the mistrust and anger.

Tears bit at the back of Marie-Thérèse's eyes. Maybe she should go home to Larissa, who was being baby-sat by Grandma Josephine, Ariana's mother. All around her people joked and laughed as though the world was still turning, when Marie-Thérèse was sure it must have stopped the moment she left Mathieu. She made her way to the refreshment table and picked up a slice of sweet bread. Maybe eating something would settle her stomach. The bread did make her feel better—until she turned and found herself face to face with Mathieu.

Her mouth opened, and an exclamation of surprise slipped out before she could clamp it shut. *Dear Father*, she prayed silently. *Please, please help me know what to do!* Mathieu had called her three times a day since he found out where she was staying. Yesterday, she had let her mother take Larissa to spend a few hours with him. Marie-Thérèse hadn't felt ready yet to face him, but had wanted him to be able to see his daughter.

"Marie-Thérèse, I'm sorry," he said, a pleading look on his face. "Please come back."

"Not here," she said, looking around at the crowd. "Let's go outside."

Mathieu obediently turned and led the way. As she followed, Marie-Thérèse caught a glimpse of Josette on the far side of the dance floor. Her sister made a fist and punched it into the air. *Be strong*, was the silent message. Marie-Thérèse's resolve strengthened. She loved Mathieu and she would fight for him, even if her opponent was Mathieu himself.

* * * * *

When they left the busy church, Mathieu took a deep breath of the fresh night air. Other than the stars shining in the night sky, he and Marie-Thérèse were all alone. He stopped walking and faced her. "I want you to come home," he said. "I'll do anything you want, anything! Please . . . I love you." In fact, the last few days had been the most miserable in his entire life.

"I love you too, Mathieu," Marie-Thérèse said softly. "That's not the problem. It never was."

He sighed with genuine relief. "I thought maybe you stopped. I thought you were so angry that you would never want to see me ever again."

"I was angry," she said. "I'm still angry."

"I'm sorry about the bed."

Now it was her turn to sigh. "Mathieu, it's not the stupid bed, it's the finances. I can't deal with it anymore!"

"Then let me do it."

"I have!" Her face tightened and turned red, a sure sign that she was about to walk away from him. He hadn't felt so desperate since the day she had decided to send in her mission papers, the same day he had asked her to marry him. He touched her shoulder. "Please, don't leave," he begged. "Maybe there is a problem. I just don't know how to fix it. But I love you, Marie-Thérèse, and I do want to make you happy."

Her face relaxed, and Mathieu thought he had convinced her. But her answer surprised him. "I'm not going back to that apartment, Mathieu, or to anywhere else unless you see a counselor about this."

"Tell our problems to a stranger?" He knew how much it would cost her emotionally to do that. For all her friendliness to people, Marie-Thérèse was very careful about sharing personal information.

"Why not, if it helps?" she cried passionately. "I just want things to be all right between us again!"

"We can work this out alone," he insisted.

"No, we can't. We can't!"

"Just come back home, and I'll show you."

She shook her head and said abruptly, "I'm pregnant."

The news sent Mathieu reeling. "You are! But that's wonderful!"

"I wish I could be happy," she said. Her voice was so soft he wondered if he heard her right. "One more doctor bill, one more mouth to feed, one more to buy clothes for." She glared at him. "Do you know how that makes me feel—to think that way about my own son?"

"Son?" Mathieu gasped. "You already know it's a boy?"

"Yes. I'm four months along."

"Why didn't you tell me?"

"Because I'm not happy about it. I don't want to have another baby."

His mind rebelled at what she was saying. "But it's not the baby, right?" he implored. "It's me—the money. Isn't it?"

She nodded once, and silent tears began to trickle down her face. Mathieu wanted to make it all better, but he didn't know how. She looked too thin to be four months into the pregnancy. He remembered how sick she'd been with Larissa. Had it been better for her this time? Had she been eating well? How had she hidden it from him for so long? He longed to ask the questions, but didn't feel he had the right. But how could he have lived in the same house with her and not known? Was he that blind? What else didn't he know about her?

Another thought tortured him even more. If he had been so blind that he hadn't recognized the obvious signs of pregnancy, then maybe he *was* blind to their financial situation as Marie-Thérèse kept insisting.

"Okay," he said, blinking fiercely to clear the tears from his eyes. "Who do you have in mind?"

She looked down at the ground and back up, hesitating. "My father," she said. "He's been the bishop for two months, and he works in banking. He cares about us both."

Mathieu would have preferred a more impartial counselor, but he didn't want Marie-Thérèse to suffer any more than she had already. "All right," he agreed. "Let's do it."

She appeared relieved. "Okay, then."

They stood awkwardly for a few moments, then Marie-Thérèse said, "I should probably go. I need to stop by Grandma Josephine's and pick up Larissa."

"Give her a kiss for me."

"I will. Good night." She backed away for a few steps, then turned and hurried into the building.

When she was gone, he stared up into the night. "Dear Father," he prayed, "I don't know what I'm doing wrong, but I think I need to change. I want to for her, for Larissa, and for my son." Now that he was alone, Mathieu let the tears come freely. "Please, help me. Help us."

*   *   *   *   *

"Having money problems is nothing to be ashamed of," Jean-Marc said, seating himself behind the desk in his office, which had once been Pauline's room. He indicated for Marie-Thérèse and Mathieu to sit in the two empty chairs in front of him. "A good percentage of couples have problems agreeing on how the money should be spent. In fact, it's one of the prime reasons for divorce."

Though her father had only been set apart as bishop for two months, Marie-Thérèse thought he fit into the role easily. Even when she had first talked to him on the night she had left Mathieu, he hadn't reproached her for not bringing it up earlier, told her it was nothing, or begun attacking her husband. The Lord had certainly chosen well. Marie-Thérèse didn't know if she could have been so open about their problem with someone else. The very thought made her stomach feel uneasy.

"Now, I know you love each other," her father continued, "and you value your relationship above all else. This is good, because we know that no matter what happens here today, there'll be no talk of divorce or similar ultimatums. So now we can get down to the heart of the matter."

He looked pointedly at Mathieu, but his words were gentle. "And there *is* a problem here, as I see it. I've prayed long and hard about the solution these last few days, and I think I may have hit on a few suggestions. But before we begin, I'd like to have a prayer. Mathieu, as patriarch of your family, would you be willing to offer it?"

"Of course." Mathieu reached out a hand to Marie-Thérèse and she held it tightly as he prayed. Hope flickered in her heart. *Maybe now things could start being all right.*

After the prayer, Jean-Marc pulled a stack of money out of his pocket and laid it on the desk. "This represents your take-home pay each month," he said. "It sure looks like a lot this way."

Mathieu nodded confidently. "It's a good wage. And I like my work."

Jean-Marc said nothing, but turned to the pile of bills Marie-Thérèse had brought. "These are your debts, including tithing but not including food, odds and ends, or impulse buying. Let's see now. Mathieu, I understand that Marie-Thérèse usually pays the bills, and I think you're right to let her. She's always been very good with numbers. If Larissa hadn't come along when she did, I would have put Marie-Thérèse in charge of one of the banks I supervise. She has the education for it and the experience. But just this once, you pretend to make the payments."

Mathieu divided the cash among the bills. After doing so, there was plenty of money left over.

"Now, how much do you need for groceries, Marie-Thérèse? Take it out of what remains. Only that much? Come on. You can't possibly be living on so little. That's not healthy. Take some more. Larissa is eating now, too."

Marie-Thérèse obeyed, though it was more money than she had been using. Is that why she always felt she only scraped by each month?

"Okay now. This is what remains."

Mathieu eyed the small stack, his smile dimmer now. "We still have enough left for our needs," he said uncertainly.

"We haven't taken out for your weekly date," Jean-Marc said. He laid a few notes to the side. "I know you go out because we baby-sit Larissa. Okay now, what about a fast offering? And diapers? Last I heard, Larissa wasn't potty-trained. Hmm, is that about right? Took out a big chunk, didn't it?"

Mathieu didn't say anything, but Marie-Thérèse began having the desperate feeling she normally got when doing the bills. She crossed her arms tightly over her stomach to stifle the churning.

"Now what can you buy with this?" asked Jean-Marc.

"Not much," Mathieu admitted.

"Certainly not enough to buy a hand-crocheted bedspread," Marie-Thérèse muttered. Mathieu glanced at her quickly, but he said nothing.

"As I see it, there's no room here for impulse buying, at least not at the rate either of you might like." Jean-Marc didn't say any names or accuse anyone, and Marie-Thérèse was glad to see that Mathieu didn't act offended. Jean-Marc looked down at the pile of debts. "We have sixteen credit card bills here, besides the rent and utilities. Let's put together the money we ordinarily have to pay on those bills and see how much we have. See? This is how much you'd have if you didn't have to pay those debts. It would be enough to buy, say, one nice piece of furniture each month. It's a good sum of money—if it wasn't already taken.

"Now, as I see it, one of your main problems is too many debts. It's not as bad yet as some couples I've seen in my years working at the bank, but it's not a good sign since you've been married such a short time." He looked directly at Mathieu. "You cannot spend more than you make. You *must* not. Our prophets have counseled against doing so for as long as I've been in the Church."

Mathieu squirmed uncomfortably. "Well, what do you suggest?"

Jean-Marc leaned back in his chair, leaving the money on the desk. "When I was serving my mission, I met an elder who would consistently run out of money the first week after receiving his stipend. It wouldn't matter how he tried not to spend it, he still did. Then he'd borrow money from his companion and ward members to last out the month. Finally, it got so bad that the president called him in for a chat. The president paid off all his debts and scheduled repayments. Then he set up a system where the missionary wasn't allowed to buy anything unless his companion agreed. The missionary was able to pay everything back before he left his mission. It took some doing, but—"

Mathieu bristled and interrupted angrily. "Are you saying I need Marie-Thérèse to approve everything I buy? I'm not a child. And it's me who earns the money. I did pretty well before we met."

Marie-Thérèse slid down in her seat and wished she could disappear.

"I think Marie-Thérèse has worked pretty hard to earn money as well," Jean-Marc said, sitting forward again. Marie-Thérèse could tell he was making an effort to control his temper. "In fact, in my analysis of your finances, her earnings are actually paying for the daily expenses. But it makes no difference who earns the money; you know that. What matters is how you spend it together. But let me explain a bit further. Don't get angry. I want all your feelings in the open, but we need to be honest. Mathieu, I want you to look through these bills and tell me the percentage of the bills you ran up before your marriage."

Mathieu looked at the bills helplessly. "I couldn't begin to say. I think I've probably got less than ten thousand francs left, that's all."

Jean-Marc opened a file on the desk. "Mathieu, I asked you to give me all your old statements."

"I know, I gave them to you yesterday."

Marie-Thérèse sat up straighter. She hadn't known Mathieu had given her father the statements.

"Well, I went through them today, and I found that over seventy-five percent of your debts, not including the apartment, were incurred before your marriage. It seems that Marie-Thérèse has had a good effect on your spending habits."

Mathieu's hands gripped the armrests on his chair. "I am an adult, I can control myself."

"I think you will be able to, but first you have to understand the problem." Jean-Marc's brow furrowed as if he was thinking deeply. "I've got an example for you. What if Marie-Thérèse spent money without consulting you?"

"So? I know she won't go overboard."

Jean-Marc snapped his fingers. "There's the key. You know that and you trust her. But can she trust you in the same way? No, don't answer; I just want you to think about it. The fact of the matter is that when you get two people together, one nearly always takes on the role of spender and the other the role of saver—to differing degrees, of course—regardless of what they did before the marriage. Take two savers, for instance, and generally, one will have to become a little bit of a spender." Jean-Marc laughed. "This actually needs to happen to some extent, or even the couple's basic needs may go ignored. But in a relationship where the spending and saving habits start out vastly different, each partner tends to view the other person as wrong and will sometimes go to extremes to try to correct the problem. The more one pulls, the more the other pushes. I see that here. Mathieu, how do you feel about Marie-Thérèse's spending habits?"

Mathieu sent a furtive glance in her direction. "She never wants to spend money. I have to get her things, or she'd never have anything new. *We'd* never have anything new."

"And you, Marie-Thérèse?"

"He spends too much," she snapped. "I'm afraid I'll never have enough to even buy a china cabinet. Or—or enough food." Marie-Thérèse felt her face color as Mathieu's gaze riveted on her. Did he hate her for what she had said? Then she felt his hand stroking her arm.

"You don't trust me, do you?"

Marie-Thérèse didn't dare respond, but he read the answer in her eyes.

"I'm sorry," he whispered. His eyes filled with tears as they had when she told him about the baby. Marie-Thérèse felt her dampness on her own face, tears driven by her guilt and her unhappiness. Her poor baby! Would her feelings of not wanting him right now affect him? No! She wouldn't let that happen. Despite the additional problems, she already loved her baby. He and Larissa were why she had to force Mathieu to admit that something was wrong.

"So there is a problem," Jean-Marc said softly.

Mathieu frowned and gave a sharp nod of agreement. "What can we do? I love Marie-Thérèse and want to make her happy. I want her back in my life, and for that I'm willing to make a change. Can you help us?"

"That depends if you're willing to do what I recommend."

"I am." Mathieu looked at Marie-Thérèse.

She wiped her face with a tissue her father handed her and smiled tentatively. "Me too."

"Well, as Marie-Thérèse's father, I can get you a good loan at the bank that will pay off all these credit cards. However, I'll do so only if you promise to cut up all the cards and never use them or any others again."

"How will that help?" Mathieu asked.

"Marie-Thérèse, do you want to answer that?"

"I've known we should do it, Dad, but I was afraid we'd just run up the cards again."

"But Mathieu will promise not to do that. And I believe he is a man of his word."

Marie-Thérèse took a deep breath and looked at Mathieu. "If we get a loan at the bank to pay off all our bills, we could pay less and still get it paid off in the same amount of time because we're paying a lower interest rate."

"But it is only valuable if you don't get back into debt," Jean-Marc emphasized. "If you go back to spending at the same rate, you'll be even worse off." He gathered all the money on the desk that represented the amount they needed to pay the bills. "The goal is to get rid of all your debts entirely. You really would need only about half of this cash to meet the new loan payment. However, I suggest you keep putting seventy-five percent down just to get rid of it faster. I would normally suggest putting one hundred percent of what you have been paying on the bills, but there is no way you can survive doing that. You'll need money for things that crop up, like car repairs, dentist bills, clothes, and the like.

"Now, there are only two rules in spending the remaining twenty-five percent or any extra money you may receive. Both of you must agree on how it is to be spent, and you do not borrow any more money, period. Let me repeat: you do not borrow any other money at all, not even a single franc. And one thing more: when you get raises, you need to calculate what the overall increase is after you pay taxes and tithing, and put that on the loan as well. Paying off that debt must be your chief concern. After you get that pretty much paid off, you can focus on getting a mortgage—which is the only debt I'll ever recommend to any of my children, because it will increase in value—especially if you pay it off early and save interest charges. For the rest, it's better to make do with what you can afford. So what do you think? Are you willing to do that?"

Mathieu sat back in his chair and sighed deeply. "I guess so, but it doesn't sound very fun."

"Oh, but I haven't mentioned the best part. Of the twenty-five percent you are now not paying on the bills, you each get a small portion." Jean-Marc counted some money onto the desk in front of them. "This is yours to spend in any way you wish, without consulting the other. You get this same amount each month. And you cannot ask the other what he or she did with the money, or in any way get an accounting unless it's voluntary. Consider it one of the monthly bills."

Marie-Thérèse stared at the money. "Anything I want?" she asked, fingering the notes.

"Anything," her father said. "Except in your case, I want you to promise that you will spend at least half of it on something for yourself. I make this stipulation only because I know that you are too likely to spend it on the bills or on an outfit for Larissa."

Mathieu laughed, scooping up the money from the desk. "That's for sure. I guess I won't have much trouble spending my share."

"There's also a support group for people who have spending problems."

"Spenders Anonymous?" Mathieu asked. Marie-Thérèse couldn't miss the humor in his voice.

"Something like that. And I want you both to go."

Mathieu's brow drew in puzzlement. "But if we follow your plan, we shouldn't need to."

Jean-Marc pushed back his chair from the oak desk and stood, stretching his back almost imperceptibly. "It isn't going to be that easy, Mathieu. Perhaps it might be for the first little while, but after that it gets hard. With a support group it'll be easier, believe me."

"Are you saying that as a bishop or as Father?" Mathieu asked, also coming to his feet.

"Both." Jean-Marc put an arm around each of them. "You guys are good kids. And I think that with a lot of prayer you'll find your way. There are much more serious problems in the world. Just remember how much you love each other, and each give a hundred percent to making it work." He dropped his arms and walked to the door. "Now, I want you to go into that room down the hall, pack Marie-Thérèse's things, and go home to your own apartment. For the last week that it's yours, anyway. I hope you've found another place."

Marie-Thérèse shook her head. "I'll start looking tomorrow."

"First, I expect to see you both at the bank."

She opened her mouth to thank her father, but he shook his head. "Don't thank me now. In a few years when you're free from your debts, or most of them, then you can thank me. Believe me, it'll be a feeling of freedom you won't be able to match. Of course, that won't let you out of the other problems life will throw at you—and this family has certainly had its share. You fall sometimes when you're hit, but as long as you keep getting up, you're not out of the game."

He hugged Marie-Thérèse, but held out his hand to Mathieu. "Uh, the money?"

Mathieu started, then grinned sheepishly as he handed back the money Jean-Marc had given them to represent the small amount of personal money they were supposed to have each month. "I almost forgot."

Marie-Thérèse tried to return her share as well, but Jean-Marc pushed her hand back, also adding the money Mathieu had returned. "Fathers are allowed some privileges," he whispered in her ear.

Marie-Thérèse tucked the money into her purse. It was amazing how a little cash made everything look brighter. She watched her father return to his office. As he closed the door, she grabbed Mathieu's hand. "We can do it, can't we?"

He pulled her into his arms, and she almost couldn't believe how right she felt at that moment. She knew her father had said that it wouldn't be easy for Mathieu to change, but she loved him and was determined to give him the chance.

CHAPTER THIRTY-TWO

The end of August came with record heat spells and a sad farewell to Brionney, who left for America and her French studies at BYU. Even with her own concerns, Marie-Thérèse noticed Marc's regret when Brionney's plane left. She wondered if he would go after her someday.

Marie-Thérèse and Mathieu had moved to a new apartment, a smaller, less expensive one, but it felt like home. They had left behind all of the old memories and much of the expensive furniture. She could only pray that the peace would last. Mathieu brought home his paycheck and, other than his monthly allotment, didn't spend a franc without consulting her. Sometimes she could tell that he was doing all he could to please her and that the effort didn't come without great cost. He did mention that they seemed to eat better now, and the small kitchen actually seemed bigger without all the ironing and clothing rods.

In her spare time, Marie-Thérèse had taken up crocheting bed covers for extra money to put toward their large debt, but she didn't point this out to Mathieu since he seemed to need to feel that he was supporting their family alone. He was doing a great job, but Marie-Thérèse worried that he might experience a relapse into his old spending habits. When could she know that he was entirely safe? Or would that day ever come?

As September passed, their baby grew and flourished inside her. She and Josette often spent the afternoons together talking and planning for their babies. Marie-Thérèse still felt guilty for wishing she wasn't pregnant during those first agonizing months. How could she have not wanted this precious life? Her situation with Mathieu had been serious, but surely not so desperate as to reject the gift of a child of God! Mathieu did his best to convince her to let the matter go, and the doctor had assured her of the baby's health, but in the back of her mind the worry simmered that she had somehow damaged her baby with her negative emotions.

Each week Marie-Thérèse attended a financial support group with a reluctant Mathieu. It reminded Marie-Thérèse of the few times she had attended the AIDS support meetings with Pauline when André hadn't been able to accompany her. Only there were many more people, most of them older.

One night in mid-October when she was seven months pregnant, Marie-Thérèse and Mathieu took Larissa to Josette's and went to the meeting. As usual, the room was too warm, but a fresh evening breeze wafted through the open window. Marie-Thérèse listened as a man in the thirty-odd member group told his story to the rest of the compulsive spenders.

"I was eighteen when I received my first credit card application in the mail," the man said. "They talked about freedom and independence and all the things I could buy to bring me joy. Build up a good credit rating, they said. It'll make it easier to buy a house someday. I sent in the application, and then when the card came I went shopping and spent up to my limit. They were right, I was very happy. New clothes, a new look—perfect to go to my new college. But they had only told part of the story." Everyone in the group nodded, some in sympathy, some in contemptuous denial.

"Same as me," another man spoke up. "You had to get another card, didn't you? To keep the same feeling."

"Exactly," the first man replied. He wasn't new to the group, but it was the first time he had spoken in front of everyone. His expression showed a mixture of relief and nervousness. "Pretty soon I couldn't pay, and that's when the court ordered me here," he said.

"They hadn't told you the truth, that's for sure," someone from the audience said in a loud voice. Murmurs spread through the rest of the group as people began to offer advice, or to ask questions. Marie-Thérèse felt her attention slipping. They had been here almost an hour already, and it looked as though it might go for one more. While she appreciated the testimonials of these men and women, she was more worried about Larissa, who had been acting cranky as she often did before coming down with a fever. Josette and Zack were competent baby-sitters, but that didn't put Marie-Thérèse's mind completely at rest.

Mathieu squeezed her hand. "Let's go," he said. "We'll come back next week."

Marie-Thérèse hesitated only an instant, then smiled apologetically at the speaker and slipped out the back door with Mathieu close on her heels.

"Did you hear anything new?" she asked. For two months they had been coming to these meetings, and for the same two months she felt as though she had been holding her breath, waiting and watching . . . and praying. Mathieu had followed her father's advice to the letter, but she felt there was some part of him that was not entirely happy about their new goals. He had shown a reluctance to attend these meetings, and even Marie-Thérèse had to admit that most of these people had problems much more severe than Mathieu's. In a way, knowing that had helped her. But had the group helped her husband at all? Each time she asked him, and each time he had said no.

She expected the same unenthusiastic reply, but today he looked at her differently, a smile playing on his lips. "Actually, yes."

"And?" She tried to hide her surprise.

Mathieu opened the car door. "I'll tell you on the way."

Marie-Thérèse remembered Larissa and hurriedly settled into the seat, buckling her safety belt. Mathieu started the engine and waited for a chance to pull into the heavy traffic.

"Well?" she asked, fidgeting with her hands.

He took one hand from the wheel and put it over hers, stilling their nervous movement. "When that last guy started speaking, I realized that he was telling my story. I remembered it so vividly—that incredible, exciting feeling of independence. At last I was a man and could do as I liked. I didn't have to wish for things as I had when my mother was too poor to take care of any but my basic needs. There was nothing before me but freedom and everything money could buy. I know they've talked about this at the group before, but it was only tonight that the Spirit told me that such an illusion of freedom is nothing more than a blatant lie Satan is using to entrap the young people. It's every bit as dangerous as alcohol, gambling, adultery—

you name it. It's another perversion he's using to make us miserable. Or even to cause divorce." His slammed one hand against the steering wheel. "It's so clear to me now—why didn't I see it before?"

"Well, if Satan's plan was that obvious, it wouldn't work now, would it?"

"You didn't believe him."

Marie-Thérèse snorted. "I'm a banker's daughter. I could add before I could read."

"That's a good thing for me." Mathieu gave a choked laugh. "You know, it's a strange thing, but as I was sitting there, suddenly I could see everything so clearly. You know, like the Spirit was talking directly to mine without having to go through the slow reflexes of my body."

Marie-Thérèse nodded to show she understood. She had felt the same thing twice before, once when she had decided to marry Mathieu and once after Larissa was born. "Like a pure under-standing," she said.

"That's it," Mathieu said. "And now I know we're going to make it. I've felt a bit resentful and angry these past months, but now it's okay." He reached over and took her hand. "I thought you'd want to know."

Marie-Thérèse felt the months of worry fade away in that moment. She squeezed Mathieu's hand and silently gave thanks to the Lord.

They didn't speak again until Mathieu drove up to their apart-ment building and opened Marie-Thérèse's door. He pulled her close and said in her ear, "Thanks for standing by me."

Marie-Thérèse met his gaze. "I guess that's what marriage is all about. You did the same for me when I kept wondering if I had done the right thing by not going on a mission."

"You had me worried," he admitted. "Until Larissa was born."

They headed to the elevator, hands linked. When they arrived at their apartment, the door flew open before they could insert the key. Grandma Simone's thin, wrinkled face grinned at them. "Thank goodness you're home," she said. "We've got to get to the hospital."

"Is Larissa okay?" Marie-Thérèse asked, feeling panic spread through her.

"She's fine; it's Josette I'm worried about. She's gone into labor. Imagine that—a week early. Come on, let's get down to the hospital before we miss all the action!"

* * * * *

Josette had heard from nearly all the women she knew that labor and delivery were the most horribly painful experiences they had ever endured. Though she knew some women tended to exaggerate their experience, she had been apprehensive enough to make sure Dr. Samain knew that she wanted an epidural when the time came, especially since Ariana had suffered difficult labors. Dr. Samain had said that a woman's labor pattern often followed her mother's. But as the labor progressed, Josette noticed that Zack seemed to be more uncomfortable than she was. He had to sit down to avoid feeling light-headed. "Some help I am," he muttered.

Josette laughed. "You can't help it," she said. "And I'm fine. I'm just feeling a little pressure, that's all."

"You're about seven dilated," the nurse informed her. "Are you sure you don't want anything for the pain?"

Josette shook her head. "I'm not feeling any yet."

"Well, I think your baby will be coming very soon. The epidural may not have a chance to work anyway."

"I'm so excited!" Josette couldn't believe this moment was here after all the months of planning and waiting. To finally hold her baby in her arms—she could hardly wait!

Another nurse came into the room. "Your mother's here. Would you like me to send her in?"

"Yes, please. And my sister, too, if she gets here in time."

"Well, there's a crowd waiting out there, but I don't think anyone mentioned a sister. I'll go ask again."

"Her name is Marie-Thérèse!" Josette called after her. A new contraction began; this time Josette did feel a little pain and had to use the breathing techniques she had been taught by the nurses.

"Here, I'll coach you," Zack said. His pale face made her want to laugh. How strange; she never thought she would laugh through labor.

Ariana came in the door, obviously hurrying but not ruffled. "How are you holding up?"

"I'm fine," Josette said. "I guess I'm pretty lucky so far. But Zack's feeling kind of bad."

Zack looked at Ariana sheepishly. "Did I ever mention I feel faint at the sight of blood?"

Ariana managed to contain most of her amusement. "There's no blood yet," she told Zack with a smile.

Fifteen minutes later the nurses called the doctor, who instructed Josette to begin pushing. Now the pressure increased, but the pain was still bearable. Then it did start to hurt, but the feeling decreased as she bore down.

"He's out!" Dr. Samain said.

Josette glanced at Zack to make sure the doctor had been talking about the baby and not her husband. Ariana had her arm around Zack, supporting him. He look battered and exhausted. Aside from a little tiredness, Josette felt great.

"He's breathing well," said Dr. Samain as he cleaned the baby. "He didn't even let out a peep. It's my bet that if it weren't so bright in here and cold compared to what he's used to, he would already be back to sleep. That was one of the easiest deliveries I've ever witnessed. Congratulations." He took a step toward Zack, then hesitated at the sight of his white face. "I usually let the father carry the baby around to the mother," he said. "But in this case, I think I'd better let the father rest."

The nurses giggled and Zack grinned. "Thanks," he said. "That's a good idea. He's so tiny I might just drop him."

"It's you falling down that he's worried about," Josette teased. She was glad her delivery had been so smooth, since Zack wasn't much help. But her discovery of this latest weakness only made her love him more. At least he had been able to conquer his queasiness enough to stay in the room!

The doctor placed the baby in Josette's arms. Zack sat next to her on the bed, and his color slowly returned. Josette couldn't believe how perfect their son was, and how tiny.

"So what are you going to name him?" one of the nurses asked.

"Emery Terrell Fields," Josette said without hesitation. She glanced at her mother to explain. "For Emeri and Zack's father." Josette felt it was appropriate for her baby to be named after good men, one who was unable to leave posterity in this life and the other whose blood flowed through the baby's veins.

"I like it," Ariana said. "And now I have two grandchildren and another on the way." She was smiling, but several tears escaped out of the corners of her eyes. "It seems like just yesterday they placed you and Marc in my arms. I was so grateful for you both. Jean-Marc was, too. It was one of the best days of our lives."

Marie-Thérèse came into the room then, followed by the rest of the family—Jean-Marc, Marc, Louis-Géralde, Mathieu, and the great-grandparents. They congratulated the new parents and discussed the presents they wanted to buy him.

After a while, Josette looked pointedly at Zack and he began to usher the family out the door. "They're not releasing her until tomorrow," he said. "So you all might as well go home and sleep."

Only Marie-Thérèse still lingered when a nurse came into the room. "We'll need to take the baby for his bath and checkup," she said. "Would either of you like to come?"

"Yeah, I'll go," Zack said. "I think I might be able to handle that much."

"I'll stay with Josette until you get back," Marie-Thérèse said. "Mathieu's still talking to my parents in the hall."

Marie-Thérèse sat down heavily in the chair next to the bed. Although she looked uncomfortably pregnant, she radiated happiness, and Josette knew it was because Mathieu's problem with money was under control, if not completely conquered. She squeezed her sister's arm. "I'm glad it's working out for you and Mathieu," she said. "You're good together."

"Thanks. I think we're going to make it. But I'm glad you're here and not in America. I don't know what I would have done without your support."

Josette laughed. "There's one for the books. Me being supportive."

"You've come a long way."

"Don't let Zack hear you say it. He still thinks I'm perfect."

Marie-Thérèse shook her head. "I doubt it—not as long as he talks about earning enough money to get you a housekeeper."

"I'm learning," Josette said, wrinkling her nose. "I never realized how much you used to clean up after me. I'm sorry."

"So is Zack happy here?" Marie-Thérèse asked after a brief lull in the conversation.

Josette thought for a moment. "I think he is. He hasn't said he isn't. And he's really trying to let me have my own space. He's taken to playing tennis with some of the guys at work. At first it was funny, seeing him running around the court, but he's actually getting pretty good. And several times he's urged me to go out alone with my friends. I think he's growing accustomed to non-missionary life here."

"Haven't you asked him if he misses his family?"

"I guess I'm afraid of what he might say. What if he's not happy? What if he wants to go back to America and live?"

"What if you're just making problems where there aren't any?"

Josette sighed. "You're right. I have to talk to him." She paused before adding, "It wouldn't be so bad, going back there now and staying. Now that Emery's here. I think I could get pretty wrapped up in him."

"It does make a difference, having a child."

"But I don't really want to go back right now."

"Maybe Zack doesn't either. Ask him."

"I will." If Marie-Thérèse could face her fears, then Josette would also find the courage. She couldn't bear to think that Zack had traded his happiness for hers.

Marie-Thérèse patted her large belly, and Josette remembered only too well the discomfort. "Your baby will be here in no time," she said. "It's so fun, both of us having boys two months apart. I bet they'll be great friends—like we are."

An odd shadow flitted across Marie-Thérèse's face. "I still hate myself for not wanting to have him," she said suddenly. "I tell him every day how much I love and want him, hoping to make up for those four terrible months. Mathieu thinks I'm a little crazy. He says the baby couldn't possibly know how I felt, and even if he did, he'd understand why. But I keep having this uneasy feeling like something's wrong."

Josette blinked at her in surprise. "But your baby is going to be fine! Don't you remember what Pauline said? She said she'd look after him till you got him. I wish she'd said that to me!"

Marie-Thérèse grabbed Josette and laughed until the tears came. "Oh, I can't believe that Pauline! She tricked me! She wasn't talking about my first child, but my second. And all this time, I've been thinking she was hallucinating."

"Well, you never know," Josette said. "I'm just saying what I feel. She could have been guessing. I mean, with as many children as you've always wanted to have, you were bound to have a boy who would give you some worry or another, don't you think?"

Marie-Thérèse shrugged. "Well, Pauline was always close to God, but I think she could have just as well been teasing me. But it doesn't really matter. I feel it's my answer. Now it seems so silly for me to have worried at all."

Josette was relieved to hear it. She had known of children acting up simply because their parents expected them to. She didn't want Marie-Thérèse's feelings of guilt to affect her son once he was born.

Zack returned with the baby, and Marie-Thérèse went to find Mathieu. It was only much later that Josette remembered to ask Zack the question. The room was dark and it was time to sleep, but they had left the bed light on to be able to see the sleeping Emery in Josette's arms. Everything was quiet in their part of the hospital, and there was a new closeness between them that gave Josette the courage to speak. "Do you regret coming here?" she asked. "I mean, to France."

Zack lifted his head to meet her gaze. "I have missed my family and my country," he said slowly. "And for a while, I think I tried to fill that void only with you—and that wasn't fair, especially to you. You didn't do that to me in America. You worked, you had school interests, a close girlfriend and more. You didn't expect me to be everything to you. That's a pretty large order for anyone. I'm sorry for that, and I hope you've noticed that I'm trying to depend more on myself."

"I did notice, and I appreciate everything you're doing. But I guess what I'm asking is if you're happy."

With a swift movement, he arose from the bedside chair and put his forehead against hers. She could taste his breath as it mingled with her own in the still air. The only sound she could hear other than her own rapid heartbeat was Emery's soft breathing underneath the arch of their joined heads.

"I told you we were twin flames," he said. "And I meant it. I don't regret anything as long as I'm married to you. And yes, I'm very happy." He kissed her fervently, and Josette could feel that he told the truth.

About the Author

Rachel Ann Nunes (pronounced *noon-esh*) is a homemaker, student, and Church worker who lists writing as one of her favorite pursuits. *Ariana: A Glimpse of Eternity* is her fifth novel to be published by Covenant and the fourth in her *Ariana* series, which has been very popular in the LDS market.

In addition to writing and family activities, Rachel enjoys reading, camping, volleyball, softball, and traveling to or reading about foreign countries. She served an LDS mission to Portugal.

Rachel and her husband, TJ, are the parents of four children.

Rachel enjoys hearing from her readers. You can write to her at P.O. Box 353, American Fork, UT 84003-0353, send e-mail to rachel@ranunes.com, or visit her web site at http://www.ranunes.com.